THE COMPLETE IDIOT'S GUIDE® TO

Bridge

Third Edition
by H. Anthony Medley

ALPHA

A member of Penguin Group (USA) Inc.

ALPHA BOOKS

Published by Penguin Group (USA) Inc.

Penguin Group (USA) Inc., 375 Hudson Street, New York, New York 10014, USA • Penguin Group (Canada), 90 Eglinton Avenue East, Suite 700, Toronto, Ontario M4P 2Y3, Canada (a division of Pearson Penguin Canada Inc.) • Penguin Books Ltd., 80 Strand, London WC2R 0RL, England • Penguin Ireland, 25 St. Stephen's Green, Dublin 2, Ireland (a division of Penguin Books Ltd.) • Penguin Group (Australia), 250 Camberwell Road, Camberwell, Victoria 3124, Australia (a division of Pearson Australia Group Pty. Ltd.) • Penguin Books India Pvt. Ltd., 11 Community Centre, Panchsheel Park, New Delhi—110 017, India • Penguin Group (NZ), 67 Apollo Drive, Rosedale, North Shore, Auckland 1311, New Zealand (a division of Pearson New Zealand Ltd.) • Penguin Books (South Africa) (Pty.) Ltd., 24 Sturdee Avenue, Rosebank, Johannesburg 2196, South Africa • Penguin Books Ltd., Registered Offices: 80 Strand, London WC2R 0RL, England

Copyright © 2012 by H. Anthony Medley

International Standard Book Number: 978-1-61564-199-4
Library of Congress Catalog Card Number: 2012930859

14 13 12   8 7 6 5 4 3 2 1

Interpretation of the printing code: The rightmost number of the first series of numbers is the year of the book's printing; the rightmost number of the second series of numbers is the number of the book's printing. For example, a printing code of 12-1 shows that the first printing occurred in 2012.

Printed in the United States of America

Note: This publication contains the opinions and ideas of its author. It is intended to provide helpful and informative material on the subject matter covered. It is sold with the understanding that the author and publisher are not engaged in rendering professional services in the book. If the reader requires personal assistance or advice, a competent professional should be consulted.

The author and publisher specifically disclaim any responsibility for any liability, loss, or risk, personal or otherwise, which is incurred as a consequence, directly or indirectly, of the use and application of any of the contents of this book.

Most Alpha books are available at special quantity discounts for bulk purchases for sales promotions, premiums, fund-raising, or educational use. Special books, or book excerpts, can also be created to fit specific needs. For details, write: Special Markets, Alpha Books, 375 Hudson Street, New York, NY 10014.

Publisher: *Marie Butler-Knight*

Associate Publisher/Acquiring Editor: *Mike Sanders*

Executive Managing Editor: *Billy Fields*

Development Editor: *Jennifer Moore*

Senior Production Editor: *Janette Lynn*

Copy Editor: *Monica Stone*

Cover Designer: *William Thomas*

Book Designers: *William Thomas, Rebecca Batchelor*

Indexer: *Angie Bess Martin*

Layout: *Brian Massey*

Proofreader: *John Etchison*

ALWAYS LEARNING   PEARSON

For my father, Harry A. Medley: A caring, generous provider,
A loving, sympathetic, and interested parent,
An honest, brilliant businessman,
Smart, considerate, and funny,
The best example a son could have,
A pal I miss every day of my life.

Contents

Appendixes

Introduction

My mother taught me how to play bridge when I was in high school, and I taught my fraternity brothers how to play at UCLA. But after graduating I played basketball, baseball, football, tennis, golf, poker, and gin rummy—everything but bridge.

Years later, after I had given up basketball and taken up tennis as my primary recreational activity, a friend of mine, Earl Cohen, called me and asked if I'd join him in a game of rubber bridge at the Marina City Club. Because I had been away from the game for so long I was afraid I'd make a fool of myself, "No way," I said. "Come on," he said. "No way," I said.

Earl is a psychiatrist, so three hours later I had spent a wonderful afternoon playing bridge by the pool. Despite my lengthy sabbatical, I remembered the game easily. Bridge is so logical. After you learn the fundamentals, you don't forget them.

After our game by the pool, Earl invited me to enter a bridge tournament with him. "Why not?" I said. We won, and I was hooked.

I played rubber bridge for several years before being introduced to duplicate bridge, a more competitive form of the game. Duplicate is different in form only. The fundamentals are identical to rubber bridge.

It was during this period that I was preoccupied with what I thought were worrisome things. I found that while playing bridge my problems receded like the tide pulling back from Mont Saint-Michel. While you're playing bridge, you think about nothing but the cards. And it's so much fun!

The trepidation I felt when Earl asked me to join him for a poolside game isn't unusual. Unfortunately, this feeling of anxiety is more normal than unique. I want to soothe the apprehension that people seem to feel at the mere mention of bridge. The wonder of bridge is that the more you play, the more you want to play.

That's the germination of this book. Bridge is such a wonderful game, and it's easy to learn and play. Although I was taught the game in my teens, because I was away from it for an extended period, I stand as a prime example of someone who took up bridge much later than many, yet became an accomplished player in a short period of time. I feel a missionary-like zeal to spread the word of what a great game bridge is and how easy it is to learn. That's what you're going to learn in this book.

I've tried all the games. Nothing compares to bridge.

Why This Book Is Different from the Others

What makes this book unique is that it is written in an easy-to-understand way by a professional writer who also happens to be a dedicated bridge player. Most bridge books are written by bridge players who write because they are bridge players. That's not to deprecate them. I admire people like Freddy Sheinwold, Charles Goren, and all the others who have contributed so much to the game. Every month I read the American Contract Bridge League (ACBL) Bridge Bulletin, a glossy-style magazine, and it's filled with entertaining and educational articles on how to play and improve their readers' game, all well written by players who love the game.

But because I'm a writer first and a bridge player second, I have the unique opportunity to produce a first-class book that is both educational and entertaining. It also allows me to give something back to a game that has given me so much joy and pleasure.

This book has a unique perspective. It's aimed at the person who wants to learn how to play bridge, but doesn't want to take lessons or read a lot of complicated books on bidding and play. I've put everything here in one easy reference. Here, at last, you'll learn everything you need to know to play the wonderful game of bridge without jumping from book to book.

How This Book Is Organized

I've broken this book into the following parts:

In **Part 1, Introduction to Bridge,** I offer an easy-to-understand explanation of the game of bridge, introduce you to basic bridge terminology, and teach you how to score. After reading these parts, you should be able to sit down at table with three other people and play some hands.

Part 2, Opening Bids, focuses exclusively on the opening bidder, the first person to make a bid. The chapters in this part tell you how to evaluate your hand in order to determine whether or not you should be the first bidder and describe the different ways you can open the bidding.

Part 3, Responses to Opening Bids, switches focus to the partner of the player who opens the bidding. Here you find out how to evaluate your hand after your partner has opened so that you can make a decision on how to bid. Your aim is to give your partner as much information about your hand as you can with a single bid.

The seven chapters in **Part 4, Rebids, Overcalls, and Doubles,** push deeper into the nuances of bidding. You find out how the opening bidder makes the first rebid after hearing her partner's response, and how that responder should in turn rebid. This part also explores the fun concept of slam, which is when you take all or all but one of the tricks. Next, we talk about how to bid if your opponents open the bidding, how to make an overcall or a takeout double, and how to respond if your opponents do the same. We tell you all about takeout doubles, defensive bidding, and penalty doubles. Finally, we touch on the all-important topic of partnership etiquette.

Part 5, Defense and Play of the Hand, is devoted to the play of the hand after the bidding has been completed. It details how a declarer plays the hand and how defenders defend the hand, and explains specific techniques—like taking a finesse, counting points in partner's hand from the bidding, and defending after the opening lead.

Extras

I've scattered the following sidebars throughout the book to call your attention to special information:

TRICKS OF THE TRADE

These are tips—nonessential extra information that will give you an edge.

ALERT

These sidebars are cautions, reminders of things for which you should always be watchful.

DEFINITION

These sidebars define specialized bridge terms to teach you the language of bridge.

BRIDGEBIT

These sidebars tell you things you might never know about bridge, such as its history and humor.

But Wait! There's More!

Have you logged on to idiotsguides.com lately? If you haven't, go there now! As a bonus to the book, we've included tons of additional winning strategies for more advanced players you'll want to check out, all online. Point your browser to idiotsguides.com/bridge, and enjoy!

Acknowledgments

Many people have contributed to my development as a bridge player and, thus, to this work. I've learned from all my bridge partners, but want to single out three for special mention: My golden partner, Luanne Leonard, was with me for 80 percent of my gold points and generously introduced me to some of the greats of the game. Millie Garrison was not only my partner for my first big tournament win—a huge victory in Palm Springs where we beat some of the best players in the world—but she also suggested Alpha Books as a likely publisher. Finally, the late E'Anne Conaway, one of the most prominent, respected, and loved bridge figures in Los Angeles, provided constant encouragement, help, and advice.

I especially want to thank Marie Butler-Knight, publisher of Alpha Books, for recognizing the need for this revised edition; my acquisitions editor, Mike Sanders, for his unfailing help; my production editor, Janette Lynn, who has had wonderful suggestions on improving the book; my development editor, Jennifer Moore, who has been understanding, cooperative, prompt, and, in short, wonderful; and my copy editor, Monica Stone, who, without mincing words, has done a fantastic job. In sum, it's been wonderful to be associated with such consummate professionals.

This is an update to the book I wrote in 1997 and updated in 2004 to teach people the best game in the world. The book has been successful beyond my wildest imagination, going through printing after printing.

The Complete Idiot's Guide to Bridge, Third Edition, was reviewed by an expert who double-checked the accuracy of what you'll learn here, to help us ensure that this book gives you everything you need to know about playing bridge. Special thanks are extended to Brad Bartol.

Trademarks

All terms mentioned in this book that are known to be or are suspected of being trademarks or service marks have been appropriately capitalized. Alpha Books and Penguin Group (USA) Inc. cannot attest to the accuracy of this information. Use of a term in this book should not be regarded as affecting the validity of any trademark or service mark.

Introduction to Bridge

Be forewarned, bridge is an addictive game. Once you get your first taste of how much fun you can have playing it, you might very well be hooked for life. In this part, I whet your appetite by introducing you to the basics of the game. Bridge has its own unique language, which you will begin to grasp as you find out about the bidding process and how to play a hand. After you finish reading these four short, easy-to-read and easy-to-understand chapters, bridge will no longer be a mystery, and you'll be firmly on the road to becoming a bridge player.

Welcome to Bridge!

In This Chapter

- Getting a basic bridge overview
- Understanding the ranking of cards and suits
- Choosing a partner and a dealer
- Shuffling, cutting, and dealing the cards

Can you add to 40? Can you count to 13? If you can do these two things, you can play bridge.

Bridge is a fast-paced four-player card game played with a standard 52-card deck. Its reliance on concentration and skill has made it popular with card players of all ages for more than 75 years. This chapter gives you a brief overview of the game and tells you what you need to play it.

A Brief History of the Game

Contract bridge as we know it today was born as a result of a game that took place on October 31, 1925, on board a ship called the SS *Finland*. While waiting to pass through the Panama Canal, Harold S. Vanderbilt and two friends needed a fourth person to play a bridge-like game called *plafond*. They allowed a woman, who was a fellow passenger, to join their game. She, however, suggested one exotic change after another, based on a game she said she had learned in China. This irritated Vanderbilt so much that the next day, during the canal crossing, he worked out the scoring table for contract bridge, which remains remarkably similar today. That night—November 1, 1925—the first game of contract bridge was played and scored under Vanderbilt's new rules. Today, the most prestigious American team trophy in bridge is the Vanderbilt Cup, named after—guess who.

Vanderbilt recalled later, "We enjoyed playing my new game on board the *Finland* so much that, on my return to New York, I gave typed copies of my scoring table to several of my Auction Bridge playing friends. I made no other effort to popularize or publicize Contract Bridge. Thanks apparently to its excellence, it popularized itself and spread like wildfire."

BRIDGEBIT

Ely Culbertson published *Contract Bridge Blue Book* in 1930, only five years after Vanderbilt's creation. That book became the recognized authority on the game. When Charles Goren popularized the methods of point-count valuation, he supplanted Culbertson as the game's premier authority. Goren's mathematical approach to bidding simplified the game, and its popularity exploded.

And grow it did! Today, contract bridge is played in every country in the world, by more than 100 million people—17 million in the United States alone. There are 3,700 individual *duplicate-bridge* clubs in the American Contract Bridge League (ACBL), and 80 sovereign countries are officially represented in the World Bridge Federation (WBF). Contract bridge is the game that most people who don't play cards want to learn.

DEFINITION

The two most popular formats of contract bridge are rubber bridge and duplicate bridge.

In **rubber bridge,** the object is to win the rubber and the bonus points awarded. The cards are shuffled after each hand. It's been called the most popular form of Contract Bridge.

In **duplicate bridge,** each hand is separate and stands on its own. Played with eight or more players, the cards are not shuffled after being played, but are passed to the next table where those players play the exact same hands. At the end of a duplicate game, the pair that has the best overall score on all the hands combined is the winner. The big advantage of duplicate is that nobody can complain about their score because "they didn't get the cards" because they are competing against pairs who played the exact same hands.

Bridge Is Easy!

When the United States Playing Card Company, which manufactures 75 percent of the cards sold in America, asked respondents what card game they wished they knew how to play, by far the most popular response was bridge.

But when asked what card games they *intended* to learn in the near future, bridge was not in the top five. The reason? They had the feeling that bridge was too complicated and that they didn't have the time to learn it.

Balderdash!

As I mentioned at the beginning of this chapter, if you can add to 40 and count to 13, you can play bridge—and play it well. In this book I show you that learning how to play bridge is easy. All you need to do is read on, learn a few principles, and then go and play.

You don't believe me? In my bridge infancy, I played with a kindergarten teacher named Nancy Kelly. Nancy was a lively grandmother who played a very old-fashioned, simple game of bridge. That was right in line with me, because that's what I played at the time. But we competed against very good players who used all the fancy systems. We had no systems. Zero. Nada. Guess what? We generally beat the socks off of everyone. Why? Because our game was very simple and we communicated very well with each other. That's all you need to do. Know the basics, which you'll learn in the first part of this book, and be able to communicate with your partner.

Believe it or not, after the first two chapters, you'll be able to play hands. The rest of the book helps you play the game better. Do you remember when you first learned to ride a bike? The only way you could learn was by actually getting on a bike (and, of course, falling off a few times); well the same goes for bridge. The only way you'll be able to master the game is to pull out a deck of cards and play!

Bridge Basics

Bridge is played by four people, comprised of two pairs. You and your partner play against two other people. At the table you are positioned opposite your partner while your opponents sit on either side of you.

In the examples throughout this book, your partner is female and your opponents are male, so references to your partner are to *she* and *her* and references to your opponents are *he* and *him*. I've adopted this convention to keep from being twisted up in pronouns, but of course, you can play bridge with any combination of either gender!

In bridge terminology, you are sitting in directions named after points on a compass. So if you and your partner are sitting North-South, your opponents are sitting East-West, and vice versa. These terms have no relevance to real compass points.

BRIDGEBIT

It is said that Bridge got its name from the Galata Bridge, which spanned the Golden Horn in Istanbul. According to this theory, approximately 14,000 British troops were stationed in Istanbul in 1854, and the officers who crossed the Galata Bridge every day to play a card game in a coffeehouse referred to the game as Bridge in honor of the bridge they crossed to get there.

Bishop Latimer referred to a Bridge-like card game in a sermon in 1529, when Henry VIII was courting Anne Boleyn and trying to figure out how to dump his longtime spouse, Catherine of Aragon. Bridge is probably of Turkish or Russian derivation. An early rendition was originally called *Khedive* when first played in the nineteenth century on the French Riviera, and that was the title of the Turkish viceroy.

A game called *Whist,* the forerunner of Bridge, was played in England starting in the late nineteenth century. It was replaced by Bridge Whist and then by Auction Bridge around the turn of the century.

The Cards

Bridge is played with a standard deck of playing cards, consisting of 52 cards in each deck.

Suits and Card Ranks

A standard deck of playing cards has four suits, with 13 cards per suit. The four suits are as follows:

- Spades (♠)
- Hearts (♥)
- Diamonds (♦)
- Clubs (♣)

Even though each suit has 13 cards, they aren't numbered 1 through 13. Numbers 2 through 10 are indeed numbered 2 through 10. The jack, queen, and king—in that order—are 11, 12, and 13. The ace is 1, and it's the highest-ranking card—even higher than a king! That's an important point to keep in mind: the ace is the strongest card in the suit, not the weakest.

So here's how the cards rank in bridge, in descending order of importance:

Number	Name	Number	Name
1	Ace	7	7
13	King	6	6
12	Queen	5	5
11	Jack	4	4
10	10	3	3 or Trey
9	9	2	2 or Deuce
8	8		

Rank of the Suits

In bridge, not all suits are equal. In fact they are, by definition, unequal. Following are the suits, ranked in descending order of importance:

Spades
Hearts
Diamonds
Clubs

An easy way to remember which suits rank where is simply to think of them in alphabetical order: C-D-H-S. Clubs is the weakest suit, whereas spades is the strongest.

The Shuffle

Before you deal the cards, you must mix, or shuffle, them so they are in random order. You shuffle the cards by dividing them into two approximately equal piles and mixing them together. Do this several times—at least three times—after each hand. You might have heard that shuffling the cards seven times will result in the most random deal, but that many shuffles aren't necessary.

Choosing Partners and the Dealer

If you don't have established partners, spread the cards out on the table, face down. Have each player pick a card and turn it over. The players with the two highest-ranking cards become a partnership, and the players with the two lowest-ranking cards become a partnership for the first *rubber*. The player with the highest-ranking card is the dealer for the first hand. After the rubber ends, you can choose partners again in the same way.

DEFINITION

A **rubber** is a unit of measurement in bridge. When a pair of players has won two games, the rubber is over. The winner of the rubber is the pair with the most points when the rubber ends. Rubbers and games are explained in more detail in Chapter 4.

The Deal

The process of delivering the cards to each player is called the *deal*. The person who deals is called the *dealer*. After the dealer shuffles the cards, he distributes them to each player, delivering one card to each player face down in turn, clockwise, until all of the cards have been distributed. By the end of the deal, each player should have 13 cards in his or her hand.

The deal rotates in a clockwise manner. If you deal first, the person on your left deals next, and then your partner, and then the person on her left, and so on.

Although bridge is played with a single deck of cards, it's standard practice to have two decks on the table. You should use decks with different colors or markings so you can easily distinguish one deck from the other. While you're dealing, your partner is *making* the other deck. This means that she is shuffling the cards for the next dealer. Once the deck is made, it is placed to the maker's right. This speeds up the game and gets rid of the dead space that can occur while the cards from the game that was just played are being shuffled and dealt.

The Cut

When the hand is over, the next dealer, the person on the previous dealer's left, picks up the cards on his left, where the maker placed them after shuffling them, and offers them to the player on his right to *cut*.

> **TRICKS OF THE TRADE**
>
> When cards are shuffled, it's very easy for the bottom card to be exposed. Because the dealer always gets the last card in the deck, if players see the bottom card, they know at least one card in the dealer's hand. Cutting the deck eliminates this possibility. The cut puts the bottom card somewhere in the middle of the deck. Such details may not seem too important now, but as you get more proficient at the game, knowing where any card is can be very valuable.

To cut the cards, pick up approximately half of them and place them toward the new dealer. He then picks up the rest of the deck and places it on top of the part that you took off, or cut. You don't have to cut the deck exactly in half. You can cut it to any depth you wish. (Note that it is card-playing etiquette—not just bridge etiquette—to place the cut *toward* the dealer. This allows the dealer to place the correct cards on top without having to ask, "Which way did you cut?") The dealer then deals the cards while his partner makes the deck that was just played.

The Least You Need to Know

- Ace is the highest-ranking card; 2 (deuce) is the lowest-ranking card.
- Spades is the highest-ranking suit followed by hearts, diamonds, and clubs. An easy way to remember ranking is to think of alphabetical order, low-to-high suits: C-D-H-S.
- The dealer picks up the preshuffled cards on his left and offers them to the player on his right to cut.
- The cards are dealt clockwise starting on the dealer's left, with the dealer receiving the last card.
- The dealer's partner makes (shuffles) the other deck while the dealer is dealing.

Basic Bridge Skills

In This Chapter

- Playing tricks
- Keeping track of tricks
- Leading
- Following suit, reneging, and revoking
- Getting acquainted with bridge terminology

Bridge has a reputation for being difficult to learn. Although it's not as simple as poker or gin rummy, its basic principles are quite simple. However, knowing how to *play* and knowing how to *play well* are two entirely different things.

Getting to the point of playing *well* is entirely up to you. This chapter explains the basics. When you're finished with Part 1, you'll be able to play the game. As you read subsequent chapters, you'll get even better. By the time you finish this book, you should be able to sit down with your bridge-playing friends without trepidation.

Be warned, however: bridge is addictive. When you know how to play bridge, you will be hooked. It's more fun than you can possibly imagine.

Tricks

The entire concept of the game of bridge is based on predicting how many tricks you or your opponents can take. A *trick* consists of the four cards in the middle of the table after every player has contributed a card. Each person can play only one card in a trick. Each person must play in order, clockwise from the person who has the lead.

To lead means to play the first card in a trick. So when someone asks, "Is it my lead?" he's asking if he's supposed to start the trick. If you tell someone, "It's your play," it means that another player has led the first card of the trick and it's his turn to contribute a card to it. Whoever has the lead is in control of that trick; he can choose what suit to lead and what card to lead. Having the lead is a very important part of the play of the hand.

A *hand* consists of 13 tricks. Each person starts with 13 cards, and the hand is over when everyone is out of cards.

ALERT

If one player runs out of cards before everyone else, or if a hand doesn't have 13 tricks in it, something is dreadfully wrong. There may have been a misdeal, or perhaps two cards stuck together and were played as one. If you can determine what happened, appropriate bridge laws apply. Otherwise, you must void the hand and deal again.

Playing Tricks

The highest card played of the suit led wins the trick. So let's say, for example, that you lead and you play the 2 of hearts. Your left-hand opponent (the person sitting on your left, often referred to as LHO, for short) plays the 3 of hearts. Now it's your partner's turn. She plays the 8 of Hearts. That leaves your right-hand opponent (the person sitting on your right, RHO for short), who is sitting to your partner's left, to play. And let's say he plays the 5 of Hearts.

Because your pair, meaning the team consisting of you and your partner, has played the highest card in the suit on this trick (your partner's 8 of hearts), your pair wins the trick. But you no longer have the lead. Why? One of the rules of bridge is that the person who plays the highest card in the suit (and who, thus, wins the trick) also wins the lead. So your partner, who won the trick with the 8 of hearts, now gets to lead.

She can lead any card she wants: she can lead another heart, or any other suit. If she leads the king of spades, your RHO plays the ace of spades, you play the 7 of spades, and your LHO plays the 6 of spades, then your RHO has won the trick because the ace is the strongest card in the suit. Because your RHO won the trick, it's his lead.

Keeping Track of Tricks

The person who wins the trick takes all the cards played on that trick and places them in front of her—all four cards as a unit—so that they look like one card. One player from each team—it doesn't matter which player—keeps all the tricks for that team.

> **TRICKS OF THE TRADE**
>
> When you win a trick, place all the cards sideways. Then when you win another trick, place that trick on top of the last trick you won, but slightly to the right of it, and at right angles to it. Keep doing this with each subsequent trick. Placing your tricks in this fashion makes it easy to differentiate one trick from another and to keep count of how many tricks your side has won.

Tricks are won (or *taken*) 13 times each hand. When the last card has been played, you count the tricks you've taken, and the tricks your opponents have taken, and that's the result of the hand. If you've played correctly, the total should add up to 13.

Two Rules for Playing Tricks

You're almost ready to start playing bridge, but before you do, you need to know a couple of important rules, which I tell you about in the following sections.

Following Suit

When playing a trick, you must follow suit. *Following suit* means that a player must play a card in the suit led if he or she has that suit in their hand. So if someone leads a heart, and you have a heart, you must play it. You can't play a spade or another card from any other suit if you have a heart when a heart is led.

If you fail to follow suit when you have a card in that suit, you are said to have *reneged* or *revoked*. For example, if a heart was led, and you have a heart in your hand but play a spade instead, you have revoked, and there are penalties for that.

A revoke is established when someone on the offending pair has either led or *played to* the next trick.

Here are the penalties for a revoke:

- If the offending player, at the end of the hand, won the trick on which the revoke took place, the trick on which the revoke occurred is transferred to the nonoffending side together with one of any subsequent tricks won by the offending side.

- If the trick on which the revoke occurred wasn't won by the offending player, if the offending side wins any subsequent trick, after the hand ends one trick is transferred to the nonoffending side.

- If you revoke and realize your mistake before your pair leads or plays the next trick, you can bring your revoke to everyone's attention and withdraw it by playing a card from the suit led. Any players who played a card to the trick after you are then given the right to withdraw the card they played to that trick and substitute a different card.

For example, if the revoking team took eight tricks during the play of the hand, when the hand is completed it only gets credit for taking six or seven tricks, depending on the circumstances above.

Discarding

If you don't have a card from the suit led, you can play any card from any suit you like. This is called a *discard*. But that card is worthless as far as taking the trick is concerned. If your opponent leads the 2 of hearts and you don't have any hearts, you can play any other card you like—even the ace of spades—but the ace of spades can't take the current trick. When a heart is led, the 2 of hearts is more powerful than the ace of spades.

Practice Playing Tricks

Now you know how tricks are played; so stop and play some. Deal out some hands and play the tricks. It's better if you have three companions, so each of you can have a hand; but if you don't, you can do it open-handed. Just deal out four hands and play the tricks, looking at each hand in turn. Do this until you're comfortable with the concept of tricks and how they're played.

The Least You Need to Know

- A trick consists of one card from each player played face up on the table. Play proceeds in a clockwise rotation.
- Each trick is won by the highest card played in the suit that was led.
- The player winning the current trick leads a card to start the next trick.
- A player must follow suit if possible. If not, he or she may discard any card.
- Completed tricks are kept by one member of the pair winning the trick.
- You and your partner as a team want to win as many tricks as possible in each hand.

The Language of Bridge

In This Chapter

- The auction and the contract
- How the trump suit is established
- More about following suit
- Declarer, defenders, and the dummy
- What is *no trump?*

Now that you know how the hands are played, you need to discover how you actually get into playing the tricks. This is the essence of bridge. The communication between the partners really sets bridge apart from other card games.

It's such a wonderful feeling to look at the 13 cards in your hand and communicate with your partner through bidding and playing. You tell her what you have in your hand without saying, "Partner, I have the ace of spades and the 2 of hearts." Based on her response, you can infer that she has the king of clubs, without her saying, "Partner, I have the king of clubs."

By polishing your bidding (communication) with your partner, you'll be able to assess the number of tricks your side can win. This is your first major step toward becoming a bridge player. In this chapter, I introduce you to the language of bidding.

Bidding

When you're comfortable with tricks, the next step to playing bridge is to predict how many tricks you're going to take before you play. Start by just looking at your hand and making an educated guess at the number of tricks that you think you can take if you have the lead. Play the hand out and see how you did. Next, let your LHO (left-hand opponent) predict how many tricks he and his partner will take, and then play that hand out.

After you do this a few times, try this: Let the dealer make a verbal prediction of the number of tricks she and her partner will take. After she makes a prediction, have the dealer's LHO make a prediction, then the dealer's partner, and then the dealer's RHO (right-hand opponent). Play the hand, with the dealer leading first, and see how you did. These predictions by each player are called *bids*.

Eventually, you will see that your prediction can help your partner make her prediction. If you predict that you can take three tricks, she can look at her hand, add what you predicted to what she can take in her own hand, and increase your pair's bid. Similarly, the second of your opponents to bid has the benefit of his partner's prediction in estimating how many tricks they will take. As you continue to do this, you'll get more accurate in your predictions.

Winning the Auction

Congratulations. As you do this predicting, or bidding, you've started to play contract bridge! Your prediction of how many tricks you think you can take is called an *auction*. You win the auction by predicting that you can take more tricks than your opponents predict that they can take. If you finally say that you can take 10 tricks and your opponents don't think that they can take more, they *pass*, in effect saying, "Okay, go ahead and try." You win the auction.

Winning the auction doesn't mean that you've won the hand, though. All it means is that you get to name the *trump* suit (explained shortly) and play the hand as declarer. (The opponents play the hand as defenders.) If you and your partner win the auction, you must take at least the number of tricks you predicted in order to win the hand. Otherwise you'll be *set*—that's not good—and your opponents will receive points for each trick you fell under your prediction.

> **DEFINITION**
>
> If you take fewer than the number of tricks you predicted, you are **set** or **down,** and your opponents get a score based on the number of tricks you took under what you predicted. So if you predicted you'd make eight tricks and only made seven, you are said to be *set one* or *down one,* and your opponents get points for each trick under your prediction, or bid.

Think of the auction as a conversation using a different language. You're communicating to your partner what you have in your hand by the way you bid. Instead of saying, "Partner, I have five spades in my hand," your bid communicates this by simply mentioning a number (not five, ironically enough) and the word *spades.* Similarly, you can communicate to your partner how strong your hand is, based on your bid.

Six Tricks Makes Book

When you score in bridge, as declarer—the person who won the auction—you don't get credit for any tricks until you've taken six tricks. After you've taken six tricks, any subsequent tricks you take count toward your bid. In other words, every trick over six is credited to you. So if you think you can take seven tricks, you don't say, "I think I can take seven tricks." Instead, you say, "I think I can take one trick."

The first six tricks taken by the declarer is called *book.* So if you say you can take one trick, you mean you can take six (book) plus one additional trick.

If you think you can take ten tricks, you don't say, "I can take ten tricks." Instead, you say, "I can take four tricks (the six tricks that constitute book, plus an additional four).

If you don't think you and your partner can take more than six tricks, then you shouldn't make a bid; instead, you should pass.

Pass

If you don't have a good enough hand to make a bid you must say, "Pass." After you pass, it's up to your LHO to bid. Passing communicates to your partner that you don't have a suit that you want to bid at this time. You may, however, change your mind and make a bid later when it's your turn again. After you've passed, you can't bid again until all three other players have bid or passed.

The Trump Suit

Now that you're familiar with tricks and how they're played, let me introduce you to a new concept: trump. The trump suit, for the duration of the hand, outranks all other suits. The deuce (2) of the trump suit will win a trick over an ace of a nontrump suit.

The trump suit is the suit in which you want to play the hand, which is generally the suit you and your partner think you have the most of between you. Because you have more cards in this suit than any other, it's to your great advantage to promote it to be the highest-ranking suit.

Getting to name trump is what the auction is all about. That's what you're bidding to win. Your team might have a lot of hearts, and your opponents might have a lot of spades, so you're dueling to see who thinks they can make the most tricks if they name trump.

During the auction, if you want to make hearts trump, you don't just say, "I think I can take seven tricks if hearts is trump." The way that you actually say this when you bid is very simple: when it's your turn to bid, you say, "One heart." This means, "I can take seven tricks—book (six) plus one additional—if hearts is trump."

When estimating how many tricks you can take, keep in mind that you can't just play a trump card whenever you please. Because you have to follow suit (see Chapter 2), you can't play trump when another suit is led, unless you don't have any of that suit. For example, if clubs is trump and someone leads with the ace of hearts, you can't play the 2 of clubs to win the trick unless you're out of hearts (also called *being void* in hearts). So if your opponents lead with the ace of hearts and you have a heart, you must play it to follow suit.

Now that you know about trump and bidding, let's try it. For the following *contracts*, convert them into bridge lingo by saying how you would bid:

1. Eleven tricks in spades

2. Seven tricks in hearts

3. Nine tricks in diamonds

4. Five tricks in clubs

Number 1 is bid by saying, "Five spades" (book plus five).

Number 2 is bid by saying, "One heart" (book plus one).

Number 3 is bid by saying, "Three diamonds" (book plus three).

Number 4? Were you tricked? You don't have a bid. If you don't think you can at least make book plus one, you shouldn't bid. Each bid means, "I can take six tricks *plus* the number I bid." Making the first six tricks is a condition of making your bid. Instead of bidding, Number 4 must say, "Pass."

DEFINITION

A **contract** is the final, winning bid of an auction. The pair that makes the contract commits to trying to take the specified number of tricks they bid at their final bid.

The Auction Revisited

To *open* means to make the first bid in an auction. The opener doesn't have to be the dealer necessarily, although the dealer gets the first chance at it.

In an auction, if your partner opens with one heart, your LHO might think he can take seven tricks if spades are trump. So he would bid one spade.

What if your LHO thinks he can take seven tricks if clubs is trump? He can't, because you can't bid an inferior suit over a superior suit at the same numerical level. Remember the rank of the suits from Chapter 1? Hearts outranks clubs. That means that he can't bid one club if you have already bid one heart. If you bid one heart before him, he must bid two clubs if he wants clubs to be trump.

You can bid one heart over a one-club bid, but you can't bid one club over one heart. So if your opponent thinks that he can do better than you if clubs is trump, and if he thinks that he can take eight tricks, he says, "two clubs" after you've said, "one heart."

ALERT

After the bidding has been opened, all bidding ends after three consecutive passes. So if you open, and your bid is followed by three passes, you don't get another chance to bid.

Your partner has been sitting there listening. She looks at her hand and sees that she has four hearts! If you think that you and she can make one heart without knowing what's in her hand, and she has almost a third of the hearts in the whole deck, there's a good chance that her hand can help you make one or two more tricks. She looks at her clubs and they're weak. If clubs is trump, the opponents might be able to make their two clubs bid. However if hearts is trump, she thinks your pair can make two hearts. So she bids "Two hearts," saying to you, basically, "Partner, if you think you can take seven tricks, I have at least one additional trick in my hand, so together we should be able to take eight tricks."

Your RHO has been listening to this, too. He looks at his hand and sees he has four clubs. He says to himself, "If my partner thinks he can make two clubs all by himself, I bet he can make at least one more with my four clubs to contribute." Based on this reasoning, he bids "Three clubs."

You listen to all this and say to yourself, "Wait a minute. I thought I could take one heart all by myself, but my partner has at least one trick in her hand. I thought I could *probably* make two hearts before I heard her bid. So, if she has enough to tell me she thinks we can make two hearts, I think we can make three hearts." So you bid, "Three hearts."

Well, the bidding has gotten a little high, and your LHO looks at his hand and says, "I don't think my partner and I can make four clubs," so he passes. Your partner is satisfied, so she passes, too. Your RHO is also a little doubtful about making four clubs, so he passes.

There it is, an auction and a contract! The bid has been auctioned. You've won the right to name trump. You and your partner have entered into a contract in which you're going to try to make three hearts. This is what contract bridge is all about.

Dummy and Declarer

No, no, this is not a newly discovered novel by Dostoyevsky. The *dummy* is the hand held by the partner of the player who won the auction. Because it was a team effort, how do you decide which of you actually won it? Well, the person who wins the auction is the person who first bid the suit that becomes trump; this person is referred to as *declarer*. In the preceding example, the trump suit was hearts because three hearts was the winning bid. You were the first person to bid hearts, so you play the hand as declarer, and your partner becomes dummy for this hand.

DEFINITION

Declarer is the first person of the partnership to bid the suit that wins the auction. Declarer is the person who plays the hand. **Dummy** is the partner of the declarer.

Displaying Dummy's Hand

After the auction is over, it's time to play. Declarer's LHO always has the opening lead. After that opening lead, dummy puts her cards face up on the table, with trumps placed on dummy's right (declarer's left). The cards are placed with the highest ranking on top as declarer is looking at them, and in descending order. Most people, when they're dummy, place the cards in alternating order of color—red, black, red, black—but this isn't required. You can place them in any order, as long as trump is on declarer's left as she looks at the cards.

The rest of the cards in dummy's hand are laid out so that everyone at the table can see each card, its suit, and denomination. While the hand is being played, dummy can't collaborate with the declarer on the correct play of the hand.

During the play of the hand, dummy can't say anything except to ask declarer if she is void when she doesn't follow suit, or to tell her that the lead is either in her hand or in the dummy if it looks as if she's going to lead from the wrong hand. Otherwise, dummy is barred from speaking. Similarly, your opponents may not verbally communicate with one another during the play of the hand, except to ask if their partner is void in a suit when he doesn't follow suit, or to say it's not his lead if it looks as if he is about to lead out of turn.

Playing Dummy's Hand

You have two options for how you play dummy's hand. The first, and better, way is for declarer to call the card she wants played from the dummy hand and for dummy to follow her instructions and play the card. So in playing the hand you see spread in the following illustration, if the declarer led a low heart from her hand and her LHO played the 9 of hearts, declarer would call out the card she wanted played, without touching it, for example, "Queen of hearts." Dummy would then play the queen of hearts.

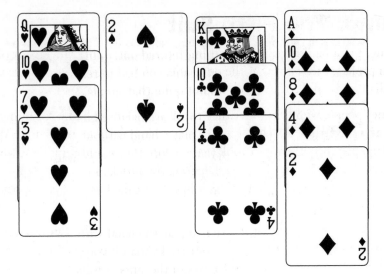

This is the way a dummy's hand looks to the declarer.

The previous figure is a graphical representation of a typical bridge hand. The following is the notation for that same hand:

♠ 2
♥ QT73
♦ AT842
♣ KT4

BRIDGEBIT

For the purposes of displaying hands in this book, the hands are always arranged in descending order of the rank of suits: spades first; followed by hearts, diamonds, and clubs; in that order. Although this notation may take some getting used to, it's a common and fairly intuitive method for displaying card hands.

The second way to play the hand, and the way most rubber bridge players play, is for the declarer to actually play the card from the dummy. In this example, dummy just sits there and watches, while declarer does all the work.

No Trump: The Fifth Suit

You thought you had the whole suit thing figured out, didn't you? I sort of tricked you. You probably thought that the only suits you had to remember were spades, hearts, diamonds, and clubs. Well, it's not quite that simple.

Sometimes people who have what they think are balanced hands, meaning a hand without any singletons or voids, want to play a hand without any trump. When people first started playing this way, it took years before they could figure out what to call a hand without any trump. Finally, they took the problem to the top of a mountain and asked the bridge guru. Since then it has been called *no trump*. Was that genius or what?

The point is that you don't always have to play the hand with a trump suit. If you play it no trump, you get more points for your tricks than if you played it with a suit as trump. This fifth suit makes the rankings of the suits as follows, with the strongest on top:

> No trump
> Spades
> Hearts
> Diamonds
> Clubs

I've already told you that you can bid one heart over one club, but if one heart has already been bid, you can't bid one club over one heart. If you want clubs as trump in this scenario, you have to bid at least two clubs.

But what if you want to play the hand without anything being trump? Then you bid "one no trump." And you can bid one no trump over any suit bid at the one level. So if your opponents have bid one spade, you can still stay at the one level by bidding one no trump.

If you win the auction with a no trump bid, you play the hand without any suit being trump, kind of like you did when you learned about tricks and were just playing the cards to see how it went back in Chapter 2. When the contract is no trump, the highest card of the suit led wins the trick.

More Practice

Practice the bidding again: Deal some hands and bid them, allowing the dealer to bid first, then proceeding clockwise around the table. Bid, enter into the contract or let your opponents take the contract. Lay down dummy's hand, and play the cards.

If you can do this, you're playing bridge! The rest of the book will tell you how to improve. But as you read you should continue to play. Each time you read, try to play in addition to reading. Each time you play you will improve and learn. Playing is as important as reading.

This chapter has just set forth the basics of the game. If you're comfortable with the concepts of shuffling, dealing, bidding, and playing, you're ready to go on to the next chapter, which will teach you how to communicate with your partner through the bidding process. This communication helps you make informed decisions about what suit should be trump (if any), at what level you should be playing the contract, and whether you should let your opponents play the contract with you defending.

The Least You Need to Know

- Bidding is the act of predicting how many tricks you and your partner may win. The dealer is the first player to bid, and the bidding proceeds clockwise, each player in turn.
- The highest bid wins the contract and determines if there is a trump suit and which suit it will be.
- The first player of the partnership that wins the contract to bid the suit (or no trump) is declarer.
- Declarer's LHO makes the opening lead, after which declarer's partner places her hand face up on the table, becoming dummy for that hand only.
- Each player must follow suit if possible. If he can't, he can play a trump if he has one, or play a card from another suit.
- No trump is designated as the fifth suit and ranks above spades. When the contract is no trump, the highest card of the suit led wins the trick.

Making Game and Scoring

In This Chapter

- Scoring the game
- Calculating the value of major and minor suit tricks and trump tricks
- Adding points above and below the line
- Scoring when you're vulnerable
- Winning the rubber

The whole purpose of bridge is to win the game, which in bridge is often simply referred to as *making game*. *Game* is when one pair of players has made a certain number of scoring points. You get scoring points based on the number of tricks you take as declarer and whether you contracted to take that number of tricks or not.

Scoring per Trick

Scoring is heavily weighted toward accurately predicting how many tricks you'll *make*. If you take all the tricks available (13), you've made seven (book, plus seven). However, if you only contracted to make three, the four additional tricks you make are much less valuable than if you had contracted *to take* seven.

> **DEFINITION**
>
> **To make** means to make the contract, which means to win the game. **To take** refers to how many tricks you take.

The value of each trick varies depending on the contract. If you're playing in hearts or spades, the major suits, the tricks are more valuable than if you're playing in clubs or diamonds, the minor suits. If you're playing no trump, the first trick is more valuable than if you are playing in a major suit.

The following table lists the values of tricks in each suit.

Suit	Points
Spades and hearts	30 per trick
Clubs and diamonds	20 per trick
No trump	40 for first trick, 30 per trick thereafter

You've won the game when you've made at least 100 points below the line (explained in the "Scoring" section later in this chapter).

Making Game in a Major Suit

If you're playing with spades or hearts as trump, you must make four tricks over book to exceed 100 points (at 30 points per trick), so you have to take ten tricks. Remember: you don't get anything for the six tricks you take to make book; you start scoring after you've made book. Then, if you're playing in a major suit, you get 30 points per trick; so four tricks over book would be 120 points—enough to make game.

Making Game in a Minor Suit

If you're playing in a minor suit—clubs or diamonds—you must take an extra trick to reach 100 points. You must take five tricks over book (eleven tricks total) because minor suit tricks are only worth 20 points each, not the 30 you get if you're playing in a major suit.

Trump determines how much each trick is worth. If you're playing a contract of five diamonds, and you lead with a spade and everyone follows suit and you win the trick, you only get 20 points for that trick—even though it's a spade trick. When the contract is reached, if it's in clubs or diamonds, declarer only gets 20 points per trick, regardless of the suit led. If the contract is in a major suit—hearts or spades—each trick is worth 30 points, even if it's a minor-suit trick. You only get these points for each trick over book.

Making Game in No Trump

If you're playing in no trump, you only need to take three tricks over book—a total of nine tricks—to reach 100 points. Why? Because the first trick you take over book in no trump is worth 40 points, then each succeeding trick is worth 30. So if you make three no-trump tricks, you get 40 points for the first trick over book and 30 for each of the other two, for a total of 100. This is one of the advantages of playing in no trump: you need one less trick to make game.

Scoring

You get different types of points: points *above the line* and points *below the line*. What's the line? The *line* is what separates above the line from below the line. A rubber-bridge score sheet looks like this:

You write the score for the tricks you contracted to take below the line and the score for the tricks you took over and above what you contracted for above the line. Only scores below the line are counted in determining whether or not you make game.

So if your contract is two spades and you make three spades, your score is 60 points below the line (for the two spades you contracted and made) and 30 points above the line for the trick you made over and above what you contracted. This extra trick is called an *overtrick*. The score below the line, if it's less than 100, is called a *partial*. You keep scoring until one pair has 100 total points below the line. It doesn't matter how many points you have above the line when determining game (those points are used to determine who is the overall winner at the end of the rubber, which we discuss later in this chapter).

After one pair has won a game, the scorer draws another line under all the points each pair scored below the line and begins scoring the new game below that line.

If you don't bid enough to make game on one hand (4 hearts or spades, 5 clubs or diamonds, or 3 no trump), you are said to have not "bid game." If you bid less than game but make your contract, you have a "partial." This is referred to as having points on. So if you bid two spades and make three spades, you get 60 points below the line and 30 points above the line. You are said to be 60 on. That means that in the next hand, you only have to get 40 points below the line to "make game," because 40 added to the 60 you already have equals 100. So if you already have 60 points below the line, the next time all you have to bid is 2 of a suit or 1 no trump to get to game. Your opponents, however, still have to get to 100 below the line before you do in order to make game. This often results in very competitive bidding that has little relationship with the quality of the hand.

Defensive Scoring

If you don't make your contract, your opponents get points instead of you; these points are added above the line. Generally, the defenders get 50 points above the line for each trick you fail to take under your contract. So if you bid four spades and only make two spades, the defenders get 100 points (50 points per trick). If declarer is *vulnerable* (see the following section), defenders get 100 points per trick for every trick you fail to make under your contract.

ALERT

If declarer was doubled (see Chapter 19 for details), the points received by the defenders are substantially increased if they defeat the contract. If the defenders don't defeat the contract, declarer's score is increased.

Scoring When You're Vulnerable

If you've won a game (you have more than 100 points below the line), you are said to be *vulnerable* for the rest of the rubber. This means that if you don't make your contract (referred to as *go set*) on any subsequent game in the rubber, your penalty is twice as severe.

However, if you go set when you're vulnerable, your penalty is doubled. So if your contract is two spades and you only make one spade, you're said to be *down* one and that penalty, instead of being 50 points, is doubled to 100. Again, those points go to your opponents above the line.

The Rubber

When one pair wins two games, that constitutes a *rubber*. Put another way, one pair must score 100 points below the line twice in order to win the rubber.

Winning the rubber entitles a pair to bonus points. If one pair wins a rubber without the other pair making a game, the winning pair gets 700 bonus points. If a pair wins a rubber after their opponents have made one game, the winning pair only gets 500 bonus points. Bonus points are posted above the line.

At the end of the rubber you add up all the points, above and below the line, and whichever pair has the most points is the overall winner. It's possible to win the rubber but not be the overall winner.

Rubber-Bridge Score Sheet

A rubber-bridge score sheet might look like this:

PLAYERS	YOU	PARTNER	YOUR RHO	YOUR LHO
FIRST RUBBER	870	870	250	250
SECOND RUBBER				
THIRD RUBBER				
TOTALS				

WE	THEY	WE	THEY	WE	THEY
⑪500					
⑦ 60	④ 20				
② 30	③ 50				
② 60	④ 80				
⑤ 40		⑥			
⑦ 60	⑧ 100	⑨			
⑩ 120					
870	250				

①

The following explanations refer to the numbers on the score sheet:

1. This is the *line* that separates above the line from below the line.

2. This means that you (or *we*) were in a major suit contract at the two level and made three. For that, you got 60 points below the line for the two tricks you bid and made, and 30 points above the line for the overtrick.

3. Apparently, you also bid a contract and went down one; that is represented by the 50 points your opponents have above the line.

4. Your opponents then bid four clubs or four diamonds and made five. They got 80 points below the line for the four that they bid and 20 points above the line for the overtrick they made.

5. On the next hand, you either bid and made one no trump for 40 points or two in a minor suit, which would also be 40. You didn't make an overtrick because you got nothing further above the line.

6. Because you made game, 100 points below the line (60 on the first hand plus 40 on the third hand), you drew a line under those hands and started another game

7. You then bid two of a major suit and made four. For this you got 60 points below the line for the two you bid and made, and 60 points above the line for the two overtricks.

8. Your opponents then made game—either bidding and making three no trump or five of a minor suit, because both of those contracts get the bidders 100 points. They didn't make an overtrick, so they got nothing above the line.

9. You then drew another line, like you did in number 6 above, and started another game. Remember, a rubber continues until one pair makes two games.

10. You bid game in a major suit—either four hearts or four spades—and made it exactly, so you got 120 points below the line for bidding and making your four. You didn't make an overtrick, so you got nothing further above the line.

11. Because you won two games in the rubber, you won the rubber; so you got a 500-point bonus. Had you won the rubber without your opponents making a game you would have received a 700-point bonus.

At the end of the rubber, add up your points. You and your partner were the overall winners because you had the most points. You move the points up to keep a running score of *each player* at the top. (Attributing scores to individual players is important only if you switch partners. In this case, each player in a pair gets the points. If you change partners, you do the same thing the next time you record the scores. If each person wants to play at least once with everyone else, you would play three rubbers, changing partners each time. At the end of the three rubbers, the person with the most points is the winner.) If you don't switch partners, when you're done playing as many rubbers as you wish, you simply add up the points each pair made and the pair with the most points is the winner.

Stop reading now and, using what you've learned in Chapters 1 through 3, play some hands before moving on to the next chapter.

The Least You Need to Know

- Your goal is to bid enough tricks to make game if possible.
- Game in a major suit is four hearts or four spades, for a total of ten tricks (book plus four).
- Game in a minor suit is five clubs or five diamonds—eleven tricks total (book plus five). Game in no trump is three no trump, or nine tricks total (book plus three).
- You get points below the line if you make the number of tricks you contracted. You get points above the line for the tricks you make over what you contracted. Only points below the line count toward game.
- You get points above the line when you are on defense for every trick your opponents fail to make under what they contracted.

Evaluating Your Hand

In This Chapter

- Sorting your cards
- Assigning value to every card in your hand using high-card points
- Counting distribution points and quick tricks
- Communicating with your partner through the bidding process

Now that you've started to communicate with your partner (Chapter 3) and you know how to score the game (Chapter 4), you need to know how to evaluate your hand so that you can tell your partner what you have. If one of you has the ace of spades, what does that mean to you? Does it mean anything more than that you might be able to take one spade trick?

You bet your sweet bippy it does. This is where bridge begins to get fun. In this chapter, you're going to find out how to determine if you have anything in your hand that you want to tell your partner.

Sorting Your Hand by Suit and Rank

When you pick up the cards that have been dealt to you, they're mixed, or shuffled, and in no particular order. The first thing you should do is arrange your hand by suit. Most people alternate the colors—red, black, red, black. This helps distinguish one suit from another and avoids confusing cards that look similar, such as the 2 of clubs and the 2 of spades.

Most players also arrange the cards by rank, with the highest card in a suit on the left, and then in descending order. Again, this is done mainly so you're less apt to play the wrong card. If you want to play the queen of clubs, for example, and you have the suit sorted as AQ943, you know exactly where the queen is. If you have them arranged randomly, however, you're more liable to pick out the wrong card and play it.

There's a disadvantage to sorting by suit and rank, however. A very astute player can watch you play and may be able to make judgments about how many cards you have in a suit and what their ranks are. I have seen players just pick up their cards, bid, and play them as they were dealt. For me, playing with a jumbled hand makes bridge confusing and inordinately difficult to play. I remember watching a guy who played like this; I asked him why. He replied that he did it so that no one could determine what was in his hand. The problem was that *he* was included in that group. I watched him make some mistakes, and I thought they were because he didn't arrange his cards. I strongly advise against randomly arranged hands and encourage you to always sort your hand immediately by suit and rank.

Counting High-Card Points (HCP)

After you've picked up your cards and sorted them, it's time to evaluate your hand. Are you going to bid or pass? What are you going to tell your partner about your hand?

In bridge each card in each suit has a *high-card point* value (HCP). These points have no bearing on scoring, but are used solely to evaluate your hand. The values, or points, are as follows:

Card	Points	Card	Points
Ace	4	Jack	1
King	3	Everything else (2–10)	0
Queen	2		

The 10, jack, queen, king, and ace are called *honors*. When someone asks you how many honors you have in a suit, you count each of these cards as one honor. For example, if you have AQT74 in a suit, you have three honors: the ace, the queen, and the 10.

BRIDGEBIT

Whenever I describe a hand in this book, I list the suits in order of rank. The first suit is always spades, the second suit is hearts, the third is diamonds, and the last suit is clubs. This is standard in the world of bridge.

Even though 10s and 9s aren't assigned numerical values, they are far better than lower-spot cards. For example, AQT98 is a better suit than AQ432. So 10s and 9s sprinkled around the hand are at least worth a plus value, if for no other reason than they may eventually take tricks ahead of lower-spot cards.

Let's take a little test. Count the HCP in the following hands. Cover up the answers that follow the hands.

	1.		2.		3.		4.
	♠ 742		♠ 743		♠ AKQ7		♠ T987
	♥ AK52		♥ J53		♥ KQJ		♥ 864
	♦ QJ9		♦ AJ52		♦ QJT		♦ 974
	♣ 432		♣ QT7		♣ KJ9		♣ T75

Hand 1: 10 points. Count 4 for the ace of hearts, 3 for the king of hearts, 2 for the queen of diamonds, and 1 for the jack of diamonds.

Hand 2: 8 points. Count 1 for the jack of hearts, 4 for the ace of diamonds, 1 for the jack of diamonds, and 2 for the queen of clubs. (Remember, 10s, although they are honors, are still worth 0 HCPs.)

Hand 3: 22 points (a powerful hand). A total of 9 for the ace, king, and queen of spades (4 plus 3 plus 2); 6 for the king, queen, and jack of hearts (3 plus 2 plus 1); 3 for the queen and jack of diamonds (2 plus 1); and 4 for the king and jack of clubs (3 plus 1).

Hand 4: 0 points.

Counting Distribution Points

Now you know how to count HCP. But hands can also have distribution points. Distribution points are determined two ways: either by adding points for length in suits (the more cards in a suit you have, the longer the suit), or by adding points for shortage in suits (the fewer cards in a suit you have, the shorter the suit). Since only experienced players use length points (even lots of experienced players don't use them), we are only going to talk about shortage points in this book. You add shortage points to your evaluation of your hand if you only have 2, 1, or 0 cards in a suit.

Shortage points are calculated as follows:

Number of Cards in Suit	Points	Number of Cards in Suit	Points
3 to 13	0	1 *(singleton)*	2
2 *(doubleton)*	1	0 *(void)*	3

DEFINITION

Bridge players use some special terminology when talking about shortage points. If you don't have any cards of a suit in a hand, you are said to have a **void** in that suit. If you have one card of a suit, you have a **singleton,** and if you have two cards of a suit, you have a **doubleton.**

If you open up a hand and see 13 cards in the same suit, after you bid it and play it, stop the game, take a picture, and save the hand. Thirteen cards of the same suit in one hand is rarer than hen's teeth.

Now, count the shortage points in the following hands.

1. ♠ A	**2.** ♠ 782	**3.** ♠ J97	**4.** ♠ T9873
♥ J9875	♥ AKQ	♥ void	♥ 853
♦ Q9432	♦ AKQ	♦ 98743	♦ 3
♣ 87	♣ 8642	♣ AKQJ9	♣ J987

Hand 1: 3 shortage points. Count 2 for the singleton spade (it doesn't matter that it's an ace), and 1 for the doubleton club.

Hand 2: 0 shortage points. This is called a 4-3-3-3 distribution.

Hand 3: 3 shortage points for the void in hearts.

Hand 4: 2 shortage points for the singleton diamond.

You give yourself distribution points because long and short suits have definite value as you play a hand. As you will learn when I discuss trump, if clubs is trump and you still have clubs in your hand as well as a singleton heart, and your opponents have the ace, king, and queen of hearts, you can trump two of their apparent winners, the king of hearts and the queen of hearts (their ace will take your queen of hearts, but after that you will be out of hearts and can play your trump). So your singleton has a value, even if it's only a deuce. Counting distribution points in this way gives you a way to evaluate the worth of the shortness as you communicate with your partner. That's the huge value of trump, to be able to take tricks you would otherwise lose, like an ace or a king, if you have no more cards in the suit, and it's why short suits are so important that they can be assigned points like you assign to high cards when evaluating your hand.

Combining HCP and Distribution Points

Combine the knowledge that you just gained and count the last four hands for both distribution and HCP.

Hand 1: 10 total points—7 HCP (4 for the ace of spades, 1 for the jack of hearts, and 2 for the queen of diamonds) and 3 distribution points.

Hand 2: 18 total points—18 HCP (2 ace, king, queen combinations) and 0 distribution points (because of its 4–3–3–3 distribution).

Hand 3: 14 total points—11 HCP (10 for the ace, king, queen, and jack of clubs and 1 for the jack of spades) and 3 distribution points for the heart void.

Hand 4: 3 total points—1 HCP (the jack of clubs) and 2 distribution points for the diamond singleton.

BRIDGEBIT

When reading bridge hands, it's common usage to list any card below honor rank as *x* when the actual rank of the card is unimportant to the discussion. Sometimes you will see a hand that looks like this: AKxxx—meaning a five-card suit headed by the ace and king with three cards under the rank of 10.

Relating HCP and Distribution Points to Goals

There are 40 high-card points (HCP) in each deck, distributed among the hands of the four players. When you bid, you're basically telling your partner how many of those points you have. She listens to your bid, looks at her hand, adds her points to yours, and tries to determine how many tricks the two of you can take. How does she do this? Over the years, the gods of bridge have realized that if a pair has a certain number of points, it will probably take a certain number of tricks.

The following table presents a generalized list showing how many total points—HCP and distribution—it takes to make game.

Contract Suit	Points Required
Hearts and spades	26 (HCP plus distribution points)
Clubs and diamonds	28 (HCP plus distribution points)
No trump	25 (HCP only)

Why the difference? Simple. You can make game in no trump by only taking nine total tricks, so you only need 25 of the total 40 HCP available. If you're playing with hearts or spades as trump, you need to take one additional trick over what you would need to take in no trump, so you need a more powerful hand. As you'll soon see, however, having this many points doesn't *guarantee* you can make game; it's just a very good indication.

If you're playing in a minor suit—diamonds or clubs—you need yet another trick to make game—five above book or eleven tricks total. This means that you need to take all the tricks but two; for this you need 28 points or more.

Quick Tricks

Another concept to consider when evaluating your hand is called *quick tricks*. A quick trick is a card or combination of cards that will probably win a trick. An ace is a quick trick. A king and a queen in the same suit comprise a single quick trick. Why? Because the ace can take only one of them. After the ace is played, the other—either the king or the queen, whichever wasn't played when the ace was played—will win the trick because it's the highest card left in the suit.

The following table shows a list of quick tricks. The card(s) listed are always in the same suit.

Card(s)	Quick Trick	Card(s)	Quick Tricks
Ace	1	AQ	1½
K (singleton)	0	AK	2
KQ	1	Kx	½

A general rule of thumb is to consider opening a hand if it contains three quick tricks, even though it might not meet the other requirements for opening (see Part 2 for details on requirements for opening).

Your Opening Bid

Your opening bid is the first communication you have with your partner. You want to communicate as much to her as you can when you state your bid. After you've arranged your cards and counted your points, you should know what your opening bid is going to be.

When you make an opening bid in a suit at the one level (like one heart) you may have as little as 13 HCP and meet suit-distribution requirements. (You'll learn about this rule in Chapter 7.) But what if you have more than 14 points? If you opened every hand with more than 13 points, one of a suit, your partner wouldn't know if you had 13 points or 25. Opening bidding has been refined so there are many bids you can make that describe the strength of your hand.

BRIDGEBIT

Charles Goren added distribution points in 1944, and became the primary advocate for what came to be known as the Goren system. In the Goren system, 13-point hands are optional, 14-point hands must be opened, and 11-point hands can be opened in third seat after dealer and dealer's LHO have passed (third seat is the third person to make a call; dealer is in first seat). Under this system, Goren determined that 26 points would produce game in a major suit, whereas 29 points were required for game in a minor suit.

The Least You Need to Know

- After receiving a bridge hand, sort the cards by suit and rank in descending order.
- High card points are assigned as follows: ace = 4, king = 3, queen = 2, jack = 1.
- Distribution points are assigned based on short suits as follows: void = 3, singleton = 2, doubleton = 1.
- Count high-card points (HCP) and distribution points. Adding HCP to distribution points gives you the bidding value of the hand.
- Requirements for game are generally 25 HCP in no trump, 26 points (HCP plus distribution points) in a major suit, and 28 points (HCP plus distribution points) in a minor suit.
- Consider opening a hand if it contains three quick tricks, even if the hand doesn't meet other criteria for opening.

Opening Bids

In bridge, you want to avoid the famous admonition to Cool Hand Luke, "What we have here is a failure to communicate!" Bridge is based on effective communication between partners. In this part, I show you how to evaluate your hand for the purposes of making an opening bid. Then I walk you through the many different types of bids that you can make to describe your hand to your partner. I also show you how to determine whether you or your partner is the captain of your pair. The strategies you discover in this part will not only help you communicate what you have to your partner, but will also enable you to interfere with your opponents' ability to communicate with one another.

Surrendering Command: Opening No Trump Bids

In This Chapter

- Requirements for game in no trump
- Stoppers
- Point count and distribution requirements for two–no trump and three–no trump openings

Now that you know how to count your hand, you need to be able to communicate this to your partner in a way that enables her to determine what the two of you can accomplish. You do this through your opening bid.

Your opening bid is the first communication you have with your partner. You want to communicate as much to her as you can when you state your bid. After you have arranged your cards and counted your points, you should know what your opening bid is going to be.

In this chapter, you're going to find out how to tell your partner what you have in your hand. She can convert what you tell her into a mathematical formula that enables her to make a fairly accurate estimate of the number of tricks you can take.

You're also going to start getting your feet wet by bidding a hand that is a very good hand, indeed—a no trump opening. When you finish this chapter, you'll be well on your way to being a bridge player.

Opening One No Trump

If you have a fairly balanced hand—no voids or singletons—and more than 14 points, you want to communicate this to your partner in your first bid. With a hand containing 15 to 17 HCP, no singletons or voids, and no more than two doubletons, you can open one no trump. This says, "Partner, I have 15 to 17 HCP in my hand, no singletons or voids, and no more than two doubletons."

ALERT

Although the modern trend is for an opening of one no trump to promise a no-trump range of 15 to 17 HCP, many rubber bridge players assume it indicates 16 to 18 HCP. Discuss this with your partner before you play to make sure you're on the same wavelength.

This is enormously helpful information to your partner because it limits your hand. You have at least 37 percent of the total HCP available; in addition, you have at least two cards in each suit! Further, you have limited your hand by telling your partner that you have less than 42 percent of the total HCP available. So she knows you have 37 to 42 percent of the total HCP available. And you've told her all this in just one bid!

Because she knows that you need 25 to 26 points to make game, if she has just 10 points in her hand, she knows that you should probably bid game (so that you bid and make either 3 no trump, 4 spades or hearts, or 5 clubs or diamonds) in some denomination.

When you open one no trump, you designate your partner as the captain of the team for the hand. Why? Because she knows an incredible amount about your hand, whereas you know virtually nothing about hers. She may want to determine if the two of you have enough cards in any suit to qualify it as trump. On many hands she will merely choose to play the hand in no trump. You can just sit back, answer her questions, and let her place the contract for the partnership.

When you open one no trump, you are giving your partner a specific description of how many HCP you have in your hand. You have between 15 to 17 HCP—no more, no less. If you open a 14- or 18-point hand one no trump, you are giving misinformation to your partner—and that's a cardinal sin in bridge.

The Distribution

An opening of one no trump not only describes the HCP in your hand, but it also promises your partner that you have a very specific distribution in your hand. It promises, basically, that you have at least two cards in each suit. You shouldn't open one no trump if you have a void in a suit, a singleton in a suit, or more than two doubletons.

If you have 15 to 17 HCP, but have a hand with a singleton or void, then you should find another bid to make other than one no trump. We'll discuss this situation in Chapter 7.

A "perfect" no trump–distribution is a hand that contains four cards in one suit and three cards in every other suit; in other words, a 4–3–3–3 distribution. You don't have to have a 4–3–3–3 distribution to open one no trump, however. You may open one no trump with any 15- to 17-point hand without voids, singletons, or more than two doubletons, with one or two exceptions. This means that you can have a hand with 5–4–2–2 distribution and open it one no trump.

Opening a bid with one no trump communicates the strength of your hand to your partner in one bid. However, just because you open one no trump doesn't mean that you're going to end up playing in no trump! Remember that when you open one no trump, you designate your partner as the captain of the hand. It's up to her to determine whether it's better to play the hand in no trump or a suit, or to defend if your opponents enter the bidding.

Stoppers

A *stopper* is a card or distribution of cards that enables you to take a trick in the suit. An ace is a definite stopper. A king and a queen comprise a stopper because, even though the opponents may lead an ace, it will only take the queen, and you'll still have the king to take a trick. Kx and Qxx are full stoppers, also called guaranteed stoppers, in spite of what might happen. Partial stoppers are Jxx or Qx. (Remember that x stands for any card of the same suit below the rank of 10.)

A king and one card in a suit or a queen and two cards in a suit is a guaranteed stopper only if your LHO leads the suit. Nonetheless, Kx and Qxx are considered full stoppers for bidding purposes.

Let's explore what happens if you have Kx. If your RHO gets the lead and he leads that suit, and your LHO has the ace and the queen, your king will be dead as a doornail. Why? Well, what are you going to play when your RHO leads the suit in which you have Kx? If you play the king, your LHO will play the ace and then you won't have a stopper. If you play low, your LHO will play the queen and then the ace will take your king. Have you figured out why the king is a stopper only if your LHO leads the suit? If the LHO leads the suit, he's leading into your hand, because your hand will be the last one to play to the trick. So if the LHO leads—no matter what he leads, and no matter what your RHO plays on the trick—your king will be a definite winner at some point. If the RHO plays the ace, your king is the high card out. If the RHO *ducks*, you can win the trick with the king. You'll be in trouble if they get the lead again and attack the suit, because your stopper will be gone. But that's why bridge is such a challenge.

DEFINITION

To **duck** means to refuse to win a trick or to refuse to play a higher card when you have the capability to play low. Ducking is covered in detail in Chapters 19 through 22, on play of the hand.

The same is true of a queen and two in a suit. Your opponents, if the ace and the king are in alternate hands, can lead through your queen and you can lose it. How? Well, let's say your LHO has the lead and he leads low. Your RHO has the ace and plays it and returns the same suit, through your queen. If you play the queen, your LHO will take it with his king. If you play low, your LHO may take it with a lower card, then lead the king and your queen will fall. But it's still considered a full stopper.

The term *partial stopper* is defined in bridge language as Qx or Jxx or T9xx (rare). Think in terms of the lead coming from declarer's left: Kx is a stopper; Qx or Jxx requires help from your partner. (True that the lead may be a different suit to RHO's ace, then back through our Kx, but this isn't a consideration when determining stoppers for no trump purposes.)

The Kx is a better stopper than the Qxx, because the Kx is a definite stopper if your LHO is on lead and leads the suit. Then no matter what your RHO does, your king will take a trick. However, with the Qxx—even if your LHO is on lead—you can be left without a stopper if your opponents defend correctly.

Exceptions to Opening One No Trump with 15 to 17 HCP

There are two basic exceptions where you should consider not opening a balanced 15- to 17-HCP hand one no trump:

- **If you have two suits without stoppers.** Especially if you're opening a hand with two doubletons, you should have stoppers in the two doubletons. But that rule only applies to the rare hand that allows you to open a hand with two doubletons with a one–no trump bid. Sometimes you'll have to open a hand one no trump with one suit that is an *unstopped doubleton*. Finally, you may open a hand with one unstopped doubleton with a one–no trump bid if the hand only has one doubleton. The rule of having doubletons stopped only applies to the hand with two doubletons.

- **If you're 5–4 or 4–5 in the majors.** If you have five cards in one major and four cards in the other, it's better to open the bidding by bidding your five-card major. If your partner doesn't support you, you can then rebid your four-card major. More on opening in your major suits in Chapter 7.

 DEFINITION

An **unstopped doubleton** is when you have only two cards in a suit and you have no opportunity to take a trick with those cards; examples of unstopped doubletons are the 5 and the 3 of a suit, or the 10 and the 8 of a suit.

Opening Two No Trump

You aren't limited to opening the bidding at the one level. You can open a hand at any level you like. But each opening transmits specific information to your partner. If opening one no trump shows a balanced hand with 15 to 17 points, what would a two–no trump open show?

It doesn't show the next level up—18 to 20—which is what you probably thought. (Another series of bids describes hands that have 18 to 19 points.) When you open two no trump you're telling your partner that your distribution is the same as if you opened one no trump, no voids or singletons, and no more than two doubletons; but your HCP are much higher. A two–no trump opening tells your partner that you have 20 to 21 HCP. Following are some typical two–no trump openings.

1.	♠ AKQ	2.	♠ JT9	3.	♠ 83	4.	♠ QJT72
	♥ KJ95		♥ KQ2		♥ Q64		♥ AQ
	♦ A75		♦ KQ5		♦ AKJT		♦ KJ
	♣ K84		♣ AKQ3		♣ AKQJ		♣ AQJ6

The first two hands are no-brainers. You have 20 HCP and perfect 4–3–3–3 no-trump distribution. The third hand gives pause because you have a doubleton—spades—unstopped. But you have 20 HCP, all but 2 in the minors. By opening two no trump, you describe your strength to your partner, and you take away your opponents' bidding room and limit their flexibility to see if they have a major suit fit.

In the fourth hand, you have a five-card major (spades); some players don't like to open no trump with a five-card major. But the problem with not opening this hand two no trump is that you mislead your partner in your opening bid, by either initially describing a hand that is weaker than you have, or one that is stronger. This five-card major is far too weak to even think about opening anything other than two no trump. If the spades were AKQJx instead of QJTxx, then you should probably open 1 spade. But with a weak five-card major, 20 points, no voids or singletons, and no more than two doubletons, you should open two no trump.

Opening Three No Trump

By now you've probably gotten the drift of this. Logic would say that a three no trump open would be 22 to 24 HCP. Wrong! There's another bid for that hand, regardless of its distribution. It's called a strong two-bid, and I cover it in Chapter 8.

If you have 25 to 26 points and no voids or singletons, and no more than two doubletons and stoppers in all suits, you can open three no trump. This tells your partner that you really don't need her, you have everything you need to make game in your own hand. It invites her to explore for *slam* or place the contract in a major suit if she has a long one. The hand is the same as the two no trump open, except it has more HCP.

DEFINITION

A **slam** is when you bid and make six or seven. Which means that you bid and take all tricks but one, in the case of a six bid (a **small slam**), and you bid and take all the tricks in the case of a seven bid (a **grand slam**). That's the best thing that can happen offensively in bridge. For details on slam, see Chapter 16.

Now deal out some hands, then bid and play them using what you've learned in Chapters 1 through 6.

The Least You Need to Know

- An opening bid of one no trump describes a hand of *exactly* 15 to 17 HCP (or 16 to 18 HCP if you are playing that system) with no singletons, no voids, and no more than two doubletons.
- An opening bid of two no trump describes a hand of *exactly* 20 to 21 HCP with the same distribution as a one–no trump opening.
- An opening bid of three no trump describes a hand of *exactly* 25 to 26 HCP with the same distribution as a one–no trump opening.
- You must be disciplined about communicating with your partner.

Clothed in Information: Opening One of a Suit

In This Chapter

- HCP requirements to open one of a suit and counting shortness
- The five-card major rule and how to determine which suit to open
- Opening in first and second position versus third and fourth position
- Evaluating hands with unusual distribution
- Ruffing

In Chapter 6 you found out how to open a very good hand, one with between 37 percent and 42 percent of the HCP in it. But what if you don't have that type of hand? If you have a weaker hand, you might be able to open one of a suit. In this chapter, I give you the guidelines for opening one of a suit.

I also talk about the importance of where you're sitting in relationship to the dealer. The evaluation of the strength of your hand changes depending on whether you're the first or second player to make a call, or the third or fourth. (A *call* is any bid, double, redouble, or pass made by a player. You will learn about doubles and redoubles in Chapter 19.)

Ah, the wonders of bridge, it's so varied.

Point Requirements for Suit Bids

To open one of a suit, you want to meet specific point-count and suit-length requirements. You should have a minimum of 13 points, combining HCP and distribution points, to open one of a suit. Generally speaking, an opening of one of a suit indicates a hand of 13 to 21 points. There are exceptions to this rule, however, depending on distribution.

> **TRICKS OF THE TRADE**
>
> You can open one of a suit with a hand that's too strong or too distributional to open one no trump. For example, if you have 15 to 17 HCP that includes a singleton or void, you can't open one no trump, but you must open it.

For instance, many experts suggest that you add or deduct a point to your hand evaluation if you have all aces or no aces in your hand, respectively. You deduct a point if you have no aces and you add a point if you have all four aces. So it would be unwise to open in the following hand:

♠ J64
♥ J84
♦ KQ7
♣ KQJ3

This hand has 13 HCP; but if you deduct a point for no aces you're down to 12 HCP. That's not attractive enough to take a chance. Subtracting a point for no aces should be limited to hands with 4–3–3–3 distribution. So passing the preceding hand above is correct. But the following hand should be opened one diamond because, although it doesn't have any aces, the doubleton limits your potential loss in hearts to two tricks; or, to put it another way, you will lose one less trick in hearts with this hand than with the preceding hand:

♠ JT4
♥ J8
♦ KQT7
♣ KQJ3

Suit-Length Requirements for Suit Bids

You should have at least five cards in the suit if it is a major (hearts or spades). (The older style was to open any suit if it had four cards, but I'm teaching you the newer, *five-card major* style of bidding.) This means, for example, that if you have 13 points, but you don't have a five-card major, then you should open a minor suit (clubs or diamonds), even though you may not have any honors in that suit, and you may only have three cards in the suit.

If you open a hand one spade with fewer than five spades in your hand, it will mislead your partner, and her reply could mislead you. You'll be progressing rapidly down the road to ruin on this hand. So when you agree to play a system, like the five-card major system I'm teaching here, stick with it and don't deviate. In other words, if you agree that your opening bid of one spade promises at least five spades, don't later decide that, for one hand, you can open one spade with only four spades. You must exert discipline in your bidding.

BRIDGEBIT

There are innumerable bidding systems. The *Official Encyclopedia of Bridge* lists 54 different systems. In this book, you are learning the Standard American system, the most widely used system in America. If you sit down at a table, despite what system your opponents are using, it would be unusual if they hadn't learned Standard American first. Regardless of what system your opponents are using, you and your partner must use the same system in order to communicate.

Opening

What if I have 13 points but no five-card major, you ask? Good question. If you have a five-card minor (clubs or diamonds), open that. But often you have one or both four-card majors and no five-card minor. What then? The good news is that you can open a minor with four or even three cards in length. For starters, here are the basic guidelines for opening one of a suit:

- You must have at least 13 points.

- An opening bid in a major suit (hearts or spades) promises at least five cards in the suit.

- If you have 13 points but no five-card major, open your longest minor.

- If both minors are four cards in length, open one diamond.

- If both minors are three cards in length, open one club.

That's it for opening 1 bids. Following are some hands. Determine whether or not you would open each and, if so, what your opening bid would be.

1. ♠ AK982	2. ♠ 763	3. ♠ JT42	4. ♠ 976
♥ QT54	♥ AK75	♥ AK642	♥ AKQJ
♦ K5	♦ 74	♦ 87	♦ A62
♣ J3	♣ 8754	♣ 64	♣ 632

Hand 1: A clear one-spade open. You have 13 HCP and a good five-card spade suit.

Hand 2: Pass; not enough points.

Hand 3: Pass. Even though you have a nice five-card heart suit, you only have 8 HCP—10 total points with distribution—and that's not enough to open. If you open this hand you're telling your partner you have at least 13 points, and even though your heart suit is very attractive, you would be lying to your partner.

Hand 4: Open one club. Sure, your hearts are terrific, but there are only four of them. If you open one heart, you're telling your partner you have at least five hearts, and you don't. Whatever you do, you don't want to lie to your partner, because she's relying on you for accurate information in evaluating her hand and making her bid. (Opening one club doesn't necessarily guide the partnership toward a final club contract. You may easily end up in hearts, your best suit, or even no trump. Subsequent bidding will determine this.)

Determining Which Suit to Open

Okay, so far it has been pretty easy. The sample hands have had fairly obvious answers. Alas, bridge isn't always that cooperative. Generally, your hands are what I call *thinkers*, because they contain elements that vary from the rules. So let's start with some thinkers now. What do you do if you have two five-card majors? Which suit do you open? Look at these hands:

1. ♠ AK964	2. ♠ JT865	3. ♠ 98642	4. ♠ 98632
♥ AK865	♥ AKQ53	♥ AJT76	♥ QT852
♦ 76	♦ 3	♦ AK	♦ A
♣ 7	♣ 96	♣ 4	♣ AK

How would you open each? I know that you don't know any of the rules yet, but just use your common sense and write down how you'd open each.

Now for the answers.

The answer to all four hands is one spade. When you have two five-card suits in a hand, major or minor, you always open the higher-ranking suit. This is true when both five-card suits are majors. So if you have five hearts and five spades, you open one spade, even if the hearts suit is much, much stronger than the spades suit.

The reason behind this is a little complicated. Let's assume the bidding goes as follows:

You	LHO	Partner	RHO
One spade	Two clubs	Pass	Pass
Two hearts	Pass		

By first bidding one spade and then following up with a two-hearts bid, you're telling your partner that you have at least five spades and at least four hearts. If your partner likes spades more than hearts, she can still remain at the two level by bidding two spades.

Think about what would happen if you had hand 2, 3, or 4 and opened hearts first. The bidding would have gone as follows.

You	LHO	Partner	RHO
One heart	Two clubs	Pass	Pass
Two spades	Pass		

Now, what if your partner is void in spades, but has three little hearts and only 4 points? Obviously you should be playing in hearts, but she has to go to the three level with her terrible hand. What to do? She's in a quandary.

> **TRICKS OF THE TRADE**
>
> Keep in mind that at all times during an auction each partner is called on to make decisions. When your partner shows two suits, she is asking you to choose which of her suits you prefer. Even though the choice isn't always pleasant, you must make a choice.

If you open one spade—even though your spades are much weaker than your hearts—and then rebid two hearts, she could pass, showing her preference to play in hearts, and you're at a much safer and lower two level instead of a three level. If her holding is reversed, and she has three spades and a heart void, she could just simply bid two spades over your two hearts, telling you, "Partner, my hand stinks, but I'd rather you play this in spades than hearts."

Regardless of how strong your hearts are, you're better off playing in a suit in which you and your partner have eight cards between you than a suit in which you only have five or six cards between you.

Opening Your Longest Suit

When opening, you should open your longest suit, regardless of its high-card strength. If you have a six-card minor and a five-card major, open the minor. Look at the following hands:

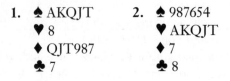

1. ♠ AKQJT
   ♥ 8
   ♦ QJT987
   ♣ 7

2. ♠ 987654
   ♥ AKQJT
   ♦ 7
   ♣ 8

Hand 1: One diamond. Your spades are nice and you should be able to show them at a subsequent bid, but you have to tell your partner that your diamonds are longer. If you open one spade and then rebid diamonds, you're telling your partner that your spades are longer than your diamonds or that they are of equal five-card length.

Hand 2: One spade. Again, even though your hearts have a lot of high-card strength, your spades are longer. If your partner has two hearts and two spades, your spades are your stronger suit and should be the trump suit. Note that even though this hand only has 10 HCP, it has 14 total points given the two distribution points for each of the two singletons (assuming a trump fit with partner), so it's a hand that must be opened.

Opening in Third Position

When you're in the first or the second bidding seat, your evaluation of your hand is different from when you're in the third or fourth seat. In the first and second seats, you haven't heard from your partner yet. In the *first seat* you haven't heard from anyone. You will be the first to describe your hand to everyone else.

DEFINITION

First seat, also referred to as **first position,** means the first player to make a call. The dealer is always in first seat; dealer's LHO is in second seat; dealer's partner is in third seat; dealer's RHO is in fourth seat.

When you're in second seat, although you haven't heard from your partner, you have heard from your RHO. If your RHO has passed, you know that he probably has fewer than 13 points. This tells you something, but not too much, about what everyone else is holding.

However, when you're in second seat and your RHO has opened the bidding, you not only know something about his hand, you know a lot about the hands of everyone else. From the RHO's bid, you know the placement of a substantial number of the cards in the deck.

If your RHO has opened one of a suit, or one no trump, you know approximately how many HCP are in his hand. Let's say he opens one no trump, and that you have 12 points in your hand. You know you and your RHO hold between 27 and 29 of the total of 40 points in the hand. That means that your partner and your LHO have a total of 11 to 13 points between them.

Easing the Requirements in Third Seat

When you're in third seat, and your partner and your RHO have passed, you can ease the stringent requirements to open your hand. Why? Because you know that neither your partner nor your RHO have an opening hand. So if you have a minimum opening hand, you and your partner probably don't have game. Because her maximum holding should be 12 points and if you have 12 points, you may have a maximum total of 24 points between the two of you ; not enough for game. If you don't bid, you will be abandoning an opportunity to tell your partner something about your hand with very little risk involved.

There is a further advantage to bidding in third seat with a less-than-opening hand. It's the only chance you will have to give your partner a suggestion of an opening lead in case you are the defending pair. What if you're sitting there with the AKJxxx of clubs, and not much else? If you open one club and your LHO does have a powerhouse and ends up playing a contract, your partner will know that you want her to lead a club. If you don't make your third seat opening bid, she'll be in the dark about your hand.

Of course, you're guessing whether your partner had a hand close to opening, like 10 to 12 points, or a *Yarborough*. You are also in the dark about your RHO's hand. Does he have 12 points, or 0? This lack of knowledge about two hands at the table leaves you in the dark about your LHO's hand.

If both your partner and your RHO have very weak hands and you have a minimum opening, your LHO could be sitting there with a powerhouse. So if you want to get in a bid, now is the time to do it. Maybe you have a good spades suit and little else, maybe 10 points. What to do? Answer: make a tactical *light opening* in the third seat.

> **DEFINITION**
>
> A **Yarborough** is a balanced hand containing no points; in other words, it's a disaster. It was named after an English lord who would give odds of 1,000 to 1 against someone coming up with such a hand, which was defined as a 4-3-3-3 hand with no card higher than a 9. The actual odds are 1,827 to 1, so, as with most bookies, he had a nice edge.
>
> A **light opening** is one that has less than the standard requirements of an opening hand of at least 13 points.

Rules for a Light Third-Seat Open

If you're opening in third seat, you should have the following, at a minimum:

- At least 10 points
- A good suit, headed by ace-king or king-queen-jack, for lead-directing purposes. (*Lead-directing* means you are making a bid to tell your partner what to lead if your LHO [her RHO] gets the contract. If you have AKxxx in a suit, you obviously want her to lead it. If, on the other hand, you have JTxxx, you don't want her to lead that suit.)

Look at the following hands and determine an opening bid when you're in third seat and the first two players have passed:

1.	♠ 975	2. ♠ QJ2
	♥ 873	♥ QJ3
	♦ 7	♦ 6
	♣ AKJT75	♣ QJ6432

Hand 1: One club. You have 10 points (8 HCP points and 2 distribution points for the singleton), but a terrific club suit. If your LHO gets the bid, you definitely want your partner to lead a club. This is your only chance to tell her. If you get the contract in one club, you won't be hurt too much. If your partner raises clubs, or bids either of the majors, you have minimal support. If she bids diamonds, you can rebid your club suit.

Hand 2: Pass. This hand contains 11 points (9 HCP points and 2 distribution points for the singleton), but has no lead-directing values. If your LHO gets the contract, do you want your partner to lead a club? If your LHO bids a major and your partner bids two diamonds, what are you going to do? You certainly don't want to be playing this in three clubs if your partner doesn't have support for you.

Your partner should be aware that you might be opening light in third seat, so she shouldn't jump to optimistic conclusions if she's holding a hand with slightly less than opening values. If you open and she has 12 points, she should proceed with caution, knowing that you might be opening a 10-point hand for lead-directing purposes.

Opening in Fourth Position

Things change again when you're sitting in fourth position. If all three players pass the bid around to you, you know that nobody has an opening hand. You may also assume that your RHO isn't very close to an opening hand because he could have opened light in the third seat.

But when the bid is passed around to fourth seat, and you're sitting with a little less than an opening hand, the odds are against you opening, because your two opponents probably have 9 to 11 points in each of their hands. Your partner might be sitting there with 5 or 6 points.

You need a full opening hand in fourth seat to open. If you don't have a full opening hand, it is wiser to pass and deal again. The danger of opening a marginal hand in fourth seat is that you might give your opponents the opportunity to get a plus score when they're ready to pass the hand out. You don't have game. What's the point of bidding in the hope that you have a fit with your partner or your partner is sitting there with points to help you out?

The situation is completely different from what you faced in third seat. There, you don't know what your opponent in the fourth seat has in his hand. He could have a powerhouse. That could be your only chance to bid a suit that is headed by the ace–king.

In fourth seat, however, you have no worry about someone bidding behind you with a powerhouse, leaving you without a bid. If you pass, the hand will be passed out, meaning that all four players have passed, so the cards are reshuffled and a new hand dealt. In rubber bridge that can never really hurt you, whereas bidding on a marginal hand and allowing your opponents to find a partial will definitely hurt you.

Opening Hands with Unusual Distribution

One of the wonders of bridge is that you can set forth all these rules, but you will constantly get hands that tax your ingenuity in applying the rules. In fact, you will rarely get a hand that will not cause you to think, and that's why bridge is so challenging and so much fun.

What we've said so far is pretty straightforward, and the hands we've given you as examples comply with the rules we've given you. But there are literally billions of combinations of cards that you can get in a bridge hand.

So how would you open the following hands, applying the rules you just learned?

	1.		2.		3.		4.	
	♠ KQJT76		♠ 97654		♠ 6		♠ 754	
	♥ 6		♥ QT985		♥ 8		♥ void	
	♦ KQT5		♦ A		♦ KQJ865		♦ QJT32	
	♣ 64		♣ A7		♣ KQT42		♣ AQJT7	

Clearly, these hands don't follow the norm; even without much help from your partner, you'll make book and then some if you play these hands.

Hand 3 only has 11 HCP, but conceivably you could lose only four tricks and make three with your partner sitting there with a Yarborough. If things are right—and they don't need to be unusually right—you lose all four aces and that's it. If you get a favorable lead, like the ace of clubs, you might make more. And if your partner has something, you might make game. Obviously, you must open this hand.

All these hands have potential, but they illustrate the value of distributional hands, which are hands that contain at least one long suit (six cards or more), or two five card suits, and a singleton or void. You'd feel very uncomfortable passing any of them, even if you're in first seat, despite their minimal HCP holdings.

Hand 1: One spade. You have 11 HCP, a singleton, and a doubleton; that's 14 points.

Hand 2: One spade. You have 10 HCP, a singleton, and a doubleton for 13 points, a minimal opening hand.

Hand 3: One diamond. You have 11 HCP and two singletons, still enough to open one diamond with 15 total points.

Hand 4: You have 10 HCP and a void; that's 13 points. But let's take a look at this hand and see what happens if you open a two-suited hand (a hand with two suits of at least five cards in length) when the suits are relatively weak.

Let's say you have Hand 4 and you open one diamond, which this hand calls for (the higher ranking of two five-card suits, remember?). What's your partner going to bid? Because the gods of bridge can sometimes be terribly cruel, often when you have a hand like this and you open, your partner bids your void. So she bids one heart. What now? Well, you mention your other five-card suit, and bid two clubs.

What does she do? Because of the perversity of the gods of bridge, she will often repeat her hearts, showing six hearts. Now your hand is extremely diminished in value. Not only is your void in hearts not going to give you any *ruffing* power if hearts is trump, but you don't have anywhere to go. She might be six hearts, four spades, and two and one in your suits. And you certainly don't want to play at the three level in a 5–1 fit. You're left having to pass her out at 2 hearts with your void. Therefore, Hand 4 is a hand you may choose to pass, even though you have 13 total points.

> **DEFINITION**
>
> **Ruff** is another word for trump used as a verb. To trump or ruff simply means that you have taken a nontrump trick by playing a trump, which you can't do unless you're void in the suit led.

If clubs or diamonds is trump in Hand 4, you can ruff, or trump, any heart that is led. Theoretically you can't lose a heart trick. But if your partner's suit is hearts, your ruffing power is diminished because she probably won't have a lot of heart losers.

Opening a 15- to 17-HCP Hand with a Five-Card Major

Many players don't like to open a hand in no trump with a five-card major. Some limit this to not opening no trump with a *good* five-card major. How you open a hand and who plays the hand can have a major determination on your result.

For the purposes of your learning, you should adopt a consistent rule to play with your partner. If you have a 15- to 17-HCP balanced hand with a five-card major:

- Open in one of your five-card major if you have an unstopped doubleton.

- Open one no trump if you have all the suits stopped.

Look at the following hands:

	1.	♠ KQJ85	2.	♠ QJT85
		♥ AQ3		♥ AT3
		♦ K73		♦ KQ3
		♣ 75		♣ K5

Hand 1: One spade. You have a good five-card spade suit and you have an unstopped doubleton club.

Hand 2: One no trump. Your spade suit isn't that great and you have all the suits stopped.

ALERT

Play with consistency. If you choose to open all hands with a five-card major with one of the major, that's fine, but then you should always open a hand with five-card majors the same way. One of the worst things you can do is be inconsistent. As long as your partner knows what she can count on when you bid, you should be okay.

If you open up a 15 to 17 HCP hand with your five-card major and your partner doesn't have support, your partnership will conceivably end up playing the contract in no trump. However, your partner could easily be the one to bid the no trump, so the strong hand will be displayed as dummy whereas the weak hand will be playing it. This isn't a disaster, but it's better to have the strong hand concealed.

Alternatively, if you open up one no trump, and your partner has a weak hand but three in your major, you're not going to find your eight-card major suit fit; so you'll be playing the hand in the wrong contract. This is the beauty of bridge. Sometimes what you do is correct. Another time with the same hand it might be incorrect.

Now, stop reading: deal, bid, and play some hands, using what you have learned in Chapters 1 through 7.

The Least You Need to Know

- Opening suit bids at the one level contain at least 13 total points.
- Open the longest suit if two suits are at least five cards in length. Open the higher-ranking suit if both are five or six cards in length.
- Open a major suit only if it contains at least five cards.
- With no five-card major, open the longer minor. If both minors are equal in length, open one diamond if both minors have four cards, open one club if both minors have three cards.
- Count HCP and distribution points to determine whether you should open a hand, deduct a point if a hand contains no aces and has a 4–3–3–3 shape.

Thou Shalt Not Pass: Strong Two Opening Bids

In This Chapter

- Opening a hand of more than 22 points
- Responding when your partner opens a strong two
- Rebidding when you open a strong two

In previous chapters, I showed you how to open hands that contain 15 to 17 HCP, 20 to 21 HCP, and hands that contain at least 13 points but fewer than 22 points. So as Peggy Lee once asked, "Is that all there is?"

No, Peggy, there's more. Sometimes you get hands that contain more than 21 points. Statistically, you'll get a hand with more than 21 points about every 200 hands that you play. The game is going to grab you, and you'll play hundreds, if not thousands, of hands a year, so you're going to get hands like these occasionally, and you have to know how to handle them.

There are two basic ways to handle big hands. The first is to open all strong hands that fit the criteria at the two level. The other is to open all strong hands that fit the criteria by opening 2 clubs.

In this chapter, I teach you the strong two-bid system for showing big hands. Most rubber bridge players play strong twos. (Check out the online Chapter 24 to find out how to use the weak two-bid system). This chapter will describe what kind of hand you need to open a strong two.

Definition of a Strong Two

A strong two is a hand that is of one of two types. It is either one of the following:

- A hand containing at least 22 points.

- A hand that guarantees 8½ tricks if trump is a major suit or 9½ tricks if trump is a minor suit. Put another way, if you have a hand with which you know you can make at least one trick less than game with no help from your partner, you should open it with a strong two-bid, regardless of the number of points you hold.

When you open a strong two-bid, your partner is required to keep bidding until one of you bids game, unless you rebid your opening suit. In that case, your partner may pass. This prevents your partner from passing the hand out short of game, thereby emasculating your big, 1-in-200 hand by playing it in a partscore.

To open a hand with a strong two-bid doesn't require any special jargon. You just bid "two Spades," for instance, if nobody else has opened the bidding before your turn to make a call. That's all you need to say.

Hands Containing 22 Points with a Five-Card Suit

If you open a strong two in diamonds, hearts, or spades, you're guaranteeing that your suit contains at least five cards, and that your hand contains at least 22 points. Look at the following hand:

♠ AKQJT9
♥ AKQJ
♦ A8
♣ 7

This 27-point monster is a typical strong two-spades opening hand.

You might be looking at this hand, remembering what you've learned, and asking yourself, "This hand is *cold* for four spades. Why not just open four spades? Why open at a lower level?"

If you asked yourself this question, I like the way you're thinking. But there are reasons why you don't just open four spades with this hand. One is that an opening of four spades shows a different hand (see Chapter 9 for details).

DEFINITION

Cold is a slang term meaning an easily makeable contract.

Another reason is something we've hinted at before—the possibility of slam. Sure, four spades is cold. But you might be able to make more. If your partner has the ace of clubs or the king of diamonds, six spades is cold. If she has both, seven spades is cold. So why bid four spades, a bid that your partner can pass? The opening bid of two spades basically tells your partner, "Look, pard, I can make four spades pretty easily with only a little help from you. I want you to tell me about your hand to see if we can make slam."

Another reason is that you don't want to constrain your ability to communicate with your partner by getting the bidding too high when you might be able to make slam with a little communication between you.

A more typical two-level opening would be the following hand:

♠ AKQ42
♥ AKQ
♦ AQ63
♣ 8

That's a 26-point hand (24 HCP points and 2 points for the singleton), but if your partner has a Yarborough and is short in spades, you only have seven cold tricks. Although with a five-card spade suit like this, you can generally count on at least four spades taking a trick, which would elevate it to eight tricks. You should open this hand two spades. Game isn't cold. You need information from your partner, but you don't want your partner to pass. Maybe your partner has five clubs including the queen-jack along with four diamonds. If that's all she has, you should make three no trump if she doesn't have three spades in her hand.

The point is this: you must tell her what you have so she can evaluate her hand and tell you whether or not she has a trick (or two) or three spades in her hand, or both. An opening at the two level allows your partner to reevaluate her hand. A hand that looked terrible when she first looked at it can suddenly look surprisingly powerful when her partner opens with a strong two. Look at the *responder's* hand:

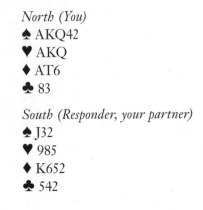

North (You)
♠ AKQ42
♥ AKQ
♦ AT6
♣ 83

South (Responder, your partner)
♠ J32
♥ 985
♦ K652
♣ 542

DEFINITION

Responder is the person who is the partner of opening bidder. Responder's call, after opener has opened the bidding, is called a *response*.

Does responder have a lousy hand, or what? But look at how responder's hand fits with your hand. Responder's king of diamonds and jack of spades make your pair cold for six spades! Because she has three spades, including the jack, in her hand, it's almost certain that you won't lose a spade trick. She can't lose a heart trick. Responder's king of diamonds ensures she won't lose a diamond trick. The only loser is the singleton club.

A two-spades opening allows you to say, "Hey, this stinkeroo is starting to smell like Joy perfume! I've got three of my partner's trump with an honor, and the king of diamonds. We could be going someplace here!" Without the two spades opening, you would just hope you get the contract in as low a spades bid as you can.

Balanced Hands with 22 or More Points

If you open a strong two-bid in clubs, your hand either contains 22 points and five clubs, or it contains 22 points and is balanced, without a five-card suit. If it contains five clubs, it's no different from the spades hands discussed earlier, and the bidding is made the same way.

If it's balanced without a five-card suit, however, there's an entirely different way to bid this. Take the following hand as an example:

♠ AQJ
♥ AK53
♦ AQ87
♣ K6

You can't open this hand in any of the no trump bids we've discussed. Do you remember why? *You can't lie to your partner,* that's why. You've agreed with your partner that an opening bid of one no trump promises between 15 to 17 HCP, no more, no less. An opening bid of two no trump promises between 20 to 21 HCP, no more, no less. An opening bid of three no trump promises between 25 to 26 HCP. When you make a no trump opening, you cannot be outside the range promised, either below *or* above.

This hand has 23 HCP, 24 total points with the doubleton clubs. You cannot open it in no trump. You cannot open it in any other suit bid because any opening in diamonds, hearts, or spades at the two level promises a five-card suit.

This is where the strong two-clubs bid comes into play. You open this hand two clubs. Then, if your partner responds with a suit you can't support, you respond two no trump.

An opening bid of two clubs, followed by a fairly standard response of two diamonds—a *waiting bid*—and a rebid of two no trump, tells your partner that opener has a balanced 22- to 24-point hand with no singletons or voids, and no more than two doubletons.

DEFINITION

A **waiting bid** is one that says nothing about the suit bid, but is forced by your partner's opening bid. A response of two diamonds to a strong two-clubs open just says to your partner, "I don't have a five-card suit headed by the king-jack, so tell me more about your hand."

Now bid the following hands:

	1.	2.	3.	4.	5.
♠	AKQJ874	J7	A	A	86
♥	A6	AKQJ	86	KQJT	KQT
♦	A5	AKQJ	AKQT9874	865	AKQ
♣	87	J76	A8	AKQJ8	KQJ98

Hand 1: Two spades. Even though this hand only contains 21 points, you can take nine tricks—seven spades tricks and your two aces—so it can be opened at two spades.

Hand 2: Two clubs. You have 22 points, but no five-card suit. Open two clubs and rebid two no trump if your partner bids a suit you can't support.

Hand 3: Three diamonds. Like Hand 1, this contains only 21 points, but you can take 10 tricks—8 diamonds and your 2 aces.

Hand 4: Two clubs. You can open two clubs with a five-card clubs suit. You tell your partner that you are not opening up a balanced hand without a five-card suit at two clubs by not bidding two no trump at your next bid. Instead, you will bid your other suit of four cards or better, two hearts, promising your partner at least four hearts and that your clubs suit is longer than your hearts suit.

Hand 5: Two no trump. This is a 21-point hand with 20 HCP. You can't make a two demand because you don't have enough points.

The difference between opening two of a suit and opening two no trump is that two no trump isn't a *demand bid*. Your partner may pass an opening bid of two no trump, but she may not pass an opening bid of two in a suit.

DEFINITION

A Strong Two is sometimes referred to as a **demand bid,** which means that the opener is demanding that your partner keep the bidding open. Some people refer to it as a two demand.

Responding to Strong Two Openings

First rule: You may not pass after your partner opens a two-bid in a suit if your RHO has passed. If you value your life, you won't pass. I once opened two spades. My LHO passed. My partner passed! My RHO passed. I almost fell off my chair. "You can't pass when I open two spades," I said. "But I only had 1 point," my partner replied. "I had 25 points and you had 1, which equals 26 and 26 equals game," I said. "I'm never going to bid a 1-point hand," she replied. We never played together again. Bridge players take this commitment seriously.

Think about it, gentle reader: if your partner has a huge hand—more than half the points in the deck—you probably won't have much. But that doesn't mean that you don't have much between you. As I told my ex-partner, "25 plus 1 equals game." *When your partner opens a two-level bid in a suit, you don't need much to make game.*

So when are you off the hook? When may you pass? You may pass once either of the following occurs:

- The partnership has bid game
- Opener rebids her suit

The corollary to this rule is this:

> If opener bids a new suit, responder must bid again.

Opener is definitely in control of this hand. Responder (the opening bidder's partner) must respect opener's bidding. No matter how terrible responder's hand, unless opener lets her off the hook by bidding game or by rebidding her suit, responder must keep the bidding open.

Responder may bid her own suit, but she must have a five-card suit with at least a king-jack. However, if she responds to an opening two-level bid with a suit bid of her own (other than a two diamonds response to a two clubs open, which is a semi-automatic bid that both have agreed says nothing about diamonds, which I'll explain later), she is making a 100 percent game-*forcing bid*. Whereas a strong two opener can stop short of game by rebidding her suit, if you, as responder, bid a new suit at your first bid, you and your partner have agreed you will not stop short of game.

DEFINITION

A **forcing bid** is a bid that requires your partner to make a bid other than pass if there is no intervening bid. It forces your partner to keep the bidding open so you can make another bid when it comes back to you.

Weak Response to Opening Two-Bids in Diamonds, Hearts, and Spades

If you have absolutely nothing, you respond to your partner's strong two-bid opening in diamonds, hearts, or spades with a bid of two no trump. This implies that it is a negative response, so your partner immediately suspects that you're holding garbage. She doesn't know it for sure, but it's a strong suspicion.

Opener *shouldn't* pass a two no trump response by you. This is important because a two no trump response doesn't absolutely promise a terrible hand. You might have a balanced hand with some points but without trump support for your partner's opening bid. What then? You would have to respond two no trump. So two no trump is a bid that warns your partner you might not have much, but still holds out the hope that you do have something. This is why your partner must bid again. A response of two no trump can be interpreted as asking your partner to bid her second suit, if she has one; but it must be a four-card suit. Let's look at a hand held by responder:

♠ 53
♥ 9864
♦ 765
♣ 8742

Phew! But your partner opens two spades—your worst fear. Not much to think about, right? You respond two no trump, saying, "My hand smells to high heaven, but do you have another suit because a five-card spades suit won't work?"

Your partner rebids three hearts, telling you she has at least four hearts. Hearts is a new suit, so you have to bid again. Since you do have hearts support, and you know you have at least eight hearts between you, you can bid four hearts.

Rules for Responding to Strong Two-Bid Openings in Diamonds, Hearts, or Spades

There are at least six things you should know about responding to a strong two-bid opening in diamonds, hearts, or spades.

- You can't pass unless your RHO bids. The obligation to bid only arises in the situation where opener's bid could be passed around to her, so if your RHO bids, you are relieved of your obligation to bid because even if you pass your partner will have another chance to bid.

- If you have a five-card suit headed by the king and jack, you should bid it.

- If you don't have a five-card suit but you do have at least one king, and if you also have three-card support for your partner's opening suit, you should raise immediately. It's worth noting here that when you have a fit, a singleton in an outside suit becomes as valuable as a king.

- The only circumstance under which you may pass after your first response is if you respond two no trump and your partner rebids her opening suit.

- If you bid your own suit in response to your partner's opening bid, you must keep the bidding open to game, even if your partner rebids her suit.

- You can't support opener's second suit unless you have at least four cards in it.

Bid these hands with your partner opening two diamonds:

1.	♠ KJ863	2.	♠ 86	3.	♠ KJ76	4.	♠ A4	5.	♠ 9865
	♥ 863		♥ QT742		♥ 874		♥ T9632		♥ Q63
	♦ J74		♦ 98		♦ JT9		♦ JT3		♦ 42
	♣ T7		♣ QJT4		♣ 842		♣ 632		♣ 8542

Hand 1: Two spades. You have a five-card spades suit headed by the king-jack and 6 points. This is a perfect hand with which to make a positive response. Your partner is promising at least 22 points, and you have 6 points. You should have game somewhere, so your bid forces opener to keep the bidding open to game, and you promise the opener that you'll keep the bidding open to game.

Hand 2: Two no trump. Even though you have 7 points, you can't bid your five-card hearts suit because it's headed by less than the king-jack. You have a very good hand and intend to tell your partner about it after her rebid. Remember, a two no trump response doesn't promise a terrible hand; it only implies it. Opener shouldn't pass your bid of two no trump.

Hand 3: Three diamonds. You can't bid your spades because you don't have five; but you do have three-card support for opener's suit, so you should tell her this.

Hand 4: Three diamonds, again. You can't bid your hearts because they aren't strong enough, but you do have three diamonds and an ace.

Hand 5: Two no trump. This is a stinkeroo. The only thing that could save it would be for her to rebid her diamonds, in which case you could pass, or for her to bid spades at her second bid, in which case you could go to four spades because you'd be assured of a 4–4 spades fit.

Bidding Sequence When You Have a Yarborough

Let's look at a bidding sequence when responder has a Yarborough (a balanced hand containing no points). This is your hand when you hear your partner open two spades:

♠ 986
♥ 875
♦ 954
♣ 9832

Partner	You
Two spades (1)	Two no trump (2)
Three diamonds (3)	Three spades (4)
Four clubs (5)	Four spades (6)
Pass (7)	

1. I've got a *great* hand with at least five spades.

2. I'm glad yours is good. Mine stinks (maybe).

3. I've also got a diamonds suit—at least four of them. I don't care how bad your hand is, I *insist* that you bid again.

4. Okay. I do have some support for your spades suit. I'm still not happy about this and would like to pass next time. Can I pass?

5. I'm glad to hear about your spades support. I've also got something in clubs. No, you can't pass because we can definitely make at least game. Can you give me any help? We may have a slam!

6. If I've said this once, I've said it a million times: I have absolutely no interest in slam. As far as I can tell we can't make anything. I have no help for you except three spades. Please, can we pass?

7. Pass. Okay, pard. I trust you.

This was your partner's hand:

♠ AKQJT
♥ A
♦ AKJ7
♣ AK8

She bid it well. She communicated with you as agreed. She could continue to bid with complete confidence that you wouldn't pass her out in either of her secondary suits (diamonds and clubs) so long as she continued to bid new suits.

After you had established spades as your agreed-upon trump, all of your partner's remaining bids were simply to tell you that she had strength in these suits. If you had anything at all in those suits, you would have supported them and she would have ended up in slam. All you needed was the queen of clubs or the queen of diamonds and the hand was cold for six spades.

This is a classic example of how partners must trust one another. Your partner trusted you to continue to bid as long as she bid a new suit. She could bid a four-card suit—diamonds—knowing that you'd bid again. She could bid a three-card suit—clubs—knowing that you'd bid again. See what a disaster it would have been if you had four clubs and passed her four-clubs bid because you thought your hand was terrible and wanted to "save" her?

You trusted her by continuing to bid. Your hand was awful, but you continued to bid in response to her forcing bids. That was your agreement. You cannot make unilateral decisions and nullify your agreements with your partner. If you've agreed upon a system, like continuing to bid when your partner opens a strong two whenever your partner bids a new suit, you must comply with that agreement, regardless of your interpretation of the strength of your hand.

Finally, she trusted your weak responses and closed out at four spades. Many people with less trust in their partners would ignore all the negative information you had transmitted, and *unilaterally* gone on to slam by themselves, to their ultimate chagrin.

Responding to Strong Two-Clubs Opening

When your partner opens a strong two in clubs, your responses change. You can still bid a decent five-card suit headed by at least the king–jack. But your negative, or *waiting* response is now two diamonds, not two no trump.

The reason you use two diamonds as a waiting bid is to keep the bidding low so opener can describe her hand at the lowest level possible. Because opener would have opened with a bid of her five-card suit, her response is almost always two no trump when you bid two diamonds. About the only time her response isn't two no trump is when she has opened a five-card or better clubs suit.

Rules for Responding to a Strong Two-Clubs Opening Bid

The following list explains what you should know about responding to the strong two-clubs opening bid:

- You shouldn't pass an opening bid of two club—unless, that is, your RHO bids. As I noted earlier in this chapter, the obligation to bid only arises in the situation where opener's bid could be passed around to her, and when your RHO bids, your partner is guaranteed another chance to bid even if you pass.

- If you have a five-card suit headed by the king–jack or better, you should bid it.

- If you don't have a five-card suit headed by the king–jack, you must bid two diamonds as a waiting bid, regardless of the strength or length of your diamonds suit.

- If opener rebids two no trump, she's telling you she has a balanced hand with 22 to 24 points. You may pass with less than 3 points.

- As long as opener bids a new suit, you must continue bidding if your RHO passes the bid to you.

- You can't support opener's second suit unless you have at least four cards in it.

- If opener responds two no trump to your two-diamonds waiting bid, the hand is treated as if opener opened a no trump bid, and you respond in accordance with Chapter 10 on no trump responses.

If opener opens two clubs and then bids a new suit after you make your two-diamonds waiting bid, what does that tell you about her hand? Think about it before you answer; this is the type of question you should always be asking yourself in bridge.

What does it tell you? It tells you that she opened up a clubs suit with at least five cards in it, that she probably has at least four of the suit she bid at her second opportunity, and that she has more clubs than she has of her second suit. She has not opened up a balanced 22-plus-point hand. That's quite a lot of information, don't you think?

Example Hands Responding to Strong Two-Clubs Opening Bid

Your partner opens with a bid of two clubs. How do you respond with the following hands?

1.	♠ KJ75	2.	♠ T974	3.	♠ KJ983	4.	♠ 3	5.	♠ 87
	♥ QT864		♥ QJ97		♥ 986		♥ 9854		♥ 863
	♦ KJ7		♦ 4		♦ 96		♦ 973		♦ T9865
	♣ 9		♣ QJ98		♣ KT8		♣ KQ965		♣ 983

Hand 1: Two diamonds. You don't have a five-card suit headed by the king-jack, so two diamonds is your only bid. Your hearts suit, which has five cards headed by two honors (the queen–10), isn't strong enough, and your spades suit, headed by the king-jack isn't long enough. So two diamonds just says, "I'm here. Tell me more."

Hand 2: Two diamonds. This bid says nothing about your diamonds suit. It just says that you're complying with your agreement to keep the bidding open, but denies that you have a five-card suit headed by the king–jack.

Hand 3: Two spades. You have a good five-card suit headed by the king–jack and 8 points. That's plenty good enough to tell your partner what you have.

ALERT

A two-diamonds response to an opening bid of two-clubs is automatic if you don't have a five-card suit headed by the king–jack. It can be negative or neutral. It just keeps the bidding open for your partner to further describe her hand.

Hand 4: Three clubs. Any five-card suit headed by two of the top three honors is worth an immediate bid even if it's clubs. The reason: if you bid two diamonds first, planning on showing three clubs later, the strong two-bidder won't realize that your suit is this good! You may be bidding three clubs for lack of anything better on QJTx4, or KT9xx.

Hand 5: Two diamonds. You're not bidding your five-card diamonds suit. You're just keeping the bidding open. If your RHO bids after your partner's two-clubs opening bid, you should pass because you have no obligation to make a free bid that would indicate a fairly good hand. The obligation to bid only arises in the situation where opener's bid could be passed around to her. Because opener will have another opportunity to bid over RHO's bid, you need not bid. Your pass after RHO's bid communicates your weakness to her.

Rebids by Strong Two-Bidder in Diamonds, Hearts, or Spades

After you've opened a strong two-bid, you must continue to describe your hand to your partner until the two of you have arrived at a decision as to what the best contract is. However, because the bidding has started at a high level, there isn't a lot of bidding space for you to communicate.

The first thing you do is evaluate your partner's response:

- Did she bid a new suit? If so, you know she has at least a five-card suit headed by at least the king–jack.

- Did she raise your suit? If so, you know she's probably working on a minimum, which, at this level, isn't much, but she has at least three cards in your suit.

- Did she bid two no trump? Then you know that she probably (but not definitely) has a hand without an ace or a king and she has less than 4 points.

Some Rules for Rebids

Here are two rules for rebid by opener in two diamonds, hearts, or spades:

1. If your partner has given you a positive response by bidding a new suit, it is *forcing to game*, so you can't pass until game is reached. Even rebidding your suit is forcing your partner to bid because she has made the bid that forces your pair to game.

2. If you bid a new suit, you're forcing on your partner for one round. The only time your partner may pass you is if you rebid no trump or rebid your own suit.

DEFINITION

Forcing to game means that both of you must continue bidding until one of you has bid game, which is either 3 no trump, 4 hearts or spades, or 5 clubs or diamonds.

Here are two rules for rebid by strong two-clubs opener:

1. If your partner has made a two-diamonds waiting bid, any bid of a suit by you shows a second suit shorter than your clubs suit. The second suit might be only four cards in length.

2. A response of two no trump shows 22 to 24 HCP and a balanced hand, whereas a response of three no trump shows 27 to 28 HCP and a balanced hand. Any no trump rebid by a two-clubs opener usually implies that opener doesn't have a long clubs suit.

With these rules in mind, look at the following hand:

♠ AKQJT4
♥ AKQ7
♦ A8
♣ 4

After your two spades opening bid, your partner responds two no trump. Now what? If you rebid your strong six-card spades suit, your partner may pass. You don't want that to occur because you have a cold game in your hand.

You can bid four spades, but you don't need to do that yet. Remember, *you are in control.* Your partner may not pass if you bid a new suit. And you have a four-card major you can bid, hearts. So you bid three hearts. This bid is forcing, but it only promises a four-card suit.

If your partner raises your hearts, she is promising a four-card suit. *Responder cannot raise opener's second suit without at least four cards in it.* If she raises hearts, then just play it in four hearts and don't worry about your six spades. They'll come in very handy after you *pull trump.*

DEFINITION

To **pull trump** or to **draw trump** means for declarer (the player who first bid the suit in which the contract is made; this is the player who plays the hand and whose partner is dummy) to lead trump until opponents have no more trump in their hands. It's a standard method of playing a hand.

If your partner responds three no trump or four of a minor suit to your hearts bid, you may return to four spades at that time. That puts you in game and is a bid that your partner may pass.

Playing Three No Trump After Opening a Strong Two-Bid in Diamonds, Hearts, or Spades

Sometimes when you have a long suit and an unbalanced hand, three no trump is still your best contract. Look at the following:

♠ 9
♥ AKQ76
♦ AQJT
♣ AK6

You	Partner
Two hearts (1)	Two spades (2)
Three diamonds (3)	Three hearts (4)
Three no trump (5)	Pass (6)

1. I've got a *terrific* hand with at least five hearts.

2. I've got something. In fact, I've got at least five spades and they are headed by not less than the king–jack.

3. I've got at least four diamonds. Do we have a fit in either hearts or diamonds? Give me a preference.

4. Okay, of the two suits, I prefer hearts to diamonds, but I'm not promising great hearts support, maybe only two.

5. I've shown you everything I have. Your five-card spades suit is interesting but I don't have more than two. I don't know how many hearts you have. I'm satisfied to play this in three no trump but if you have three hearts, take the bid to four hearts. Because you know my hand is exceptionally good, I am relying on you to take it to a higher level if you have more in your hand than the decent spades suit you have already told me about.

6. I've told you all I can. I only have two hearts. Let's play it in three no trump.

Your partner's hand?

♠ KQ986
♥ 75
♦ 97
♣ Q873

In three no trump you have three hearts tricks, three diamonds tricks, three clubs tricks, and spades stopped twice. You should make at least four no trump, but you will definitely make three.

Stop reading. Deal, bid, and play some hands using what you've learned in Chapters 1 through 8.

The Least You Need to Know

- A strong two-bid is a hand containing at least 22 points or that can take 8 tricks in a major suit or 9 tricks in a minor suit.

- An opening bid of two clubs may either be a clubs suit or a balanced hand with 22 to 24 HCP.

- Strong two-bids are forcing to game unless the suit opened is repeated at the three level. A rebid of two no trump after a strong two-clubs opening is nonforcing.

- If responder's first bid to a two demand in diamonds, hearts, or spades is a new suit, it's game forcing.

When Weakness Is a Weapon: Preemptive Openings

In This Chapter

- What is a preempt?
- Making preemptive bids at levels higher than two
- Rule of two, three, and four
- Responses to preemptive opening bids

In the previous chapters, I showed you how to evaluate and open hands that contain at least 13 points. However, sometimes you have a hand that doesn't have 13 points but contains qualities that you want to communicate to your partner. This chapter tells you what these hands are, how to evaluate them, and how to bid them.

We're talking preempts now! This is real down and dirty because a preempt is a defensive bid. Essentially, you're trying to foul-up your opponents. Basically, you don't have a very good hand, but your hand does possess the qualities that can allow you to throw a monkey wrench into your opponents' bidding. Ah, preempts are a lot of fun!

A Concise Description of a Nonopening Hand

You should now be able to deduce what kind of hand *not* to open at the one level. You shouldn't open if you don't have at least 13 points. If you pick up your cards and count your points and they don't add up to at least 13, you're probably going to pass.

But what if you have a long suit, and not much else? Is there any value in communicating this to your partner? And if so, how do you do it? "Pass" doesn't tell her much, except that you don't have 13 points.

But what happens if one of your opponents has 13 points and a five-card club suit headed by the ace–king, and you open three diamonds in front of him? He had a hand that he would have clearly opened one club; but you've bid three diamonds! What's he to do? Is his hand worth bidding four clubs when he has no idea what his partner has? It puts him in a terrible dilemma. You could steal a bid at three diamonds when they could, conceivably, have a game. You've kept them from finding the game by starting the bidding at a level that makes it dangerous for them to bid.

What Is a Preempt?

A *preemptive bid* is one that's made at a high level. It's made with a hand with a long suit and not many HCP. Its purpose is to constrict opponents, who may have most of the HCP, and make it more difficult for them to find their contract. Plus, if your partner has the right cards, a preempt can let you play a game your way!

Point and Suit Quality Requirements

When you're in first or second seat, your preempts should be fairly disciplined. You should promise at least a good suit, headed by two of the top five honors in the suit, and some values, but not much.

You shouldn't preempt when you have more than 9 HCP. Why? What you've learned here is that you should open a hand at the one level if you have 13 points. If you have a seven-card suit and 10 HCP, you must have at least 13 points, which would require an opening at the one level instead of a preempt. Look at the following hand:

♠ AKQJ873
♥ 87
♦ 75
♣ 52

You have 10 HCP. You have three doubletons, each of which is worth a point. That's 13 points. Open one spade. Even if the six nonspades cards are changed around so you have a different combination of singletons and voids, your hand will always add up to 13 points. A hand with 10 HCP that includes a seven-card suit will *always* have

13 total points. Thus any hand with a seven-card suit and 10 HCP must be opened at the one level. Look at your partner's possible hand:

♠ 973
♥ AK432
♦ 9
♣ 9876

That's only 9 points, so she passed originally. If you open three spades, she'll probably pass again. If you open one spade, however, she's going to support you because she has 9 points and three spades. And you're cold for four spades. If you bid your 10-point hand preemptively, you're preempting yourselves out of a cold game. You must have all of the following in order to open a suit at the three level:

- A seven-card suit

- A suit headed by at least the queen–10

- 4 to 9 HCP

- No *outside* ace

- Not more than one outside king

- When opening in a minor suit, no four-card major

 DEFINITION

Any honor in a suit other than your long suit is said to be **outside**. So if your long suit is hearts and you have the ace of spades, it's an outside ace.

Making an Opponent's Life Miserable with Preempts

Think how you feel when you look at a terrific, 15-point hand with five hearts. You're in the second seat and you're just salivating to get into this hand, when you hear your RHO say, "Three spades." Wow! What do you do? You know he's weak with seven spades, but where are the HCP in this hand? Do you just bid four hearts—game—with 15 points? Maybe your LHO is sitting there with 15 points, too, and he's just waiting to pounce on you.

This is an example of how preempting can really throw the next bidder (in this case, you) for a loop! Your RHO really caught you off guard; you're not sure what to do now.

That's the value of a three-level preempt. It makes life miserable for the opponents because it raises the level of the bidding so high. Because you are opening on a seven-card suit, and some values, you might be set a couple of tricks if you get the contract. But you might find your partner with some values, and make three, stealing a game from your opponents.

First Position Opening

Any preemptive bid constrains subsequent bidders, including your partner. When you're in first seat, you should be aware that nobody—including your partner—has bid yet. So if you make a preemptive bid, you're not only constraining your opponents, but your partner as well.

As former UCLA and Los Angeles Rams coach, Tommy Prothro once said, "When you put the ball in the air, three things can happen, and two of them are *bad* for your side." When you are in first seat, the odds are at least two-to-one that a substantial portion of the remaining points are in your opponents' hands. Therefore, you have more to gain by making a preemptive bid when you're in first seat than when you're in second seat.

Second Position Opening

The numbers change when you're in second seat and your RHO has passed. Now you are preempting only two people, one of whom is your partner. You know that your RHO doesn't have 13 points, and you have a weak hand, so there are probably at least 25 HCP distributed in the two remaining hands, one of whom is your loving partner. She might be waiting over there across the table from you, eager to open this hand one no trump, or maybe even a strong two demand. Can you imagine the look you're going to get when you preempt *her* and open three diamonds? Because you already know that one of your opponents, your RHO, has less than an opening hand, a preempt in second seat is less effective than a preempt in first seat. You can do it, but be prepared for your partner's reaction if she's the one with the points.

Third Position Opening

Here's where you can really take a chance. Your partner has already passed, so you know she doesn't have an opening hand. She was in first position and didn't bid. So if your RHO has passed, and you have a seven-card suit and only 5 points, you can rest assured that your LHO has a very good hand indeed. While it's true that both your partner and RHO might have passed 12-point hands, it's not highly probable. So this is where your three-level preempt is called for, no matter what the strength of your suit.

In third position, the only person you're constraining is your LHO. You need have no fear that your partner is sitting there with a good hand because she's already told you she doesn't have one. So basically, the sky's the limit.

ALERT

The weaker your hand in the third seat, the more incentive you should have to make a preemptive bid.

Let's say that you're looking at a hand with 4 HCP and seven spades headed by the queen–10. How many points are in the other three hands? Did you say 36, subtracting your 4 HCP from the total of 40 HCP? Well, if you did, you were wrong. You forgot to distinguish between distribution points and HCP.

Sure, there are 40 HCP in a hand, but if you have seven spades (or seven of any suit), then there are 3 extra distribution points spread around the table. There are only six spades spread among three hands. That's an average of two per hand. So how many points does that give each of the three other players? If they're evenly divided, 2 points per hand (each of the other players will have 1 HCP point and 1 distribution point). No matter how you divide the cards among the other three players, there must be 3 distribution points in this hand, in addition to the HCP, if you have seven cards in one suit.

So there are 39 points divided among the other three players. Because your partner and RHO have passed, they can't have more than 12 points each—a total of 24. This means that your LHO must have at least 15 points in his hand (39 minus 24). What a great time to preempt!

Fourth Position Opening

All the rules change in fourth position. There's no need to preempt because nobody has much of a hand. So why open up a weak hand at the three level when you might go set? Why open up at all? If you open at the one level you might force your opponents into bidding, and they might find a partscore. Better to pass the hand out. Remember this rule: *Don't open in the fourth seat unless you have a legitimate opening hand.* A corollary to the rule is this: *Don't preempt in fourth seat.*

> **TRICKS OF THE TRADE**
>
> When you're in fourth seat and nobody has opened in front of you, you have total control of the hand. If you bid, bidding continues and your opponents will each have another opportunity to discover a contract with their subopening hands. If you pass, however, the hand is over; nobody will have another chance to bid.

Preemptive Openings at the Four Level

If you need a seven-card suit to open a weak hand at the three level, how long must your suit be to open at the four level? Did you say eight cards? Right on!

You can open any eight-card suit at the four level if it meets all of the following requirements:

- At least eight cards in length (is this redundant, or what?)
- At least two of the top four honors (at least king–jack) in your long suit
- 4 to 9 HCP
- No outside ace
- Only one outside king
- If opening a minor suit, no four-card major

Again, you must be sensitive to the seat in which you're sitting. In the first or second seat you'll be preempting your partner, as well as your opponents, so you must tell her what you have. There's no problem with preempting at the four level in first or second position—just be certain that you have what you say you have. If your partner has a big hand, she can decide whether or not to make a higher bid.

Possible Double

One thing you should be sensitive to when opening at the four level in hearts or spades is that opponents are more liable to *double* you than if you open at the three level. When you open at the three level, they would be *doubling you into game*, which, if you made it, would give you a huge bonus.

> **DEFINITION**
>
> **Double** is a call that increases the scoring value of the number of tricks declarer is set or the number of tricks he makes . You make it when you believe the opponents have bid too high and that you can set them.
>
> **Doubling into game** means that your opponents have doubled what would only be a partial, like two hearts. If you make it, you get the equivalent of four hearts, which makes game. Doubling into game is risky, and the penalties for failure are severe. For details on doubling, see Chapter 19.

There is no such fear if you open up in a major at the four level because you're bidding game, so the penalty to the opponents for failure is much less. For example, if you're nonvulnerable and bid and make three hearts, if doubled, you would get 530 points above and below the line. Whereas if you were undoubled, you would only get 90 points below the line—a difference of 440 points!

However, if you bid and make four hearts doubled you would get 590 points above and below the line, versus 420 above and below the line undoubled—which is only 170 points more. So the difference between *doubling into game* versus doubling a game bid is huge. If you open up a preemptive hand at the three level, your opponents will be reluctant to double you because of the huge penalty they will suffer if you make your contract. But if you open up a preemptive hand at the four level in a major suit, your opponents will feel freer to double because the penalty for failure is much less. The risk of being doubled is something you should take far more seriously when you open up a preemptive hand in game than if you preempt below game.

Why the requirement that the hand be weak to open up at high levels (four level for majors and five level for minors), especially when you're opening at game? The reason is because of the possibility of a slam. You don't want to preempt your partner because you don't want to preempt yourselves out of finding a slam.

Preemptive Openings at the Five Level

Okay, class, if you need a seven-card suit to open a weak hand at the three level, and an eight-card suit to open a weak hand at the four level, how long must your suit be to open at the five level? Can you say "nine cards"?

Well if you did, you should have qualified it. You can open preemptively at the five level only in a minor suit. You shouldn't open a major suit at the five level preemptively. Why? Because game in a major suit is only four, so if you have a nine-card major suit and otherwise satisfy the requirements for a five-level opening, just open at the four level. Why overbid if you don't have to?

Requirements to open a suit at the five level are as follows:

- Must be clubs or diamonds
- Nine-card suit
- Suit must be headed by at least two of the top four honors (at least king–jack)
- 4 to 9 HCP
- No outside ace
- Only one outside king

Rule of Two, Three, and Four

One simple way of determining whether or not to make a preemptive opening is to count your tricks. The *rule of two, three, and four* may be used as a guide for you; here's how it works:

If you're vulnerable and your opponents aren't (this is called *unfavorable vulnerability*), you can overbid your hand by two tricks. That is, if your hand shows that you can take seven tricks with your long suit as trump, you can make a preemptive three-level opening.

If you and your opponents both have the same vulnerability—either you're both vulnerable or you are both nonvulnerable (this is called *equal vulnerability*)—you can overbid your hand by three tricks. That is, if your hand shows that you can take six tricks with your long suit as trump, you can make a preemptive three-level opening.

If you aren't vulnerable and your opponents are (this is called *favorable vulnerability*), you can overbid your hand by four tricks. That is, if your hand shows you can take five tricks with your long suit as trump, you can make a preemptive three-level opening.

> **TRICKS OF THE TRADE**
>
> As a general rule of thumb, you can figure that a good seven-card suit should take five tricks, and eight- and nine-card suits should have a maximum of two losers, regardless of their high card strength. So an eight-card suit should take six tricks, and a nine-card suit should take seven tricks. It doesn't always work out like that, but it will most of the time.

Example hands follow:

Unfavorable Vulnerability	Equal Vulnerability	Favorable Vulnerability
♠ 98	♠ QJT9874	♠ QJT9852
♥ 7	♥ KQ	♥ J85
♦ QJT9642	♦ 865	♦ 74
♣ KQJ	♣ 6	♣ 3

In the unfavorable vulnerability hand, you should have five diamonds tricks and two clubs tricks. That's seven tricks, so you can open three diamonds in any seat.

In the equal hand, you have five spades tricks and a hearts trick for six total tricks, so you can open three spades.

In the favorable vulnerability hand, even though you only have 4 HCP, and only 7 total points, you should have five spades tricks, so open this hand with three spades. There are 36 HCP spread among the other hands. If your partner has a substantial number, she knows that you have seven spades and can go to four spades if she has outside power and even as little as one spade in her hand. If the points are in your opponents' hands, however, you have constrained their bidding substantially. The worst that can happen is that you miss making your contract by two ticks (called being "down 2" or "set 2"), for 100 points above the line for them, undoubled.

Counting Sure Tricks

A *sure trick* is a trick you know you will definitely take, like the ace of trump. You count sure tricks the same way you count quick tricks (see Chapter 5). But in this instance, for the purposes of evaluating your hand under the rule of two, three, and four, you can also count any four-card suit as a trick. So look at the following hand:

♠ QT97653
♥ 7
♦ 8754
♣ Q

This has 4 HCP, but you can count your seven-card trump suit as capable of producing five tricks, and your four-card suit should produce an additional trick, so this should be a six-trick hand that you can open three spades with favorable or equal vulnerability. In fact, in third seat, you shouldn't hesitate to open this three spades, because it could cause your RHO in fourth seat, who is undoubtedly salivating to open his huge hand with a demand bid, to go ballistic.

Opener's Subsequent Bidding

Under no circumstances should a preemptive opener bid again unless your partner makes a forcing bid. You've described your hand to your partner. You have no idea what's in her hand. She knows your hand much better than you know hers. You've told your story. Leave it up to her. If she bids, fine. If she bids a new suit below game, you are forced to bid (see Chapter 8). Otherwise, stay out of it! It's up to her to place the contract. If she doubles opponents, trust her. If you haven't lied to her, she should know what to do.

Let's try bidding some hands:

1.	♠ 5	2.	♠ 75	3.	♠ 873	4.	♠ QJ98643	5.	♠ J876543
	♥ 9832		♥ 84		♥ KJ985432		♥ 76		♥ KQ
	♦ KQJ9832		♦ 6		♦ KJ		♦ void		♦ 97
	♣ 7		♣ KJ986532		♣ void		♣ KQ87		♣ 87

ALERT

Remember that whenever you make a preemptive bid, even if you're bidding game, you are showing a weak hand, a hand that doesn't have enough points to open at the one level.

Hand 1: Pass in the first or second seat because you have a four-card major. However, I'd open three diamonds in third seat. You have four hearts, but only 6 HCP. In third seat your LHO probably has a good hand. It's worth the risk that you and your partner might miss a heart fit to preempt this hand in third seat only. There is a total of 37 points—34 HCP and at least 3 distribution points—in the other three hands. If your partner and RHO have the maximum of 12 each, that leaves 13 for LHO. But the odds are that both your partner and LHO don't have 12 each, so your LHO is sitting there with a big hand. Hit him with a preempt now while you can.

Hand 2: Four clubs. Again, count the points. There are 36 HCP and 4 distribution points in the other three hands (five clubs distributed among three hands equals 4 distribution points no matter how you slice it). So that's 40 points in the other three hands. Because you know your partner and RHO can't have more than 12 each, that leaves a minimum of 16 points in your LHO's hand. Your LHO is undoubtedly sitting there with a big hand.

Hand 3: Four hearts. The difference between this hand and Hand 2 is that this hand has *side strength*. And you're opening up in game.

DEFINITION

Side strength means strength in a suit other than the trump suit or the suit you are bidding. For instance, if you're bidding clubs, the ace of hearts would be side strength in hearts.

Hand 4: Open this three spades at all levels of vulnerability and in all seats. This is a maximum preempt, because you have 8 HCP and 4 distribution points (1 for the doubleton and 3 for the void) for 12 total points. You don't need much help from your partner for game. If your partner has only the ace of hearts and the jack of clubs, you have a very good shot at game. But if you open one spades, you'd be lying to your partner because you don't have 13 points. A danger in opening Hand 4 with one spades is not that you don't have ample "playing tricks" to make some number of spades, but that, when the opponents compete, which they surely will, your partner will "double" them, counting on you for more defensive values.

Hand 5: Pass in first and second seats. Open three spades with equal or favorable vulnerability in third seat. Pass with unfavorable vulnerability. Your suit is very weak, but you can still count on five tricks from it, plus a heart trick.

Everyone listens to the bidding. When you make a preemptive opening you tell *everybody*, not just your partner, that you have a weak hand. So what you have is no secret.

Responses to Preemptive Openings

How do you respond if your partner makes a preemptive opening? Because responses to preempts are completely different from responses to normal openings, I explain them here

If your partner opens with a preemptive bid and you bid anything other than game or to support her suit, she should bid again. If you bid game in a major or three no trump, your partner should pass. If you raise her suit, she can pass. In other words, a raise is the only nonforcing bid you can make when your partner opens with a preemptive bid. That's all you need to know. Next subject.

Okay, okay, I'll show you some hands, because you can get into real trouble when you have a good hand and your partner opens with a preempt, especially when it's short of game. In the following hands, your partner opens three diamonds:

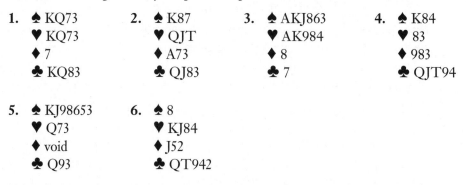

1.	♠ KQ73	2.	♠ K87	3.	♠ AKJ863	4.	♠ K84
	♥ KQ73		♥ QJT		♥ AK984		♥ 83
	♦ 7		♦ A73		♦ 8		♦ 983
	♣ KQ83		♣ QJ83		♣ 7		♣ QJT94

5.	♠ KJ98653	6.	♠ 8
	♥ Q73		♥ KJ84
	♦ void		♦ J52
	♣ Q93		♣ QT942

Hand 1: Pass. Surprised? Are you saying to yourself, "Wait a minute, I have 15 HCP. This is a terrific hand. I've got all the other suits stopped twice! We can make three no trump." If this is what you're saying, then you have a lot of company. I have partners today who would want to bid three no trump with this hand; but it would be a big, big mistake. Why? Because you have no source of tricks from your partner, that's why. Are you saying, "But she opened three diamonds! She's got diamonds tricks!"? Wrong! She is telling you she has a *weak* hand! Because she opened in first or second seat (you would have opened if you were bidding before her!), she is only promising you a suit headed by the king–jack and 4 points. That's her minimum. Would you want to play this in three no trump and see the following hand from her?

♠ 652
♥ 8
♦ KJ86542
♣ 62

Can you make three no trump with these two hands? If so, you're ready for the Bridge Hall of Fame. But this hand is all your partner is promising you when she opens three diamonds in first seat. Never lose sight of the fact that the primary message your partner is sending you when she makes a preemptive opening is "My hand is *weak!*" She might be at the top of her bid, 9 points, but you can't count on that. You have to count on her having a minimum when you respond.

In addition to the fact that you will have a hard time making three no trump, you've got a terrific defensive hand. If opponents compete and bid anything else at the three or four level, you have a great chance of setting them because you've got length and strength in all the other suits. So just sit back and reap the rewards! This is a hand where you pass and pray that your opponents bid. You want them playing this hand.

Hand 2: Three no trump. Fooled you! Now you must really be confused. Why can't you bid three no trump on the first hand, that has 15 HCP, but can bid three no trump on this hand with only 14 HCP? The answer is because you have good diamonds support for partner's bid. She has promised *at least* KJxxxxx of diamonds. You have Axx. You should be able to take at least six diamonds tricks, probably seven if the rest of the diamonds don't split 3–0 between your opponents. And you have *transportation*, because, in addition to the ace of diamonds, you have two small diamonds to lead to dummy.

DEFINITION

Transportation is the ability to get the lead back and forth between declarer's hand and the dummy. In Hand 1 you have no transportation to dummy, because you only have one diamond and no other way to get back to dummy, because dummy has no other entries.

An **entry** is a card that enables you to get the lead into a specific hand.

Hand 3: Three spades. This is a hand where you want to contract to play in game, either four hearts or four spades. So you bid three spades. This forces your partner to bid again because if you bid a new suit it is *forcing*, remember? Therefore, unless your partner bids four spades, you're going to bid four hearts at your next call. This tells your partner, "I want to play this in four hearts or four spades, so take your pick." If she has two in one suit and one in the other, she'll pick the one in which she has two. If her best suit is hearts, she passes four hearts. If it's spades, she bids four spades. If she has relatively equivalent holdings in both, she should choose your first bid suit—spades—because you should have an equal number or longer spades. Under no circumstances can she take the contract to five diamonds.

Hand 4: Four diamonds. Remember that a raise is the only nonforcing bid when your partner makes a preemptive opening. You have a five-card club suit that might be able to be developed as a source for tricks; shortness in hearts; the king of spades; and three trumps. Therefore, you should make a competitive bid to restrict your opponents' bidding space. And your partner has a fair chance of making it.

Hand 5: Pass. Sure, you'd rather play this as three spades than three diamonds. But you can't make a preemptive bid over your partner's preemptive opening. If you bid three spades, it's a forcing bid that tells your partner you have a big hand. You don't. That's the risk one takes when making a preemptive opening. Your partner may have a better preempt. If your partner makes a preemptive opening and you have this type of hand, you just have to ride it out and let her play it in a less favorable contract.

Hand 6: Four diamonds. There are two instances in which a raise of her suit is a good idea. The first was Hand 4, where you had a nice outside five-card suit you might be able to develop and three-card trump support. The second is if you have a singleton with at least three trump, which is what you have here in Hand 6. Shortness in an outside suit doesn't help you much if you're also short in trump. But if you have at least three trump, your partner should be able to get at least one, maybe two tricks by trumping your short suit in dummy.

The Least You Need to Know

- Use rule of two, three, and four to determine whether to make a preemptive open.
- A three-level opening bid shows a seven-card suit headed by at least the queen–10.
- An opening three-level preempt contains no outside ace and not more than one outside king.
- A three-level preempt contains 4 to 9 HCP.
- A raise is the only nonforcing response when your partner opens with a preemptive bid.
- If you make a preemptive opening bid, you should not bid again unless your partner makes a forcing bid.

Responses to Opening Bids

3

After your partner has made her initial description of her hand, it's up to you to respond.

If her opening bid is a no trump bid, your response tells her that you have taken control of the hand. Instead of telling her what you have, you'll be asking her for a more specific description of her hand so that you can place the final contract. This part explains how to evaluate your hand in light of her opening no trump bid.

If your partner's opening bid is in a suit, the purpose of your response is to tell her the most about your hand that you can with one bid. You will find out how you must respond depending on the values in your hand and the opening bid she has made. You'll also learn about forcing bids, weak bids, bids that show support for your partner's opening bid, and bids that deny support.

Taking Control: Responses to No Trump Openings

In This Chapter

- When to pass
- Invitational bids and forcing bids
- The captaincy principle
- Natural bids versus conventional bids
- How to deal with interference by your opponents

Enough about opening. Now we start to delve deeper into the interaction that takes place at a polite bridge table, the actual communication with your partner. Up until now we've been talking about what you tell your partner with your first bid.

In this chapter, you learn about responses—how you, or your partner, take the information imparted by whoever opened, evaluate it, and then communicate back what you have in your hand. This chapter is limited to responding when your partner opens the bidding by telling you she has a pretty big hand: 15 to 17 HCP and no trump distribution.

Basic Arithmetic Prevails

You have two basic goals in bidding in bridge:

- Bid game if you have it.
- Stop at as low a level as possible when you're certain you don't have game.

When bidding in a no trump contract, arithmetic is more important than when bidding in a suit contract. In a suit contract, you can take an ace with the two of trump. In no trump, you're stuck with the suit that was led. High cards are much more valuable, because the highest card in the suit led will always take the trick.

> **TRICKS OF THE TRADE**
>
> Remember that when evaluating no trump hands, you don't count distribution points, only HCP.

When you're bidding no trump you always have 25 points in mind, because that's typically the minimum number of points required to make game in no trump (see Chapter 6). When your partner opens one no trump, remember that she's telling you that she has between 15 and 17 HCP, no singletons or voids, and no more than two doubletons (see Chapter 6). There are some simple rules to start. If you, as responder, have a balanced hand, add up your HCP and make one of the following bids:

HCP	Bid
0–7	Pass
8–9	Two no trump
10+	Three no trump

A Discussion of Yes, No, and Maybe

In evaluating your hand to respond to a no trump opening, you may think in terms of three little words: they aren't *I love you*, they're *yes*, *no*, and *maybe*.

Yes

If you have 10 or more points, what should you do? Of course, you bid game by responding three no trump. Why? Even if your partner's at the bottom of her bid with 15 points, when added to your 10 you should be able to make game. This tells your partner, "Great! You have at least 15 points, and I have at least 10 points; we should definitely be playing this hand in game."

No

When you have 0 to 7 points, you must pass. Why? Go back to your basic arithmetic. What's the maximum amount of HCP your partner can have when she opens one no trump? Seventeen HCP, right? How many points do you need for game? Twenty-five. If you have a maximum of 7, add that to her maximum possible of 17. What do you get? Twenty-four. That's not enough for game. So you don't want to bid further. You communicate to your partner by your pass that you have 7 or fewer points. You're telling your partner, "Well, it's nice that you have such a pretty hand, with at least 40 percent of the points in the deck, but my hand is too weak for us to make game, so let's stop bidding."

Maybe

If you have 8 to 9 points, you might be saying, why not bid three no trump, because 17 plus 8 equals 25? Because when evaluating whether or not to bid with 0 to 7, you were looking to see what would be the best thing that could happen if you were both at the top of your bid. The best thing that could happen was that you wouldn't make game with your total maximum points. So what's the purpose of bidding?

When you have 8 to 9 points, you look at it the other way. Your partner might have 17, but she might have 15 or 16. And if she has 15 or 16, your 8 points won't be enough for game. If you have 9 and she only has 15, you still won't have enough for game. Therefore, because her hand is undefined between 15 and 17, you must tell her what you have by making an *invitational* bid of two no trump. This tells her that you have 8 to 9 points. And it says to her, "Partner, if you're at the top of your bid with 17 points, go on to game. But if you're in the middle or at the bottom, just pass and we should be able to make two no trump."

Forget algebra, geometry, and computer programming. When your partner opens one no trump, all you need is simple arithmetic. You add your points to hers and decide whether it is *yes, no,* or *maybe.*

Understanding the Captaincy Principle

When your partner opens one no trump, in addition to describing her hand to you, she's telling you, "That's it, partner. You now know what I have. You're the captain of this hand. Place the contract where you think we have the best chance."

One no trump is one of the most descriptive bids in bridge by an opener because it severely limits her hand. Most other bids in bridge are slightly limiting, but have a varying range, and the differences are communicated by subsequent bidding. But one no trump limits the hand to what we've discussed. Never could (or should) your partner open a hand one no trump without having the precise qualities we've discussed: 15 to 17 points, no singletons or voids, and no more than two doubletons.

Because of this severe limitation, the opener designates responder as the "captain" of the hand. Because you know what she has in her hand, it's up to you to use your knowledge of bridge and your own hand to place the contract. Your partner will be trusting you to either place it in a suit or to leave it in no trump, but at the proper level. You might ask her more about her hand, but in the end, it's up to you to determine where the contract will be played; there is no bid that responder can make that's as limiting as partner's one no trump open.

Natural vs. Conventional Bids

A *convention* is a bid that means something different than what it appears to mean. A *natural* bid is one that means what it says. One no trump—meaning 15 to 17 points and a balanced hand—is a *natural* bid. Two clubs, on the other hand, when it means a huge hand as discussed in Chapter 9, is a *conventional* bid because it doesn't say anything about clubs.

Many conventional bids have been developed as responses to a partner's opening bid of one no trump. You only need to learn one of them—the *Stayman*—at this stage. It has become so widespread that it is considered to be standard.

The Stayman Convention

Because your partner can open a hand one no trump but still have one or two four-card major suits (spades or hearts), it's quite possible that you may also have at least four cards in one of the major suits. You should be playing this hand in the major suit and not in no trump.

It's conventional bridge wisdom that if you and your partner hold at least eight cards in a major suit combined, you should be playing the hand in that suit and not in no trump. Because you control most of the trumps, you should be able to get one more trick than if you were playing in no trump.

But how do you get this sort of information out of your partner? And how do you find out which suit your partner holds four cards in?

The answer is Stayman, which is a very simple conventional bid. It says, simply, that if your partner opens one no trump and you have four cards in a major suit and at least 8 points, you respond with a bid of two clubs. This says absolutely nothing about the clubs you're holding in your hand. When you respond two clubs to your partner's opening bid of one no trump, you are saying to your partner the following:

"Partner, I promise you I have …

- At least four cards in at least one major suit.

- At least 8 HCP.

Please further describe your hand to me."

That's all it says. You could be void in clubs and still bid two clubs if you have a four-card major and at least 8 HCP.

How to Respond to Stayman

If you're the opening bidder and your partner responds two clubs to your one no trump opening, Stayman requires you to answer her question. If you have a four-card major, you bid it. If she responds two clubs and your hand contains three spades, four hearts, three diamonds, and three clubs, your next bid must be two hearts.

Now under the captaincy principle, responder knows as much about your hand as she needs in order to place the contract. If she has four hearts and 10 points, with her four hearts and your four hearts, she will bid game—four hearts. If she has 8 to 9 points without four hearts, she'll bid two no trump; if she has 8 to 9 points with four hearts, she'll bid three hearts. Both of these bids say *maybe*. If you've opened with 17 points and she bids three hearts, you should accept her invitation and bid game. If you're at the bottom of your bid and opened with 15 points, you would just pass her bid of three hearts and play the hand in three hearts.

What if you, as opener, don't have a four-card major? Then Stayman requires you to bid two diamonds. Again, this is a conventional bid. It says nothing about the diamonds in your hand. The response of two diamonds to a Stayman bid of two clubs simply denies a four-card major. You have no choice in this matter. If you're playing the Stayman convention (and just about everybody does), you must respond two diamonds if you don't have a four-card major.

Responder then places the contract. If responder has 10 points, she bids three no trump (answering *yes*); if she has 8 to 9 points, she bids two no trump (telling you *maybe*). And that's where the contract is played unless you have opened the bidding at the top of your bid with 17 points. In that event, you can close out the contract at three no trump. Responder has promised at least 8 points, and added to your 17, you should have game. Responder's bid of two no trump is considered invitational, inviting you to go to game if you are at the top of your bid.

So the basics for responder to bid Stayman are the following:

- At least one four-card major
- At least 8 HCP

If you're responder and your partner opens one no trump and your hand satisfies these two simple rules, you should bid two clubs.

The last thing to discuss is what you do if you have at least 8 or 9 HCP but don't have a four-card major. The answer is simple: regardless of where your points are, you bid two no trump. A bid of two no trump over opener's one no trump says the following:

- I have exactly 8 to 9 HCP, but less than 10 HCP.
- I don't have a four-card major.

Your partner now knows your hand pretty well. If she opened a 17-point hand or an attractive 16-point hand, she goes to three no trump. Otherwise she passes and you play the hand at two no trump.

That's all there is to it. And for now, that's all you need to know.

Now, bid these hands as responder after your partner has opened one no trump:

1.	♠ 9765	2.	♠ 743	3.	♠ JT86	4.	♠ J643
	♥ AQ73		♥ Q65		♥ 85		♥ J965
	♦ K763		♦ 62		♦ AK864		♦ K3
	♣ 6		♣ KQJ73		♣ 86		♣ 985

5.	♠ J84	6.	♠ J753
	♥ Q93		♥ J642
	♦ K632		♦ J9732
	♣ Q52		♣ void

Hand 1: Two clubs. You have 9 HCP and two four-card majors. It doesn't matter that you only have a singleton clubs. Your two clubs bid describes a hand that has at least 8 HCP and at least one four-card major, which is what this hand has.

Hand 2: Two no trump. You have 8 HCP, but you don't have a four-card major, so you can't bid Stayman. Although you have a very nice clubs suit, you can't bid clubs, because that would be Stayman. Remember, bidding two clubs in response to your partner's one no trump opening doesn't say anything about clubs! Instead, it's asking your partner to bid a four-card major. You'd much rather play a hand in no trump because no trump tricks are worth more than a minor suit trick.

Hand 3: Two clubs. You have a nice diamonds suit and your clubs are terrible. But you have 8 HCP and four spades. This is a hand that requires a bid of two clubs if you're playing Stayman.

Hand 4: Pass. Even though you have two four-card majors, you don't have enough points to bid. It is better to let your partner play this in one no trump. This is a hand where you must be disciplined. I know a lot of players who are tempted to bid two clubs on this hand on the outside chance that they'll find their partner with a four-card major and they'll be able to play it in a 4–4 fit at the two level. The problem with this is, what if your partner responds two diamonds, denying a four-card major? You can't pass when you only have two diamonds. Your partner might have opened up the following hand:

♠ KQ7
♥ KQ3
♦ 98
♣ AK764

When you bid two clubs, she must bid two diamonds. Because she doesn't have a four-card major, she must comply with the rules of the Stayman convention you agreed to play. She can't respond anything else, so if you pass, she'll be playing in a 2–2 trump fit and you'll be looking around for a new partner because she's never going to want to see you again. If she bids two diamonds in response to your bid of two clubs, your only choice is to bid two no trump and hope and pray that she wasn't opening up a 17-point hand. If she was, she's going to be in three no trump with two chances—slim and none. So the result of your gamble will probably be that your partner will be playing a hand in two no trump or three no trump that she could have played in one no trump. She might have made one no trump but will have very little chance at the higher level. You must be disciplined when you bid. If you have two four-card majors, but not enough points to bid, pass.

Hand 5: Pass. This is the one hand with 8 HCP that you should pass, when distribution is 4–3–3–3.

Hand 6: Two clubs. When you bid two clubs, you know that your partner must respond with a bid of two diamonds, two hearts, or two spades. This hand is terrible, but you want it played in your eight- or nine-card trump fit. So when you bid two clubs, you're forcing your partner to bid one of your three suits. No matter which suit your partner bids, you pass and you're in a better contract for your pair than one no trump would be, considering your horrible hand. Sure, she might only have two diamonds, but you have five, so she will be playing in a 5-2 fit with the ruffing power of your void.

Weak Responses

If you have a lousy hand—one with less than 8 points—but a five-card major, it's probably better for the hand to be played in two of the major than to have declarer play it in one no trump. Remember that your partner cannot open one no trump without at least two cards in every suit. So if you have a five-card major, you should bid it at the two level. This is called a *drop dead* or *sign-off* bid, and your partner must pass.

ALERT

Eight cards is the magic number when determining a trump fit.

So if your partner opens one no trump and you bid two diamonds, hearts, or spades, you're telling your partner that you have a weak hand with at least five cards in the suit you bid, so she should pass. This applies whether or not you're playing Stayman.

Invitational Five-Card Major Responses

If a direct bid of a major over your partner's one no trump opening is weak, how do you show an invitational or game-going hand with a five-card major? If your partner has at least three cards in your suit, you should be playing it in your 5–3 major-suit fit instead of no trump.

The answer is that you must first bid two clubs, and then if your partner responds in your major, you're in good shape. If she responds with two diamonds or two of the other major, showing four cards in that suit, you just bid your suit. That shows her you have at least five and at least an invitational hand. Then it's up to her whether to bid again and, if so, what level or *strain*.

DEFINITION

Strain refers to spades, hearts, diamonds, clubs, or no trump.

Game-Forcing Five- or Six-Card Major Responses

If you have 10 points and a five-card major, you should bid two clubs; then if your partner denies four cards in your suit, jump to three of your suit. That tells her that you have at least 10 points and five cards in your major. It's then up to her whether to play it in three no trump, or four of your suit. If she has three-card support for your suit, she'll bid four of your suit, game. If she only has two cards in your suit, she'll bid three no trump.

If you have at least 9 points and a six-card major, you should immediately jump to game in your six-card major.

Interference and Stayman

What if you have a four-card major and your RHO bids two clubs? You can't say, "Wait a minute; that's what I was going to bid!" Too bad, too, because that would tell your partner what you wanted her to know. But unfortunately, bridge won't allow you to do that. So you must have some response. How do you let your partner know you have a four-card major if opponents interfere?

Just about everybody in this situation (when you intended to bid two clubs and your RHO took it away from you) plays a double to show that your RHO took your bid. So, since you can't bid two clubs, you say "double." This is not a double that tells your partner you want to defend two clubs doubled. Rather, in this situation a double of two clubs says, "Partner, I was going to bid two clubs but this jerk did it before I could."

That's pretty easy. But what if you intended to bid two clubs and your RHO bids two diamonds? Not too pretty, but never fear, it has come up, and the bridge gods have figured something out. If you want to bid Stayman but your RHO bids a higher-ranking suit than clubs before you can bid, there is a way to handle it: You *cue bid* RHO's suit.

DEFINITION

A **cue bid** is a forcing bid in a suit in which it's obvious that bidder cannot wish to play. A bid of the opponents' natural suit bid is a cue bid and forces your partner to bid again to further describe her hand. At a lower level like this, you use it to get more information from your partner.

A bid of your opponents' naturally bid suit is a *cue bid*. Clearly, if you're of sound mind, you probably don't want to play the contract in a suit that your opponents felt so good about they wanted to play the contract in that suit—so why would you bid your opponents' suit? The only reason would be to tell your partner something other than suggesting that it might be a good idea to play the hand in this suit yourself.

When using a cue bid after interference after your partner has opened the bidding one no trump, you're telling your partner that you wanted to bid two clubs as Stayman, but the intervening bid kept you from it.

You must have at least 10 HCP to make a cue bid as Stayman because it's a game-forcing bid. You shouldn't do it if you don't have a hand in which you're willing to have your partner play in three no trump if she doesn't have a four-card major, or if her four-card major isn't your four-card major. If it isn't, you'll have to bid three no trump after she bids her four-card major.

If RHO bids a major suit at the two level, and you cue bid that suit at the three level, you're promising four cards in the other major. You shouldn't do this unless you have at least 10 HCP and are willing to have your partner play the hand in either three no trump or four of your major suit.

As you can see, interference by your RHO when you are responder causes severe problems. Because of this, it's a good idea when trying to bid Stayman over interference, not to continue unless you have a game-going hand. You're going to be forcing the bidding to the three level, and your prospects are not too good if you have a weak hand. If opponents interfere and you have a weak hand, don't try to find the 4–4 major card fit. Just pass and defend. You might find that your results are much better than if you try to play the hand.

So, over interference, you can bid Stayman two ways:

- If RHO has bid two clubs, by doubling

- If RHO has bid a suit higher than two clubs, by cue bidding RHO's suit at the three level

Requirements for bidding Stayman over interference follow:

- At least one four-card major
- At least 8 HCP if you are doubling two clubs, or
- At least 10 HCP if you are cue bidding RHO's suit at the three level

Jump Bids

A *jump bid* is one that skips one level of bidding, like if opener bids one no trump and your first response is three diamonds, instead of two diamonds.

What if your partner opens one no trump and you have an unusual hand? Maybe six cards in a minor suit, but not many points? The *jump bid* over your partner's opening of one no trump can give you some solutions.

Invitational Jump Bids

What would you think a bid of three clubs would mean over your one–no trump opening?

Well, it could mean whatever the partnership agrees that it means. But the way I play it, and the way a lot of the better players play it, is that it means your partner has a *broken* six-card suit. By broken, I mean that she has some honors, but there are some cards missing. Like maybe she has AQTxxx of clubs, missing the king and the jack. The jump bid in this case is *invitational*; it is telling you, "Partner, I have a six-card club suit and nothing else. But my suit contains several honors with holes. If you can fill in the holes, then you can probably take six tricks in clubs; so if you have stoppers in the other suits we could make three no trump." It's a great way to get to three no trump with responder only having 6 points, but a suit that makes the contract cold.

DEFINITION

An **invitational bid** is one that suggests to your partner that your pair might want to play the hand in game or slam. As the word implies, it "invites" a game or slam bid.

Weak Jump Bids

If you bid Stayman—two clubs—in response to your partner's one no trump opening, and then rebid three clubs or three diamonds over whatever she bids, you're demanding that your partner pass. This bid shows a bad six-card or longer suit and a very weak hand. Remember that when your partner opens one no trump, she's promising at least two cards in every suit. So if you have a six-card suit, you are assured of at least an eight-card fit between you. If you have a truly terrible hand, maybe it's better to play it in your minor with the ruffing power it will have, instead of forcing your partner to play it in one no trump, a contract in which you can give her little or no help at all.

Note: If you have a very weak hand, you can bid Stayman *without* a four-card major. It's just a way of telling your partner that you have a weak hand with a six-card minor and that it's better to play it in the minor. You might get lucky. Your long suit might be diamonds and she might respond two diamonds, denying a four-card major. Then you can pass and she'll be playing the hand in two diamonds, your weak six-card suit, instead of the three diamonds you thought you might be forced into if she bid two hearts, or two spades, or two no trump. If you're not that lucky and your suit is clubs or she bids hearts or spades, your rebid is your six card suit at the three level and she should pass because you are describing your hand as weak with a bad six card suit.

Practice Hands: Jump Bids

Take a look at the following hands, which you open one no trump, and decide what you'll do with your partner's jump bid:

	1.	2.	3.	4.	5.
♠	T54	AK	KQ7	KQT7	A6
♥	AK7	QT7	643	K752	64
♦	K742	875	KJ4	A84	QJ65
♣	AQ8	KQJ65	AQ42	QJ	AKJ83

What if your partner responds to your one–no trump open with a bid of three diamonds and you're playing it as invitational?

Hand 1: This is a tough call because if you get a spades lead you could be down before you get the lead. I'd take the chance and bid three no trump because there's a good chance spades will split 4–3–3–3 among the players, and you may not even get a spade lead. Remember, with you holding the king of diamonds, your partner is promising the ace–queen and probably the jack, so you will have six diamond tricks plus two heart tricks for sure. If your opponents lead a club, you're in good shape.

Hand 2: Pass. You are probably not going to be able to get more than four tricks in diamonds, if that, because you can't fill in your partner's diamonds. If you bid three no trump, hearts may be a problem, and you will certainly lose the ace of clubs. You have four losers for sure: ace of clubs, ace–king of hearts, and the diamonds, and maybe more if your opponents play the hearts correctly.

Hand 3: Three no trump. Take a chance on a heart lead and *bad split*. Maybe you'll get a clubs lead into your ace–queen.

DEFINITION

A **bad split** means that a suit doesn't split evenly between your opponents. For example, if the opponents hold five cards in a suit, a bad split would be if one is holding four of those cards and the other is holding one of them (a 4-1 split) or one is holding all five (a 5-0 split). A "good split" would be a 3-2 split.

Hand 4: Pass. Even though you have the ace of diamonds for six diamonds tricks, there are too many holes in the hand. You could get killed in both clubs and hearts. Forget game and let your partner play it in three diamonds, which should give you a pretty good score.

Hand 5: Pass. You almost certainly are going to get a lead of a major suit, and if it's hearts you're probably dead meat. If you get a clubs lead, you can run off all the tricks (in other words, to take all the tricks you can without losing the lead) before they get in to cash their major suit tricks, but this hand is too risky.

Responses to an Opening of Two No Trump

As we've seen, an opening bid of two no trump shows that your partner has 20 to 21 points and no trump distribution. Stayman applies over a two no trump open just as it applies over a one no trump open. The only difference is that you need fewer points to respond.

Always assume that when your partner opens two no trump she has 20 points. Then add to that the HCP you have in your hand. If they total 25, you should be in game somewhere. That means that you can bid with as few as 4 to 5 points.

The problem is that you don't really have the room to make an invitational bid, so you must make a decision based on your hand and what you know about her hand.

If you have 5 HCP but no four-card major, you respond three no trump. Know why? She has at least 20 points in her hand; you have 5. Together they equal 25, game in no trump. The point to remember is that when your partner opens two no trump, you should respond with a much weaker hand than when she opens one no trump. Against a one–no trump opening you had to pass unless you had a long major suit or at least 8 points. With a 0- to 7-point hand and no five-card major, you pass. When your partner opens two no trump, you should pass only if you have 0 to 4 points. You should bid with 5 points or more.

> **TRICKS OF THE TRADE**
>
> When you play rubber bridge (a form of contract bridge), which is what you're learning here, always keep the following goals in mind:
>
> - When bidding, reach game if possible.
> - When it is determined that a game is not possible, stop at as low a level as possible.
> - When playing, maximize the number of tricks you take, whether you're defending or declaring.

The Least You Need to Know

- After a one–no trump opening, if you hold a balanced hand …
  Pass with 0 to 7 points.
  Bid two no trump with 8 to 9 points.
  Bid three no trump with 10 or more HCP.

- When raising no trump, only count HCP.

- Bid two clubs (Stayman) to investigate for a major-suit fit.

- A Stayman bid promises at least one four-card major and 8 or more HCP.

- A jump to three of a minor suit is invitational to game showing a broken six-card suit.

Simple Responses to Opening One-Bids in a Suit

Chapter 11

In This Chapter

- Evaluating your hand for a response to a suit opening bid
- Describing your strength
- Knowing when to pass

Responding to opening one–no trump bids (see Chapter 10) is much easier than responding to an opening of one in a suit. That's because a one–no trump opening is such a specific bid. You know your partner has between 15 to 17 HCP and no trump distribution. However, when she opens one of a suit, all you know is that she has anywhere from 13 to 21 points (including distribution points) and, if she opens a major, that she has at least five cards in that suit.

When you respond to an opening of one no trump, you become the captain of the pair because you know so much about your partner's hand. When you respond to an opening of one in a suit, however, you're not in position to take control because your partner hasn't told you enough for you to be able to take control. So instead of taking control and placing the contract, you must communicate with your partner what you have in your hand. She told you that she has an opening hand, but not the requirements for a one–no trump open; in return, she's asking you for a description of your hand. This chapter tells you how to tell her what she wants to know.

Reading Your Partner's Strength Quickly

When your partner opens the bidding, she tells you approximately how many points she has. However, if she opens in a suit, her bid isn't as specific as when she opens one no trump. Basically all you know about her hand is that she has between 13 to 21 points, and the minimum number of cards in the suit she bids. You don't know her distribution. If she opens one club, it could be 4–3–3–3 or it could be 0–1–4–8 (meaning no spades, one heart, four diamonds, and eight clubs). You just don't know. All you know, if she opens a minor, is that she has at least three cards in that suit. If she opens a major, she has at least five cards in that suit. In a nutshell, when your partner opens, this is what you know about her hand:

- She has at least three cards in the suit if she opens in a minor suit.

- She has at least five cards in the suit if she opens in a major suit.

- She has between 13 to 21 points (including distribution points).

Not much to go on, is it? But that's what you've got. And actually, it's quite a lot. You know she has at least 13 points, you can start determining what cards they are by listening to the bidding of your opponents. Now your job is to tell her what you have.

Evaluating Your Hand

As you've seen, when you open the bidding you count shortness. But in responding to a suit opening, you can't count shortness unless you have a trump fit, meaning that between you and your partner, you have at least eight cards in the suit. You can establish a trump fit quickly by your partner's opening bid. If she opens one spade and you have three spades in your hand, you have a trump fit.

When your partner opens the bidding with one of a major, she's promising you that she has the following:

- At least 13 points

- At least five cards in the suit bid

So if your partner opens one spade, and you have three spades, you know that she has at least five spades, so you have a fit. As a result, you can use shortness, (or distribution points) in determining your first bid, which is your response to her opening bid.

When you know you have a trump fit, you may give yourself more points than when evaluating your hand for the purposes of making an opening bid. When you're making an evaluation to open the bidding, you have no idea if your partner has a fit for you in your suit, so you count your shortage points (or shortness), as I discuss in Chapter 5—3 points for a void, 2 points for a singleton, and 1 point for a doubleton. But when you respond, you know what your partner has. So if you have a fit, you can give yourself more points, as follows:

Distribution	Points
Void	5
Singleton	3
Doubleton	1

TRICKS OF THE TRADE

Shortness is only an asset if you can use it to ruff losers. If you're playing in spades and you have four losing diamonds in your hand but dummy has a singleton, you can ruff three of your losers in dummy, but only if dummy has enough trump. Without a trump fit, the shortness isn't an asset because you don't have enough trump to take advantage of it.

You Must Bid with 6 Points

If you have at least 6 HCP points, you *must* bid if your RHO passes. If you pass your partner's bid when your RHO has passed, you are specifically telling her that you have less than 6 points in your hand.

Why are you required to bid with 6 points when your RHO has passed? Because your partner can open a 15 to 21 point hand with an opening bid of only one of a suit.

You've already learned that a 20-point hand is opened two no trump. However, there are specific suit distribution requirements for a no trump bid, remember? What if your partner has 20 points, but a singleton? She can't open up two no trump. She can't open up two clubs because that requires 22 points. So what's she to do?

She can't lie to you, so she's left with opening up the hand with one of a suit. Even though you only have 6 points, you must keep the bidding open for her, in the event that she has a strong hand. Look at the following.

♠ AKQ75
♥ 874
♦ AKQJ
♣ 7

That's a 21-point hand; but it can't be opened at two no trump for two reasons: First, it contains a singleton. Second, it only has 19 HCP. (Remember: you don't count distribution points for no trump bids.) Therefore, she must open one spade. But look at the hand; she has seven sure tricks if spades is trump (AKQ of spades and AKQJ of diamonds). If you have three spades in your hand, she probably won't lose a spades trick, so she has nine sure tricks. That means she only needs one outside trick from you for game. Look at your possible hand:

♠ J86
♥ KQ
♦ 8532
♣ 9765

That's 6 points. She has game cold. She's not going to lose a spade trick (unless she has an unlucky 4-1 spade break), she has four cold diamond tricks, and you give her a sure heart trick. So when she opens this hand, all she's waiting for is for you to give her an absolute minimum response of a simple raise in her suit and she's jumping to game. If you pass because you don't like your 6 points, your LHO is probably going to pass, too.

Why? Count the HCP. You have 6, your partner has 19. That leaves 15 spread between both of your opponents. Your LHO would have to have 80 percent of the remaining points to have a bid at the two level. Although it's possible that your LHO will make an overcall, it's unlikely, and you can't take the chance that you'll leave your partner in the lurch with a big hand by passing.

Just remember, when your partner opens a suit bid at the one level and the bid is passed by your RHO, you *must* make a bid if you have 6 HCP—regardless of your estimation of the quality of those points.

Pass

That said, the first call you learn is *pass*. This tells her, "Partner, I really have a lousy hand—less than 6 points. Don't count on me for much help." It's important that you pass at your first opportunity if you have less than 6 points; then if you join the bidding later, your partner will know that you're just competing to interfere with your opponents, and have no thought of making a very high contract.

TRICKS OF THE TRADE

Believe it or not, passing seems to be the hardest call to learn and conquer. For some reason, when someone's partner opens the bidding, people feel an almost irresistible urge to respond, no matter how weak the hand. Remain unemotional. If your hand doesn't meet the requirements for a minimum response, pass.

When I was still learning (actually, I'm always learning!), I was playing with one of my partners while one of the best players in Los Angeles, Earle Ziskin, was watching me. My partner opened one club. I had 3 points, two clubs, but four spades. I bid one spade. After the hand, Earle said, "Tony, you misbid that."

"But I had such a terrible hand," I replied. "I was afraid she was opening up with only three clubs. If it's passed out, she's playing in a 3–2 trump fit."

Earle replied, "You don't have your bid. You don't have enough points. Think about what might happen next. You only have 3 points. Someone might have a lot of points and it might be your partner. She might be sitting over there just waiting to hear from you. All of a sudden she makes a jump shift, bidding three diamonds. That's a forcing bid. You *have* to bid. What are you going to say?"

I didn't have anything to say to that. I knew I was in trouble in this discussion, so I kept quiet and listened.

Earle continued, "The worst thing that could happen would be that your partner would be playing the hand in a 3–2 trump fit in a one-club contract. So what? She has to have some values to open. She's going to take a few tricks. So you're down a few in one club. That's not a disaster. What would be a disaster is playing the hand in three no trump, doubled, down 3. *That* would be a disaster. One club isn't going to be doubled, so that might be your best contract in this hand."

I've never forgotten that lecture. Don't feel forced to bid when your partner opens a minor and you have a very weak hand with no support for the suit she opens. Just bid your hand. If you pass and the bid is passed out, your opponents probably have the majority of the points between them and have probably missed some sort of partscore, if not game. Maybe they could have made three hearts. If your partner plays it in one club down two, you've probably traded 100 points above the line to keep your opponents from getting 140 below the line. I'll take that any day of the week.

Additionally, if your partner has the aforementioned huge hand, with 20 points, she's going to listen to your response; remember that when you responded you *guaranteed* that you had 6 points in your hand, and might jump to game. When your hand comes down and she goes set, you'd better hope the game never ends, because the conversation afterward isn't going to be a walk in the park on a nice spring day.

Want to know how that conversation will go? Read on:

> *Partner (dripping in ice):* You didn't have your bid.

> *You (sickly smile):* I thought you'd like to know I had four spades.

> *Partner (venom in her voice):* You didn't have your bid.

> *You (starting to sweat):* I didn't want you to be in a 3–2 trump fit.

> *Partner:* You didn't have your bid, and if you make another bid like that, you won't have your partner.

The moral of the story is: *pass.* I think pass is the best bid in bridge. Learn it. Don't forget it.

Describing Strength

You want to tell your partner as much about the strength of your hand as possible in one bid. This is easier if your hand is weak. The most descriptive bid you can make is one no trump. This tells your partner two things:

- You have at least 6 points, not more than 9 points, specifically limiting your hand.

- You don't have a four-card suit higher in ranking than the suit your partner opened. If your partner opened one diamond and you responded one no trump, you deny having either four hearts or four spades.

When your partner opens and you have a weak hand, your first obligation is to show a fit. So if you have 6 to 9 points and at least three cards in her opening major suit, you should simply raise her bid to the two level. If your partner opens in a minor, you can't raise her suit unless you have five cards in it. Why? Because she only promises three cards in the suit when she opens a minor (refer back to Chapter 4 for a detailed explanation).

Your next obligation is to tell her whether or not you have a four-card suit higher ranking than the suit she opened. If she opens one heart and you have 6 points and four spades without at least three hearts, your response is one spade.

> **TRICKS OF THE TRADE**
>
> With a very weak hand your *first* obligation is to tell your partner if you have a fit in her major-suit opening bid. So if she opens one heart and you have 6 to 9 points and at least three hearts, you should immediately raise her bid to the two level by bidding two hearts. This shows her your fit.

If your partner opens one heart, and you don't have at least three hearts, but you have 6 points with less than four spades, your response is one no trump.

Knowing this, respond with the following hands to your partner's opening bid of one club:

1.	2.	3.	4.	5.
♠ AK85	♠ 9865	♠ AKQ	♠ K64	♠ 86
♥ Q74	♥ AKQ	♥ 863	♥ K65	♥ KJ972
♦ 854	♦ 832	♦ 9652	♦ Q98	♦ 853
♣ 987	♣ 742	♣ 874	♣ 9653	♣ 872

Hand 1: One spade. This is a clear bid. You have 9 HCP and four spades.

Hand 2: One spade. Your strength is in hearts, but you only have three of them. Your partner is looking for an eight-card fit. Because she can't open a major suit unless she has five of them, she must open a minor suit with only four cards in the majors. Your bid of one spade tells her that you have four spades. If she has four spades, you have an eight-card trump fit, which is what you're looking for.

Hand 3: One diamond. Despite your HCP strength in spades, you only have three of them. You do have four diamonds, even though they're weak.

Hand 4: One no trump. You have 6 to 9 HCP, but you don't have a four-card suit of higher rank than the suit your partner opened. This bid tells her that information specifically.

Hand 5: Pass. Sure, your hearts look okay, but you don't have enough points to bid. If you bid this hand, and your partner has a very strong hand, she could make a forcing bid, requiring you to bid again, and you could find yourself at a much higher contract than you should be.

Which Suit to Show First

If you have a five-card suit and a four-card suit, which do you bid? Generally, your *longest suit is your strongest suit.* To take the most extreme example, xxxxx is stronger than AKJT. If your partner opens one club and you have five spades, four hearts, and enough points to bid, you bid the spades—even if your hearts are AKQJ and your spades are Qxxxx.

Bidding with Two Four-Card Suits

If you have two four-card suits, the rule is simple: bid the lower-ranking suit first. This is called bidding *up the line.*

> **DEFINITION**
>
> Bidding a lower-ranking suit before you bid a higher-ranking suit is called bidding **up the line.** Conversely, bidding a higher-ranking suit before you bid a lower-ranking suit is called bidding **down the line.**

If your partner opens one club and you have four diamonds and four hearts, you bid one diamond. If you have four hearts and four spades, you bid one heart. This allows your partner to bid one spade if she has four of them. If you were to bid one spade and your partner has four hearts, she would be forced to bid at the two level, and she probably wouldn't want to bid a four-card suit for the first time at the two level unless she had a very strong hand.

Remember: a new suit bid by responder is forcing on opener. This means that opener must bid again if her partner responds to his opening with a new suit.

Bidding with Two Five- or Six-Card Suits

If you have two five- or six-card suits, you should *not* bid them up the line. Rather, you should bid the higher-ranking suit first, or bid *down the line*, and then rebid the other if your partner doesn't support you.

Why? There are several reasons. These are suits that demand they both be mentioned. If you bid them up the line, you might have to go to the three or four level to mention the other at the second bid. For instance, if you have five diamonds and five hearts and your partner opens one club, if you were to bid up the line you'd bid one diamond. Then if your partner bids one spade or one no trump or two clubs, you have to bid two hearts. A new suit bid by responder is forcing on opener for one round, so your partner must bid again. Basically you're asking her to make a choice, and whatever she chooses she has to go to the three level.

If, on the other hand, you bid the higher ranking first in response to her one-club opening, the bidding could go like this.

Partner	You
One club	One heart
One no trump	Two diamonds

If she's got a minimum hand with heart support, she can express her preference by bidding two hearts, staying at the lower two level.

Another reason to bid down the line for two five- or six-card suits is that this is the only way you can indicate your length to partner. If you bid them up the line, how is she to know how many you have in your first suit? You might only have four. So if you bid a higher-ranking suit first, like hearts, and then bid a lower-ranking suit at your next opportunity, you might only have four of the lower-ranking suit, but for sure you have five of the higher-ranking suit, which was your first bid suit.

Responding at the Two Level

To respond at the two level to your partner's opening bid of one in a suit, you must have the following:

- At least 10 HCP

- A five-card major suit, or a four-card minor

If your partner opens one spade and you have five clubs and 10 HCP, you can respond with a bid of two clubs. Whenever you make a two-level response to your partner's opening one-level bid, you're promising her at least 10 HCP.

Bidding two clubs over a one spade open does *not* deny that you have trump support (which would be at least three cards in spades). So if you have at least 10 HCP and five clubs, along with three spades, you can, and should, bid two clubs first, then support your partner's spades at your next bid. Your first bid shows the strength of your hand, that you have more than a minimum. Don't forget, when you, as responder, bid a new suit, it is 100 percent forcing on opener to bid again; you can't be passed out at two clubs. When your partner bids again, no matter what she bids, you can bid spades to show her that you have spade support.

This information is important to her, because if you just bid two spades over her opening bid of one spade, she would think that you had a minimum hand, maybe only 6 points, and might pass. But if you show her that you have at least 10 points and at least four clubs first, when she learns that you *also* have three spades, she can better evaluate where to place the contract.

Raising Your Partner's Major-Suit Opening

The one exception to this rule of a two-level response to partner's opening one-level bid (that you must have at least 10 HCP and a five-card major suit/four-card minor suit before responding) is if you raise your partner's suit. For example, she opens one spade and you respond two spades. A raise of your partner's opening major suit bid promises the following:

- 6 to 9 points
- At least three cards in your partner's suit

Next to responding one no trump, this is the *weakest* positive bid you can make. Responding one no trump is weaker because it denies trump support. Raising her suit promises at least three cards in the suit, and therefore informs her that you have trump support for her, which is information she can use to further evaluate her hand. This is a bid that definitely limits your hand. You can't make this bid with three trump and 10 points. Responding two spades to your partner's opening bid of one spade tells her you don't have more than 9 points.

Raising Your Partner's Minor-Suit Opening

Note that I emphasized that you may support your partner's *major*-suit opening if you have three cards in it. This is definitely not true for a minor-suit opening by your partner. Why?

- When your partner opens in a major suit, she's promising at least five cards in that suit. So if you have three, you have the desired eight-card fit.

- When your partner opens in a minor suit, she's only promising three cards in that suit. So if you have three and she only has the three that she promised, you're in a dismal six-card fit and disaster is looming.

Because of this, you can't support your partner in a minor-suit opening unless you have five cards in the suit. Occasionally you will be in a fix where you can't respond one no trump and only have four of your partner's minor suit; then you're forced to raise her with only four. But try to avoid this. Of course, when you raise your partner's minor suit opening, you're giving her the weakest response possible. If she opened on a three-card suit, and you're raising on a four-card suit, she'll probably pass, unless she opened a strong hand. That's the beauty of the auction. Each bid means something. When she opens a minor, it means she doesn't have a five-card major. If you respond by raising her suit, it means you not only don't have a four-card major, but your hand is weak and her suit is your strongest suit. Even if she only has three, if she's on just a standard opening hand—nothing special—she will probably pass. You shouldn't be in too much trouble playing in a 3–4 fit at the two level.

Enough talking, let's bid some hands. Your partner opens one club:

	1.		2.		3.		4.	
	♠ 98743		♠ AKQ4		♠ AKQ		♠ J865	
	♥ AKQ6		♥ 8764		♥ 9754		♥ 76	
	♦ 64		♦ 863		♦ 872		♦ AJ765	
	♣ 54		♣ 85		♣ 984		♣ 75	

	5.		6.		7.		8.	
	♠ 64		♠ A64		♠ 876		♠ K873	
	♥ AK98		♥ K98		♥ J86		♥ Q985	
	♦ AJ952		♦ 854		♦ AJ		♦ JT86	
	♣ 87		♣ 8754		♣ 97652		♣ 7	

Hand 1: One spade. Your hearts are terrific, but you only have four of them. You must bid your longest major, and that's spades.

Hand 2: One heart. Your spades are terrific, but when you have two major suits of equal length, you bid the lower ranking first, bidding up the line.

Hand 3: One heart. You have 9 points and four hearts.

Hand 4: One diamond. It's the longest suit, and therefore your strongest.

Hand 5: One diamond. You have enough points to bid twice. Remember that when you bid a new suit it *forces* opener to bid again. So you bid your one diamond. No matter what your partner bids, you can bid your hearts at the two level, describing your hand as more than 10 HCP with five diamonds and four hearts.

Hand 6: One no trump. You have 7 HCP and both major suits stopped once and only have four clubs. You're not promising stoppers in all three unbid suits when you respond one no trump, so the fact that you don't have diamonds stopped doesn't preclude you from responding one no trump.

Hand 7: Two clubs. This is pretty clear. You have 7 HCP, no stoppers in the majors, and five clubs.

Hand 8: One diamond. You bid suits of equal length up the line. You don't deny a four-card major by bidding one diamond in response to your partner's one club opening.

Your partner opens one heart:

	1.	2.	3.	4.	5.
♠	J643	AKJ	742	K8	QT65
♥	AK4	752	A5	862	65
♦	753	85	J632	Q62	98
♣	752	K8653	Q964	JT754	J7642

Hand 1: Two hearts. Your spades are too weak to not show your very strong hearts support immediately.

Hand 2: Two Clubs. You have 11 points and a five-card clubs suit. You show your hearts support at your next bid.

Hand 3: One no trump. You have a minimum hand without hearts support, even though you have the ace. If your partner bids another suit at the two level, you can bid two hearts, showing a minimum hand with two hearts.

Hand 4: Two hearts. This is a bare minimum hand, but you do have three hearts. You must tell your partner what you have, and a simple raise of your partner's opening suit only promises three trumps and 6 points. That's what you've got. Any other bid she makes will be her problem, because you've warned her that your hand stinks. But you have an obligation to keep the bidding open with 6 points. Why? Your partner might have opened a 20-point hand with a bid of one heart. All she needs to know is that you have 6 points and three hearts and she'll bid game. This is a classic hand where your partner must be able to trust you to bid correctly.

Hand 5: Pass. Only 4 points, no hearts support. You don't want this to get any higher. You must show your partner your weakness. You might have a 4–4 spade fit, but if you don't, what are you going to do when your partner bids three diamonds—a forcing bid—at her next call?

Responses over Interference

So far we've been talking about bidding when your opponents docilely pass at their turn. Alas, this doesn't always happen. When your opponents are bidding, it changes the meanings of your responses. When a player opens and opponents bid, that's called *interference*. Opponents are interfering with opener's bidding by bidding themselves.

You have two obligations in responding to your partner's opening bid:

- Tell her what you have as quickly and accurately as possible.

- Keep the bidding open for your partner if you have at least 6 points in case she opened at the one level with a huge hand. This obligation is removed if you have less than 6 points.

Your first obligation doesn't change when your opponents interfere. Your second obligation does.

When your opponents interfere, you're relieved of one of responder's obligations: the commitment to keep the bidding open for your partner. Why? Because when your RHO passes, you don't know what your LHO is going to do. He might pass, too. If this happens, and you haven't taken a call, the bidding will pass out and partner will be playing the hand in her opening bid. So if your RHO passes, you must bid if you have 6 points so that your partner, whose hand is basically undefined unless she's opened one no trump, will get another chance to bid. She might have opened a 20-point hand at the one level because she didn't have anything else to bid. She's just waiting to find out if you have 6 points to place the contract in game.

But when your RHO bids, your obligation to bid with at least 6 points is removed because your partner will definitely get another chance to bid, even if you pass. If you take a bid right after your RHO bids, it's called a *free bid* because you have no obligation to bid.

Free Bid of a Suit at the One Level

A free bid of a new suit at the one level tells your partner that you have a better than minimum hand. So with 6 or 7 points, you should pass. If you take a free bid after your RHO bids, you're telling your partner that you have one of the following:

- At least 8 points with a four-card suit
- At least 7 points with a good suit

If you pass, you're denying one of these holdings and telling your partner that if she bids again she can't count on much help from you.

Free Bid of a Suit at the Two Level

A free bid of a new suit at the two level promises the same 10 points it promises without interference, but implies game interest. Why? Because opponents have shown a biddable hand and some points. You're telling your partner that despite the fact that opponents may have some points and a good suit, you think the contract should be yours and want to explore it more. This bid is 100 percent forcing on your partner to bid again.

Free Bid of No Trump

A free bid of one no trump over RHO's *overcall* promises the following:

- 8 to 10 HCP
- A stopper in RHO's suit

DEFINITION

An **overcall** is any bid after an opponent has opened the bidding. So if your pair opens the bidding and opponents make a bid, it's an overcall. If your opponents open the bidding and you or your partner make a bid, it's an overcall.

Therefore, if your partner opens one club and RHO bids one spade, what would you bid with the following hands?

1.	♠ Q65	2.	♠ 86	3.	♠ 86	4.	♠ KT65
	♥ K97		♥ K94		♥ K94		♥ T94
	♦ 865		♦ Q842		♦ Q84		♦ Q82
	♣ Q975		♣ Q752		♣ Q9752		♣ J97

Hand 1: One no trump. You can properly respond one no trump because you have 8 HCP and a stopper in spades. It's not a great stopper, but it is a stopper.

Hand 2: Pass. This tells your partner that you have a minimum hand, 0 to 9 points, without a stopper in opponent's suit. Had your RHO overcalled one heart, your pass would also tell your partner you don't have four spades, because with 8 to 9 points and four spades, you should bid your spade suit over RHO's *overcall* of one heart. You can't make a simple raise to two clubs because your partner might only have three cards in the suit.

Hand 3: Two clubs. You have 8 points. Even though your partner opened a club, she may only have three cards in the suit, so you need five clubs to make a simple raise. You have five clubs and 8 points. This bid effectively tells your partner that she can count on you for only 8 to 9 points and five clubs.

Hand 4: Pass. You would have bid one spade without interference, but your RHO bid it first! Even though you have a good spade suit, you only have 6 points. A free bid of one no trump would tell your partner you have a stronger hand. A pass tells her you have less than 8 points. If she has extra values, she'll bid again. Then, if she makes a forcing bid, you can tell her about your spades. (For example, if your partner doubles to get you back in the bidding, you'd bid one no trump.) If your partner has a minimum opening hand, and given your weak hand, it would be better to defend opponents in one spade than to bid to a contract where you might have a lot of trouble.

RHO Bids Your Strong Suit

If .you have a very good suit and RHO beats you to bidding it after your partner has opened, what do you do? What if your partner opened one club, your RHO bid one spade, and you have the following hand?

♠ AK987
♥ K64
♦ 75
♣ 865

You have three possible calls here:

Bid no trump. You can clearly bid no trump here. One no trump would be fine, but here your hand is so strong you could jump to two no trump to tell your partner that you have 10 HCP and your RHO's suit stopped twice.

Double for penalty. Your partner opened the bidding, so you know she has at least 13 points. You have 11 points with your doubleton. That's 24 points, plus you have a very strong spade suit, with at least two sure tricks to make the contract. But your partner has power enough to make an opening bid, and you have a good enough trump suit to be playing the hand in spades yourself. Ask yourself, "If my RHO didn't bid, would I think that my partner and I could make one spade?" If so, you should double. This is especially true because you're sitting behind declarer.

Pass. If you're playing *negative doubles*, which you will learn about in Chapter 19, you can't make a penalty double because a double in this situation means something else. So you would pass and hope your partner would proceed as set forth in Chapter 19.

To recap, your pass over opponent's interference generally means one of two things:

- Your hand is too weak for a convenient bid over the specific interference that occurred, or

- Your RHO bid your suit and you're not strong enough to double for penalty or bid one no trump.

Your partner should be aware that your pass after interference means one of these two things.

The Least You Need to Know

- After your partner opens with one of a suit, you must respond if you have at least 6 points.

- Bid your longest suit first, provided you can still bid it at the one level. With two five- or six-card suits, bid the higher-ranking suit first.

- With four-card suits, bid the lowest ranking, if possible, at the one level. Suit quality is unimportant; length is the primary factor.

- After your partner opens a major, raise bidding to the two level with 6 to 9 points and at least three of her suit. You need at least four, and preferably five or more, to raise partner's minor-suit opening. Raising to the two level also shows 6 to 9 points.

- With 6 to 9 HCP, bid one no trump if you don't have a higher-ranking four-card suit to bid at the one level.

- A suit response at the two level shows 10 or more points and at least a four-card suit. It doesn't deny support for your partner's major suit opening bid.

Glad Tidings of Great Joy! Jump Responses

In This Chapter

- Limit raises
- Jump shifts
- Jumps to no trump
- Responses by a passed hand

Sometimes you open your hand and start looking for your calculator so you can add up all the points you hold; next thing you know, you hear your partner open the bidding! How can this be? You have a lot of points yet she's already bidding. What now?

Obviously you want to describe your good fortune to her as soon and as accurately as possible—but how?

This is where jump bids become useful. In this chapter, you learn how to use jump bids to describe hands that are better than what you can communicate by a simple response.

Limit Raises

A *limit raise* is a raise that shows a hand with trump support and not less than 10 points, but not more than 12 points. It's called *limit raise* because the bid confines the hand to these parameters. You can make other bids if your hand isn't within these boundaries. This section describes the various types of limit raises.

How do you make a limit raise? You jump your partner's suit. A *jump* is a bid that passes a level available to you.

Limit Raises When Your Partner Opens a Major Suit

What if you have four of opener's major-suit opening—10 points—but don't have a suit to bid at the two level? Take a look at the following hand, after your partner has opened the bidding at one spade:

♠ KQJ5
♥ A76
♦ J96
♣ 984

Not a bad hand, but what do you bid? If you just raise her one-spade bid to two spades, she'll think you have a minimum and will almost certainly pass. (It's possible that she had to open a 20-point hand with a bid of one spade because her distribution didn't allow her to open it two no trump. If she has such a strong hand, she will quickly jump to four spades when she finds out that you have at least 6 points.) You're too strong just to reply with two spades; what do you bid?

You give her a limit raise. A limit raise in your partner's opening major suit is a bid that says you have the following:

- 10 to 12 points

- Three or four cards in opener's major suit

For example, if your partner opens one spade, you could bid two spades, but that would show a fairly weak hand. If you bypass bidding at the two level, and make a bid of three spades, instead of two spades, it's called a *jump*. If you play that a jump in your partner's opening major suit at your first opportunity is a limit raise, then it shows at least three-card support and 10 to 12 points.

This is a very good bid because it tells your partner so much. It limits your hand to no more than 12 HCP, but promises at least 10 HCP, and it promises at least three-card trump support. It's one of the most specific bids in bridge, even more specific than the opening of one no trump. From your limit raise, your partner should be able to determine if she should bid game. If she opened with a minimum, she'll pass and the contract will be three spades. With more than a minimum she'll bid game, at least.

Limit Raises When Your Partner Opens a Minor Suit

When your partner opens a minor suit, there are slightly different conditions when you make a limit raise. In the first place, because your partner has opened with a minor, you don't know how many cards she has in her suit. Because of that limitation, a limit raise in a minor suit should promise five cards in the suit. If you give a limit raise with a four-card suit and she has opened a three-card suit, you could find yourself playing at the three level on a 3–4 fit—not an attractive prospect.

Furthermore, you should not make a limit raise of a minor-suit opening if you have a four-card major. The requirements for a limit raise in a minor suit are as follows:

- No four-card major
- 10 to 12 points
- Five-card support

If your partner has opened a three-card suit looking for a major-suit fit, and you give her a limit raise in her minor-suit opening, she'll probably either pass your limit raise and play it in three of the minor, or try three no trump if she has strength in the other suits.

Jump Shift Responses

As we've seen, a jump is a bid that passes a level available to you. A shift is a change of suit. So a *jump shift* occurs when you make a jump bid in a suit different from the suit your partner opened. For example, if your partner opens one club, you could bid any other suit at the one level. If you bid a new suit at the two level when you could have bid it at the one level, it's called a *jump shift*. For example, if your partner opens one club and you bid two diamonds instead of one diamond, you've made a jump shift. There are two ways to play a jump shift response. A lot of players play them weak; however, most rubber bridge players play them strong. That's what you're going to learn here: strong jump shifts.

Strong Jump Responses

A strong jump shift shows a very good hand and is game forcing on your partner. If you open one diamond, your LHO passes, and your partner bids two spades, that's a jump shift. She could have bid one spade; however, she skipped the one level and jumped to the two level, and she shifted from your suit of diamonds to a new suit: spades.

When your partner does this, you must keep the bidding open until you've reached game, then—and only then—you can pass. The following chart shows what each bid means.

Partner	You	Meaning
One heart	Two no trump	13 to 15 HCP, balanced hand, stoppers in the three unbid suits, denies four spades
One heart	Three no trump	16 to 18 HCP, balanced hand, stoppers in the three unbid suits, denies four spades
One heart	Two spades	16 or more points, game forcing, looking for slam, does *not* deny four hearts, could be totally unbalanced

When I started playing bridge again after a hiatus of several decades after college, I was playing the game I played at UCLA: strong two bids and strong jumps. One day I picked up my cards and saw that I had 22 points. I was ready to open two spades—which is game forcing on my partner—but my RHO opened two hearts. I was stunned. How could she have a strong enough hand to open two hearts when I had more than half of the points in the deck in my hand? I thought about it a while and decided to pass, thinking that we could get them for a good set. Alas, my opponent was playing Weak Twos, so they stole the bid and we got a terrible result; that was my introduction to modern bridge. Just be aware that if you're playing Strong Twos and strong jump shifts, your opponents might be playing Weak Twos and weak jump shifts. So when an opponent jumps the bidding and you don't know what they're playing, always ask what the bid means before you assume you know.

ALERT

You can always ask what an opponent's bid means when it's your turn to bid by asking the bidder's partner. (You must ask the bidder's partner because a bidder isn't allowed to say what his bid means.) He must give you an accurate and complete description of the meaning of his partner's bid. You can't be forced to bid without an explanation of a bid you don't understand.

Preemptive Jump to Game

Look at the following hand, after your partner has opened the bidding with one spade:

♠ QT863
♥ 8
♦ Q653
♣ QT4

What's your bid? You have nice spades support for your partner, but there's not much else that looks good except the singleton heart.

Regardless of what your RHO does, this hand suggests a jump to game with a bid of four spades. You can make a preemptive jump to game with a hand that satisfies the following requirements:

- Your partner opened a major.

- You have five-card trump support for her, or more.

- You have between 6 to 10 points.

- You have a singleton or void.

The reason for this is that your partner will have a fair chance of making the contract because you have so many trump between the two of you. If she goes set, it shouldn't be by more than one or two. And you want to stifle your opponents' ability to find the game they might have by communicating with one another. You have only 6 HCP. Your partner might be opening up a minimum with five spades, a singleton, and 12 total points, which would translate to 10 HCP. That means that your opponents would have approximately 24 HCP between them. They might very well have a hearts game between them. If you jump immediately to four spades, they don't have the time to communicate.

The prospects in this hand are twofold: You might very well have a game between you and your partner. If not, your opponents might very well have a game between them, and you've kept them from finding it or bidding it. You might have traded 100 points above the line to keep them from getting 120 points below the line and 300— or 500—points above the line. Alternatively, your opponents might bid hearts, which might be one trick more than they can make.

Also by making a quick preemptive strike, you've prevented your opponents from communicating to see if they have enough power between them to double and penalize you for your bid. Any double by them at this point would be a guess, because you obviously have a distributional hand.

Another thing to remember is that your opponents are listening to your bidding, too. If they're knowledgeable players they'll know that your bid is preemptive, so you might be doubled for penalty. (Especially if your RHO has made an overcall and your LHO has a good hand.) But that's just the chance you take. If you only go down two doubled and they can make game in their suit, you will have made a good bid—a "save" against their game.

TRICKS OF THE TRADE

The preemptive jump to game isn't strictly limited to a major-suit opening, but it's riskier in a minor suit because you must take all but two tricks. Opponents will be more inclined to double a jump to a five-level contract than a jump to a four-level contract.

Jumps to No Trump

Many jump bids to no trump don't fit any of the patterns discussed so far. Generally, all jump bids to no trump show a strong hand.

ALERT

When you're jumping from a suit to no trump, remember that you count HCP only—not shortness points—when evaluating your hand.

Remember also, when you bid no trump as a qualitative bid—that is to suggest playing the hand without trump—you designate your partner as captain of the hand. This applies to responses and rebids as well as opening bids.

Jumps to No Trump After a Minor-Suit Opening

A jump shift to two no trump after a minor-suit opening by your partner promises the following:

- Between 12 to 15 HCP
- No four-card major

- Stoppers in all suits unbid by your partner
- No trump distribution

This is a very good bid because you already know that you have more points than they do. If your partner opened the bidding, she has at least 13 points and you know that you have 12 to 15 HCP; therefore, you have at least 25 total points between you. Of course, at this time you don't know if your partner's points are HCP or distribution points, but you'll find that out when she bids.

This bid also tells your partner that you can't have an eight-card major fit between you. Can you figure out why?

Answer: Because your partner opened a minor, she probably doesn't have a five-card major, or she would have opened by bidding it. Because you jumped to two no trump over her minor-suit opening, you don't have a four-card major. This shows how you deduce what you have between you by what *wasn't* bid.

If she doesn't have a five-card major, you can't have an eight-card fit unless you both have a four-card major, but your bid denies a four-card major. Therefore, if she doesn't have a five-card major and you don't have a four-card major, you can't have eight cards in a major between you.

You both know that if you have game it will probably be in no trump. This puts it in opener's corner because only she knows whether her points are HCP or distribution points.

Finally, what if you have 12 to 15 points, no four-card major, but an unstopped, unbid suit? In this instance, you must make a two-over-one response to tell your partner what you have. Look at the following hand:

♠ 872
♥ K4
♦ AQ76
♣ KT86

ALERT

Don't forget—you shouldn't jump to no trump over your partner's minor-suit open if you have a four-card major.

If your partner opens one diamond, you don't have a four-card major to bid and you can't jump to two no trump because spades is unstopped. In this instance, you should respond two clubs. This tells your partner that you have at least 10 points, at least four clubs, and no four-card major. It's forcing your partner to bid again; you'll have a better idea of where to play the contract when you learn more about her hand. When she bids again, you can tell her that you have more than 10 points. You don't have to tell everything in one bid. It's nice when you can, but sometimes you can't.

Jumps to Three No Trump over a Minor-Suit Open of One

A jump to three no trump over a minor-suit open of one shows the next level—16 to 18 HCP—and denies a four-card major. There is sound arithmetical reasoning behind this. If you have at least 16 HCP and your partner has at least 13 points, you should probably be able to make three no trump (which generally requires 25 HCP between you both). If she has 2 or 3 shortness points—which is a possibility—that still leaves her with at least 10 HCP; this, when added to your 16 HCP, should offer a good play for three no trump.

As I said previously, if you don't have a four-card major, and your partner's opening hand doesn't have a five-card major, there's no hope of an eight-card fit in a major. That said, if you're going to be playing the hand in game, it should probably be in three no trump. If your partner opened a distributional hand, like 6–5 in the minors, she can jump to game in the appropriate minor because your bid promised at least two cards in each suit.

The following shows the HCP requirements for jumps to no trump after your partner makes a minor suit open of one of the suit:

Response	HCP
Two no trump	12–15
Three no trump	16–18

Responses When You're a Passed Hand

When your partner opens the bidding in third or fourth seat, it means that you passed at your first opportunity to bid, so you don't have an opening hand. This is called a *passed hand*. When it comes time to bid again, some of your responses remain the same, but some change. You must remember that the standards for opening in third seat are less than they are for opening in first or second seat. Now that you're responder, you must remember the standards you learned for opening the bidding in third seat and follow those standards here (see Chapter 7).

Your partner could have a perfectly good opening hand—one that she would have opened with in the first or second seat—but then again, she might not. She might be *opening light*.

DEFINITION

Opening light refers to when you open a hand with less than 13 points.

A **passed hand** is one that could have opened the bidding but the player passed instead of making an opening bid with it.

When you have 6 to 9 points, your responses are the same: You bid your four-card majors. You bid up the line. And, if you don't have a four-card major and can't support your partner, you bid one no trump.

Jump Shift by a Passed Hand

When you're a passed hand, a jump shift obviously doesn't mean that you have a hand strong enough to make a game-forcing bid, as you learned earlier in this chapter. If you had an opening hand with the values to make a strong jump shift, you would have opened!

When your partner opens a minor, you make a jump shift when you are a passed hand to show that you have a six-card near-independent major suit. If your partner opens one club or one diamond and you have the following type of holding in hearts or spades with nothing else, opposite a singleton or void, you should make a jump shift to your long suit:

> AQT9xxx
>
> AKTxxx
>
> AJT9xx

This bid invites your partner to pass. If she opened with a minimum 13 to 14 point hand, you'll be better off playing the contract in your suit—even if she has a void in your suit. You are specifically describing a hand that you feel should be played at the two level in your suit.

Unless she makes a forcing bid at her next turn to call, you have told her that you intend to pass. It's up to her to place the contract. Your strong suggestion is that she place the contract by passing and allowing you to play it at the two level in your suit. Any action she takes after this bid is on her shoulders. You have done the best you can to describe your hand.

The Least You Need to Know

- A jump raise in your partner's opening suit is called a *limit raise*. It shows 10 to 12 points and invites your partner to bid a game.
- A limit raise contains three or more cards in your partner's opening suit after a major-suit opening, and five or more cards in your partner's opening suit after a minor-suit opening.
- After a minor-suit opening, a limit raise denies a four-card or longer major.
- A jump shift shows 16 or more points and is at least invitational to slam. A jump shift is 100 percent game forcing.
- A jump shift to a major suit by a passed hand after a minor-suit open shows a strong six-card major suit with no high-card strength in any other suit. Partner is invited to pass.

Rebids, Overcalls, and Doubles

After you and your partner have made your initial bids, you continue to communicate and describe your hands to one another. This part shows you how to complete your communication and make a determination whether to play or defend.

If your opponents open the bidding, you still have a chance to bid by making an overcall or a takeout double. You'll find out about overcalls, takeout doubles, and responses to your partner's overcalls and takeout doubles.

Just because your opponents get the contract, you aren't finished. If you don't think they can make it, you can challenge them by doubling! You'll learn how to do this here, along with getting a solid grasp of the risks and rewards of making a penalty double.

Aye, Aye, Sir! Rebids by No Trump Opener

Chapter 13

In This Chapter

- Rebids after your partner responds to an opening bid of no trump
- Rebids after your partner bids Stayman
- Rebids after your partner responds over interference

As you learned in Chapter 5, when you open the bidding with any no trump bid, you designate your partner as captain of your pair. You have specifically described your hand as one that's balanced and contains a number of HCP within a very narrow range: 15 to 17 HCP for a one no trump open, and 20 to 21 for a two no trump open.

Your partner has heard you and has responded, either by asking you a question or by describing her hand to you. This chapter tells you how you respond, depending on what's in your hand and the question she has asked.

Rebids When You Get an Invitation

You've opened the hand with one no trump, which means that you have a balanced, 15- to 17-HCP hand. Your partner bids two no trump. What do you do? This is pretty easy. Your partner has said maybe by making an invitational bid. She has 8 to 9 HCP and a balanced hand. You don't know where her HCP cards are, but you know she has them. This is simple arithmetic. Your partner, who is the captain at this point, has given you a specific instruction. She has said, "Partner, if you're at the top of your bid—17 points, or a good 16 points—bid three no trump; otherwise, pass."

Why? If she has 8 points—the minimum she could have—and you have 17 points—the maximum you could have—you have 25 HCP between you; that's usually enough for game. However, even if she's just 1 point below her maximum, when added to your 17 points this only totals 24 points. That's generally not enough for game, so you should pass.

This little game of math works remarkably well. Generally, when I ignore the arithmetic and go to game with a bad 16-point hand, I get burned because I've been set the one trick that the math said I couldn't get. Sometimes you can make three no trump with 24 points or less, but the percentages are very much against you.

What constitutes a "good" 16? Even though the 10 is considered an "honor," you only give yourself points in counting the hand for honors of the rank of jack and above. But 8, 9, and 10 have value because they can often take tricks. For example, look at the following holdings:

> *North*
> ♠ K2

West
♠ Q43

East
♠ A765

> *South*
> ♠ JT98

Which hand is the most powerful? Answer: South, even though South has the fewest points. When you lead your jack of spades, West covers with the queen, you cover with the king from North, and East takes the trick with the ace. After this trick, South's 10, 9, and 8 of spades are all winners.

This shows that when you evaluate a hand—especially when playing in a no trump contract—you should take into consideration your 10s and cards just below honor rank. A good 16 points is a hand that includes lots of 9s and 10s, like the following:

> ♠ AT93
> ♥ KJT
> ♦ AT95
> ♣ AT

This hand has only 16 points. Even though you don't have 17 points, you have all four 10s and only two cards below the rank of 9! You should accept an invitational bid of two no trump by your partner and go on to bid three no trump. This hand is worth a bid of three no trump because this is a "good" 16 points. Look at the following hand, which appeared in a national tournament:

♠ AT95
♥ KT4
♦ AQ7
♣ JT7

This hand has 14 HCP, but many experts opened it one no trump because they elevated it to 15 HCP due to the *body cards*, which include three 10s and one 9. The hand contains only four cards that aren't honors or body cards. Compare it with the following hand:

♠ A432
♥ A32
♦ A32
♣ A32

 DEFINITION

8s, 9s, and 10s are called **body cards.**

Such a hand is called *aces and spaces*, and it can be a disaster because you only have four tricks: the four aces. You would still open this hand one no trump because you must describe your hand to your partner, but you're going to cringe and sweat until the bidding is over, praying that it's not passed out and that you're not stuck playing it in one no trump. The previously described hand with the body cards and 14 HCP is far more powerful than aces and spaces. Sometimes you have to be flexible in counting your points and analyzing your hand.

Change the former hand by making the 7 of clubs the queen of clubs, so it looks like this:

♠ AT95
♥ KT4
♦ AQ7
♣ QJT

This is a good 16 HCP, and you would accept an invitation to game by bidding game. In the aces and spaces hand, the invitation should be declined.

Let's look at some maybe hands, where your partner responds two no trump to your one no trump opening bid:

1. ♠ J32	2. ♠ KJ7	3. ♠ AQ2	4. ♠ A2
♥ J432	♥ KJ8	♥ 543	♥ K32
♦ AQ32	♦ AQ87	♦ KQ6	♦ AQJ54
♣ AK	♣ K87	♣ KQ65	♣ Q65

Hand 1: Pass. Simple arithmetic prevails. You have 15 HCP. By her two no trump response your partner has said, "Pard, if you have 17 HCP, go to 3. Otherwise, pass because I only have 8 or 9 HCP." With 15 HCP in your hand and a maximum of 9 HCP in your partner's hand, you have a maximum of 24 HCP, not enough for game.

Hand 2: Three no trump. You are at the top of your bid: 17 HCP. Even if your partner only has her minimum—8 HCP—8 + 17 = 25, which is enough to bid game.

Hand 3: Pass. This is the tempting hand, but it's not a good 16 points. "Well," you say to yourself, "I'm only 1 point shy. If my partner is at the top of her bid—9 HCP—we have 25 between us and that's enough for game." Don't succumb to this temptation. You must assume that your partner is at the bottom of her bid—8 HCP—and 8 + 16 = 24, not enough for game. Better to bid two and make three than to bid three and make two!

Hand 4: Three no trump. Did you miss this one? You only have 16 HCP, but you have a very good five-card suit that should give you four tricks by itself. When you have a five-card suit headed by at least one of the top three honors, and you receive an invitation from your partner, accept it and take it to game. A good five-card suit is valuable when playing in no trump.

Rebids When Your Partner Gives a Weak Response

When you open one no trump and your partner bids a suit other than clubs directly at the two level, it's a sign-off bid and you should pass. She's telling you that she has a weak hand with five or more diamonds, hearts, or spades, and the contract should be played in her suit.

Rebids When Your Partner Gives an Invitational Response in a Suit

When your partner bids two clubs (Stayman), and then bids a suit different than the one you bid, she's telling you that she has an invitational hand—8 to 9 points—and a five-card suit. Suppose the bidding goes like this:

You	LHO	Partner	RHO
One no trump	Pass	Two clubs	Pass
Two diamonds	Pass	Two spades	Pass

Your two diamonds bid tells her that you don't have a four-card major. Her two spades bid tells you that she has at least a five-card spades suit with 8 to 9 points. Your response should be along the following lines:

- Pass if you have a minimum hand with three spades.

- Two no trump with minimum hand and only two spades.

- Three spades if you have at least three spades and 17 points or a good 16.

- Three no trump if you have only two spades but a maximum hand with 17 points or a good 16. If she has six spades, she'll bid four spades because she knows you should be playing in game in the major suit if you have an eight-card fit. Your bid of three no trump tells her that you have a maximum hand but only two spades.

Rebids When Your Partner Jumps to Three No Trump

If responder has bid three no trump, opener *must* pass. It doesn't matter if opener is head over heels in love with her hand, if opener has a long suit (a five card major or a six card minor), if she's at the maximum, or whatever. Opener has described her hand to her partner so she knows, within a couple of points, what opener has. Bidding is about trust. You must trust your partner. Responder is telling opener that, based on what she knows about the two hands, three no trump is the proper contract—no more, no less. So when opener hears her loving partner say, "Three no trump," opener should say, "Pass."

Responding to Stayman

When your partner bids two clubs, she's asking you if you have a four-card major. If you do, bid it. But what if you don't? What if you have a good four- or five-card minor in clubs? Do you raise her two clubs bid to three?

Not in this lifetime. As I explain in Chapter 10, if your partner bids two clubs and you don't have a four-card major, you *must* bid two diamonds. A bid of two diamonds is conventional and denies a four-card major. It says nothing about your diamond suit. When your partner bids two clubs (a conventional bid, saying nothing about clubs) in response to your opening bid of one no trump, she's asking, "Do you have a four-card major?" You can answer one of two ways: two hearts or two spades (yes), or two diamonds (no).

If your hand contains two four-card majors, you respond hearts first. If you respond two spades to two clubs, you're showing four spades and denying having four hearts. However, the response of two hearts to two clubs guarantees having a four-card heart suit but does not deny having four spades.

Also, remember that when you open one no trump you have designated your partner as the captain of your pair for this hand. So her first question may be to find out if you have a four-card major. When she discovers the answer to this question, she'll either place the contract, or tell you something about her hand by making an invitational bid. Then it will be up to you to place the contract, but so far you don't know much about her hand, except that she has a four-card major. So just answer no by saying two diamonds and leave the rest of it up to her. Let's look at some hands and see how to respond after you opened one no trump and your partner responded two clubs:

1.	♠ A32	2.	♠ A432	3.	♠ A43	4.	♠ AKJ9
	♥ KJ9		♥ KQ6		♥ KQ3		♥ 5432
	♦ KJ8		♦ KQ5		♦ KQ92		♦ A9
	♣ K984		♣ K32		♣ K98		♣ AT9

Hand 1: Two diamonds. No four-card major. Your answer is no.

Hand 2: Two spades. You have one four-card major—spades—so you bid it. This rebid absolutely denies a four-card heart suit.

Hand 3: Two diamonds. This is a strong hand with 17 HCP. Despite that, you must respond two diamonds. Your partner is now the captain for this hand. She has asked one simple question, "Do you have a four-card major?" That's all she wants to know. She doesn't care, at this point, whether you have 15 HCP or 17 HCP. All she wants to know is whether or not you have a four-card major, and your answer is no.

Hand 4: Two hearts. You have two four-card majors, consisting of a terrific spade suit and a terrible heart suit. You *must* bid your hearts first. That's your agreement. She has at least one four-card major. It might be hearts. You'd rather play in a 4–4 heart fit with your hearts than a 4–2, or worse, spade suit with your spades, wouldn't you? If you wouldn't, you'd better go back and reread the chapters on suit bids and responses. Also, remember that bidding your four-card heart suit doesn't deny a four-card spade suit. If she then bids two no trump (telling you that her four-card major is spades, not hearts), you can rebid four spades to tell her that you have four spades as well as four hearts. Because her bid of two no trump is invitational, and you have enough to play in game in a suit (your diamond doubleton gives you 17 points in a suit contract), you should bid game. If you bid three spades, your partner is allowed to pass.

Rebidding over Interference When Your Partner Responds

Two types of interference can occur when your partner responds to your opening bid of one no trump. Interference can occur *before* your partner bids, or it can occur *after* your partner bids. We've already covered how responder handles interference before she bids (see Chapter 10), but how does opening bidder respond when interference occurs after her partner bids?

Opponents take a chance in bidding a suit after your partner has bid two clubs: Stayman. This gives you information about their hands and cards that you wouldn't have otherwise.

For example, your partner bids Stayman—asking if you have a four-card major—and RHO bids two hearts. If you have four hearts, you probably don't want to be playing this hand in hearts. If you have hearts well stopped and don't have four spades, you can respond two no trump—telling your partner that she needn't worry much about hearts if you play the hand in no trump. But you might want to double for penalty. Look at the following auction.

You	LHO	Partner	RHO
One no trump	Pass	Two clubs	Two hearts
?			

1. ♠ AQ65	2. ♠ A72	3. ♠ 5432	4. ♠ KQ2	5. ♠ 32
♥ 32	♥ AQ	♥ AJ9	♥ 98	♥ AQ65
♦ KJ9	♦ KT73	♦ KJ8	♦ AJ98	♦ KJ9
♣ AQ98	♣ QJ98	♣ KQJ	♣ KQ64	♣ AQ98

Hand 1: Two spades. You bid what you would have bid had there been no interference. If your partner's suit is hearts, she can bid two no trump or three no trump depending on the strength of her hand. If her suit is spades, then you've found your fit and she'll place the contract or give you an invitational bid of three spades.

Hand 2: Two no trump. You don't have four spades, but you do have the hearts suit well stopped. That's what this bid tells your partner: "Don't worry about hearts, pard, because I can take care of them."

Hand 3: Two spades. Your spades are terrible, but you do have four of them. If that's your partner's suit, you'll be okay because you'll be in a 4–4 fit.

Hand 4: Pass. You have a minimum no trump opening, no hearts stopper, and you don't have four spades. Both you and your partner have bid and have nice hands, but this doesn't mean you have to continue in the auction and play the hand. If your partner doesn't have any hearts, you could lose six heart tricks off the top in no trump. On the other hand, if your partner just has two aces—the ace of clubs and the ace of spades, or one ace and the king or queen of diamonds—you have a good chance to set a bid of two hearts.

Hand 5: Double for penalty. Your hearts are terrific. You're telling your partner that you have no fear of opponents' hearts and you're willing to defend. It will be up to your partner to decide whether to defend or play.

The Least You Need to Know

- With a maximum hand, you rebid game after an invitational bid by your partner.
- With less than a maximum hand, you play at the lowest level available.
- Respond to Stayman by bidding your lowest-ranked, four-card major or two diamonds, if you don't have a four-card major.
- Pass if your partner jumps to three no trump.
- If responder bids Stayman and then a major, she's showing a five-card suit.

We Can Work It Out: Rebids by One of a Suit Opener

In This Chapter

- Reversing
- Rebids with a minimum hand
- Rebids when your partner passes
- Rebids when you have more than a minimum opening hand
- Rebids over interference after your partner responds

Opener's first rebid is the bid that many experts feel is the most descriptive and most important bid in the auction. When you open one of a suit, you tell your partner only that you have between 13 and 21 points. It's with your first rebid that you more specifically describe your hand to your partner.

What Type of Hand Do You Have?

When you open one of a suit, you can have three types of hands.

Type	Points
Minimum	13–15
Extra values	16–18
Big	19–21

DEFINITION

Extra values refers to a hand that is more powerful than the minimum indicated by your partner's open. If your partner opens a suit bid at the one level, her minimum values are 13 to 15 points. If she has opened up a hand that has more than 15 points, she has extra values.

Reevaluating Your Hand When You Have a Fit

When you find through the bidding process that you have an eight card fit in one suit (preferably 4-4, but at least 5-3; a 6-2 fit isn't that valuable because the two trumps may quickly disappear through opponents leading trump), you may reevaluate the points in your hand. Instead of giving one point for a doubleton, two points for a singleton, and three points for a void, you give three points for a singleton and five points for a void. The reason is that with a fit you know that you will be able to ruff losers in the suits that have the shortness. If you don't have a trump fit, that means that you won't have enough trump to ruff the losers. So the fit in trump makes the shortness more valuable.

Rebidding a Minimum Hand

If your partner (responder to the opening bidder) bids a new suit, even if it's only at the one level, you're required to bid again. If your partner doesn't describe a hand with extra values by making some sort of jump response, you have to describe your hand as minimum. This is how you do it.

Partner Responds with a Bid of One of a Suit at the One Level

If your partner bids a higher-ranking suit than the suit with which you opened and stays at the one level, her hand is basically undefined. All you know for sure is that she has at least 6 points and at least four cards in the suit she bid. That could be all she has, but she could have a lot more. Therefore, you must describe what you have to her.

Bidding a Second Suit as a Rebid. Generally, your first choice as a rebid is to bid a higher-ranking second suit at the one level, if you have it. When you bid a second suit in your first rebid, you're promising that you have at least four cards in that suit. You're not sticking your neck out much because your partner can't support opener's second suit unless she has four cards in that suit.

A very important rule that you must remember is that *responder may not support opener's second suit unless responder has four cards in that suit.* If you're responder and you only have three cards in opener's second suit, you can't support it. This should be imprinted on your brain.

Supporting Your Partner's Suit. If your partner (responder) bids a new suit at the one level after your opening bid and you hold a minimum without a higher-ranking four-card suit, you may support it *only if you have four cards in her suit.* You may not support your partner's new suit response with only three-card support. Why? Because she can bid a four-card suit—you're looking for an eight-card fit. You don't know whether she has four cards in the suit or more. But if your first rebid is to support her suit, you're absolutely promising her that you have four cards in her suit.

Rebidding When You Can't Support Your Partner's Suit. If you don't have four cards in her suit, you have three possible rebids:

- **One no trump.** You may do this with a balanced hand. It tells your partner that you have no singletons or voids, and probably only one doubleton at most. It also tells her that you have a minimum hand, and implies stoppers in the unbid suits.

- **Rebid your opening suit.** Rebidding your suit usually implies that you have six cards in it, but sometimes you have no choice but to rebid a five-card suit.

- **Bid a new suit at the two level that is lower ranking than your opening suit.** For example: if you open one heart and your partner responds one spade, you may rebid two clubs if you have a four-card club suit. This bidding sequence would generally show that you had five hearts and either four or five clubs.

If you make a rebid at the two level of your second suit lower ranking than your opening suit, you are asking your partner to make a choice between the two suits you bid. If you opened a major and rebid a minor she should go back to the major if she has two cards in your major suit, even if she has four cards in your minor suit.

Here's a summation of your rebids when you open one of a suit and your partner responds by bidding one of a higher-ranking suit:

Your Holding	Rebid
13 to 15 points, a four-card suit higher than your partner's suit	Bid your higher-ranking, four-card suit at the one level.
13 to 15 points, less than six cards in your suit, less than four cards in responder's suit, balanced hand	One no trump.
13 to 15 points, six cards in your suit	Rebid your suit at the two level.
13 to 15 points, less than six cards in your suit, a four-card suit lower ranking than your opening suit	Bid your lower-ranking, four-card suit.
13 to 15 points, less than six cards in your suit, but four cards in your partner's suit	Raise your partner's suit to the two level.

An Introduction to the Reverse

In bidding a second suit at the two level in your first rebid, you must be careful not to reverse unless you have the points to justify a reverse. A *reverse* is when opener rebids a suit at the two level that is higher ranking than the suit that she opened with at the one level. Example: You open one club. Your partner responds one spade. You bid two diamonds. Diamonds is higher ranking than clubs and you have bid diamonds at the two level, so you have reversed. If you open one diamond, partner bids one spade, and you bid two clubs, you have not reversed because clubs is ranked lower than diamonds.

A reverse promises that you have at least 17 points and is *forcing* on your partner for one round. In other words, if you reverse, your partner *must* bid again, no matter how weak her hand.

BRIDGEBIT

One of my partners, LuAnne Leonard, was trying to explain the concept of the reverse to her boyfriend, who was just learning. When he had a hard time understanding it, LuAnne turned to another of my partners, Marilyn Mitchell, and asked her to explain it. Marilyn gave one of the best definitions I've heard: "It's a helluva hand!" she said.

Now I'm going to give you a caveat. Many rubber bridge players don't know the concept of the reverse. However, playing reverses is very good bidding procedure, so you should learn them and be aware of them. Try to avoid reversing unless you have the proper hand. You will be a better player for it.

Practice Rebidding

Okay, let's look at some hands. You open one diamond and your partner responds one spade. What's your rebid?

1.	♠ 7	2.	♠ KQ8	3.	♠ 4	4.	♠ QT84
	♥ KQJT		♥ 65		♥ KQJT		♥ 3
	♦ A973		♦ AQJ42		♦ AQJ84		♦ AQJ74
	♣ K874		♣ J98		♣ AK3		♣ AQ6

5.	♠ QT84	6.	♠ 86
	♥ K86		♥ KQ83
	♦ A832		♦ KJT7
	♣ A9		♣ A83

Hand 1: Two clubs. You should not rebid one no trump with a singleton. A new suit here—lower ranking than your first bid suit—shows a minimum, but doesn't deny extra values. It tells your partner to choose between the two suits you have bid.

Hand 2: Two diamonds. This hand poses a very difficult decision for you. Your spades, although only three, are very good. You would like to have four-card support, but this is a hand with which you could bid two spades instead of two diamonds and your partner wouldn't have much to criticize. She'll undoubtedly play you for having four spades if you raise her, but you're giving her two of the top three honors, so this will mute most of her objections if she bid a four-card spade suit—which is all she's promising. Either bid would be acceptable and would show a minimum hand.

Hand 3: Two hearts. This is a classic reverse by you and shows a hand with extra values. After opening one diamond, you rebid two hearts, a higher-ranking suit bid at the next level. The bid implies that your second bid suit, hearts, is shorter than your first bid suit, diamonds. Here you open with the five-card suit and rebid the four-card heart suit. It's forcing on your partner to keep the bid open for at least one more round.

Hand 4: Three spades. After you reevaluate your hand by giving yourself 3 points for your singleton now that you know you have at least a 4–4 trump fit, you have 17 points. The jump in your partner's suit shows a hand with extra values (see Chapter 12 for details on jump bids). The bid is invitational only to game. Your partner may pass you.

Hand 5: Two spades. This is what you were looking for, a 4–4 fit in your major suit. But you only have a minimum hand, so you just make a minimum raise to the two level.

Hand 6: One no trump. You can't support your partner's spades with only two cards. You can't rebid your diamonds because you only have four. You can't bid clubs because you only have three. You can't bid hearts because that would be a reverse, showing extra values. You may bid one no trump. You have a minimum hand, no singletons or voids, and have all the other suits stopped.

Finally, look at these hands when you open one club and your partner responds one diamond:

1.	♠ AQ76	2.	♠ 54	3.	♠ 87	4.	♠ 94
	♥ 8642		♥ 7642		♥ AKQ		♥ A6
	♦ 87		♦ AKQJ		♦ 87		♦ A953
	♣ AK7		♣ A64		♣ KQT983		♣ KQJT3

Hand 1: One heart. You bid your higher-ranking four-card suits up the line, so even though your spades are much stronger, you rebid one heart. Your partner might have five diamonds and four spades. If so, she'll respond with a bid of one spade and you can still find your 4–4 spade fit.

Hand 2: One heart. You could support diamonds, but you're looking for a major-suit fit. You must tell her you have four hearts. If you were to support diamonds at your first rebid, you would be denying a four-card major.

Hand 3: Two clubs. You have a six-card suit and don't have a four-card major; you can bid at the one level over her one diamond response.

Hand 4: Two diamonds. Your clubs are nice, but she might not have any. Because you have four cards in her suit, and you don't have a higher-ranking four-card suit to bid—and you don't have spades stopped—two diamonds is your only call. Incidentally, this is *not* a reverse because, even though you're bidding a higher-ranking suit at the two level, it's in support of your partner's suit. This takes it out of the realm of reverses.

Your Partner Responds One No Trump

When your partner responds to your opening bid of one of a suit with a response of one no trump, she's denying that she has a four-card suit higher ranking than the suit you opened. If you opened a four-card suit, then you can't have a hand with two doubletons, although you could be 4–4–4–1. In any event, if you open a four-card suit you can't rebid it. If you open one diamond and your partner responds one no trump, she has denied four hearts or four spades. If she had five diamonds, she probably would have raised your bid to two diamonds; therefore, she must have at least three clubs in her hand. If you don't like your chances in no trump after the bidding has gone one diamond — one no trump, you can chance a rebid of two clubs if you have four of them in your hand. This tells your partner that you have a minimum hand but don't want to play in no trump and asks her to pick which suit she would like to play at the two level: diamonds or clubs.

If you have a balanced hand without any voids or singletons and no more than one doubleton, you should pass her bid of one no trump and let her play it there. She's telling you that she has a weak hand. Keep it at a low level before you get into trouble in a contract you can't make.

Your Partner Makes a Simple Raise of Your Opening Bid

If your partner raises your one bid to the two level, you should pass if you have a minimum opening. Why? You have no more than 15 points in your hand. She has no more than 9 points in her hand. The math is simple, 15 + 9 = 24. You have little chance for game, so why go on?

Your Partner Responds in a New Suit at the Two Level

Finally, your partner is showing a hand that's better than the minimum. In all the examples we've seen so far, your partner has either shown a minimum hand by making a simple raise or by bidding one no trump, or made an ambiguous bid of a suit at the one level that might be minimum—or it might not.

When she responds in a new suit at the two level, she's promising at least 10 points—maybe more. If you have a minimum, you have to tell her this. Her bid is forcing on you to bid again. You can't pass.

Look at the following hands where you opened one heart and your partner responded two diamonds:

1.	♠ A7	2.	♠ AQ	3.	♠ KJ	4.	♠ A3
	♥ KQJT3		♥ KJ865		♥ KQ963		♥ KQT963
	♦ Q7		♦ J42		♦ 84		♦ 874
	♣ JT74		♣ QT8		♣ AK93		♣ AK

Hand 1: Two hearts. You're not strong enough to bid three clubs. Your heart suit is good and you show a minimum hand. If you were to bid three clubs you would show a hand with extra values, which this hand doesn't possess.

Hand 2: Two no trump. You could raise diamonds, but a two no trump bid is a better description of your hand. It also shows a minimum and allows your partner to pass. At this point you may be asking yourself, "What's the difference between Hand 1 and Hand 2 that allows you to rebid two hearts in Hand 1 but says you should bid two no trump in Hand 2?" You rebid two hearts in Hand 1 because of the quality of your heart suit and the unbalanced nature of the hand. You only have one spade stopper and one club stopper. You bid two no trump in Hand 2 because your heart suit isn't as good as it is in Hand 1—you have two spade stoppers, and the hand is more balanced, with only one doubleton. Both bids, however, tell your partner that you have a minimum hand, and this is vital information that you want to convey.

Hand 3: Three clubs. This is a hand with extra values, unlike Hand 1. When you raise the level of the bidding with a new suit in your rebid, you're showing extra values. This bid is forcing on your partner to keep the auction open to game.

Hand 4: Three hearts. Again, this shows extra values and at least six hearts.

Here's a summary of what to do if your partner bid a suit at the two level.

Your Holding	Rebid
13 to 15 points, a five-card opening suit, less than three cards in your partner's major suit or less than four cards in your partner's minor suit, unbid suits stopped, no singletons or voids.	Two no trump.
Same, but with support for your partner's suit.	Raise your partner's suit.

Here's a summary of what to do if your partner responded one no trump.

Your Holding	Rebid
13 to 15 points, balanced hand.	Pass.
13 to 15 points, with a singleton or void.	Bid a lower-ranking four-card suit at the two level or rebid your five-card opening suit.
13 to 15 points, less than six cards in your suit and less than four cards in your partner's suit.	Raise your partner's suit to the two level.

Rebidding After Your Partner Passes

If your partner passed, what does that tell you? It tells you several things:

- If there was no intervening bid between you and her, she doesn't have 6 points.

- If there was an intervening bid between you and her, she might have more than 6 points but your LHO might have bid her suit. However, if she passes after an intervening bid, then either one of two situations exist:

  - Your LHO bid her suit.

  - She has less than 6 points.

One thing you can count on is that you probably don't have an eight-card trump fit. It's possible she has three cards in your suit but less than 6 points; although you can't count on it. If she passes, you should assume she has less than 6 points and less than three cards in your suit. If you make these assumptions, you won't get hurt by rebidding based on a false expectation of support when she indicated none. Hope springs eternal, but it shouldn't in bridge. If your partner says, "Pass," take her at her word and don't count on her for anything. If your opponents have bid and it's passed around to you, you should pass—unless you have more than a minimum, shortness in your opponents' suit, or some other reason to bid.

How to proceed when you have opened and your partner has passed is an important aspect of the game. Let's look at some minimum hands after the following bidding.

You	LHO	Partner	RHO
One heart	Pass	Pass	Two clubs
?			

1. ♠ K43
   ♥ AK763
   ♦ A6
   ♣ 863

2. ♠ AJ75
   ♥ QJ872
   ♦ A
   ♣ 984

3. ♠ 86
   ♥ AKJ943
   ♦ K84
   ♣ 74

4. ♠ 98
   ♥ JT9854
   ♦ AQJ9
   ♣ A

5. ♠ 4
   ♥ KJ9753
   ♦ K83
   ♣ AQ9

Hand 1: Pass. You don't have anything else to bid. You can't rebid your hearts because you only have five, and you don't have a four-card suit to bid. Furthermore, your partner has denied 6 points and probably doesn't have hearts support. If you take another bid you're just going to get in trouble.

Hand 2: Pass. Again, you shouldn't rebid your weak five-card hearts suit. You can't bid spades because that would be a reverse showing at least 17 points, which you don't have. Anyway, if your partner had 6 points and four spades, she would have responded one spade to your one-heart opening. Remember this before you fall in love with your spades. Your partner's pass tells you a lot.

Hand 3: Pass. You might rebid your hearts if you're not vulnerable, but this hand looks like trouble. Your partner doesn't have much help for you and you don't have any outside source of tricks. What are you going to do for tricks, especially if your LHO has the ace of diamonds? You'll probably take five heart tricks only for down three. So even though you have six hearts and could rebid them, pass would be the prudent move. However, if your 9 of hearts were a 10 of hearts instead, you might be tempted to make a two hearts bid. Do you know why? Because you would have 100 honors, four of the five honors in the trump suit, which would give you 100 points above the line if you get the contract in hearts. Even if you were to get the bid and go down two, undoubled, you would break even. Your opponents would get 100 points above the line, but so would you for your 100 honors. However, don't succumb to this temptation. You shouldn't make a bad bid simply because you have 100 honors.

BRIDGEBIT

You get bonus points for having at least four honors in the trump suit in one hand. If trump is spades and you hold four of the five honors, you receive 100 points above the line. This is called *100 honors*. If you hold all five honors, AKQJT, you get 150 points above the line, called *150 honors*. The honors all have to be in the same hand, but it doesn't matter if they are in declarer's hand or in dummy. You don't have to get the contract to be awarded the bonus. All that's required is that you hold at least four honors in the trump suit in one hand.

Hand 4: Two diamonds. Your six-card heart suit is woeful to rebid when your partner passes, but this distributional hand could be nice if you find your partner with four diamonds in her hand. If it's passed to your partner, it's up to her to make a preference at this point between hearts and diamonds. You will clearly pass on your next turn no matter what she does.

Hand 5: Two hearts. Your heart suit is not terrific, but you do have six along with a singleton spade and high cards that could be sources for tricks in both clubs and diamonds. Even without much help from your partner you should bid again at the two level. However, if they go to three and your partner remains silent, let them have it.

There are several points I want you to take from this exercise:

- **Listen to your partner.** If she passes without an intervening bid, when considering your rebid you should assume she has nothing.

- **You should strain to rebid a six-card suit.** This is crucial information for your partner. If she has two of your suit, she knows that with a maximum pass in her hand—5 points—she might be able to compete to the three level in your suit; something she'd never do if she thought you only had a five-card suit. Furthermore, in a distributional hand you want ruffing power. In Hand 5, you have a good chance of getting two club tricks, depending on the location of the king, regardless of what's trump. You want to be able to ruff spades with your little hearts!

- **Count your tricks.** Even if you have a terrific six-card suit—like you do in Hand 3—if you have no outside source of tricks and your partner has no help, you could be in big trouble if you rebid your suit.

What Does Your Partner's Response Mean?

If she responds, she's telling you a lot. First, if she supports your major-suit opening she's telling you a couple of things:

- She has at least three cards in your suit.

- She has a minimum hand—not more than 9 points and not less than 6 points—and will probably not bid again unless you force her. Even if she bids another suit, she doesn't necessarily deny support for your suit. She might just be telling you she has another suit or the number of points in her hand, before she tells you she has support.

If she (responder) bids a new suit, it is 100 percent forcing on you to bid again. This means that you may pass your partner's response to your opening bid only in the following three instances:

- She bids one no trump in response to your opening suit bid.
- She raises your opening suit bid to the two level.
- Your RHO makes an intervening bid.

These things should be going through your mind when you hear your partner bid and it comes back to you to make a rebid.

Analysis of Your Partner's Response

When your partner bids a suit (refer to Chapters 11 and 12 on responses), you'll see what your partner has told you. To recap, if she bids at the one level, she's promising only a minimum hand and four cards in the suit she bid. If she bids at the two level without a jump, she's showing at least 10 points and five cards in the suit if she bids a major, but only four cards in the suit if she bids a minor. If she jumps, she's showing a more powerful hand.

Let's say you open one club and she bids one spade. What do you know about her hand? She has at least 6 points and at least four spades. Anything else? You know at least two more things about her hand. What are they?

Answer: her hearts and diamonds are not longer than her spades. Remember, you bid your longest suit in response to your partner's opening bid; if two suits are four cards, equal in length, you bid the lower-ranking suit or *up the line*. If you have two five-card suits, you bid the higher ranking or *down the line*. So you know for an absolute fact that your partner has at least 6 points—at least four spades—and not more cards in each of hearts and diamonds than she has in spades. That's quite a lot to know from one bid, don't you think?

What if you open one diamond and she bids two clubs? This time she's telling you a little more. First, she is promising you more points, at least 10. Second, she's telling you that she has at least four clubs and that her clubs are longer than her hearts and her spades.

What if you open one heart and she bids one no trump with no intervening bid? Well, you know three things for sure:

- She has at least 6 points. She shouldn't bid unless she has at least 6 points.

- She doesn't have four spades. If she had four spades she would bid one spade after your opening bid of one heart, with one exception: if she has an absolute minimum hand with four spades and three hearts. In that event she would only have one bid she could make and it should be to support your hearts, so she'd *bypass* her four-card spade suit to bid two hearts.

- She doesn't have three hearts. If she had three hearts, she would support you immediately by bidding two hearts, especially if she had a minimum hand.

So, with that one bid of hers, you can forget about trying to find an eight-card fit in a major if you opened a five-card suit!

The point of all this is that bidding requires deductive reasoning—listening to what your partner has *not* bid to determine what she has in her hand. You must take negative inferences.

Analyzing for a Rebid

You shouldn't open if you don't have a rebid. As I said in Chapter 7 on opening bids of one of a suit, when considering opening, you should always ask yourself, "What am I going to bid if my partner bids thus and so?" "Thus and so" being the worst response you could hope for with your hand, probably bidding your singleton or void. If you don't have a rebid, you shouldn't open.

When I was a bridge tyke I had heard this maxim. One day I looked at a 14-point hand and didn't see a rebid, so I passed and the hand was passed out. When we looked at the cards, it was clear that we could have made game because my partner had 12 points and we had a fit. They asked me why I didn't open. "I didn't have a rebid," I replied. They all laughed … and they weren't laughing *with* me.

A 14-point hand always has a rebid. Remember that. And often it's one no trump.

Rebidding One No Trump

What does one no trump rebid by opener tell partner? Several things:

- Opener has no more than 14 points.

- Opener has a balanced hand.

- Opener doesn't have four cards in responder's suit.

- Partner becomes captain of the hand, just as if opener opened with one no trump (which would, of course, show a stronger hand than a rebid of one no trump).

You can't make a one–no trump rebid as opener if you have a singleton or void. If you have a singleton or void, however, you must have at least two four-card suits; so your rebid would be your lower-ranking four-card suit, if you can't support your partner's response. Let's look at some hands, all of which you open one club and your partner responds one heart:

1. ♠ AK74	2. ♠ AK7	3. ♠ QT94	4. ♠ K8	5. ♠ 85
♥ 74	♥ 7532	♥ AK9	♥ Q7	♥ KJ
♦ Q84	♦ 983	♦ 75	♦ KJ32	♦ KJ3
♣ A832	♣ AK9	♣ A942	♣ AT432	♣ AJT643

Hand 1: One spade. You have four spades. When you open one club, you generally deny having as many as five spades, so you're telling your partner that basically you have a maximum 18-point hand with four spades. She might have bid a four-card heart suit up the line and have four spades, too.

Hand 2: Two hearts. Sure, your hearts aren't pretty, but you have the correct number—four—so you will be in a 4–4 at worst if you play in hearts.

Hand 3: One spade. You certainly have nice hearts support, but you don't have four cards in the suit; so tell her about your spades now. Her hand might be a minimum. She might have four spades. She might have five hearts or more. You just don't know. The best thing to do is to describe your hand as accurately as possible and let her take it from there.

Hand 4: One no trump. You can't support hearts. You can't bid diamonds because it would be a reverse. (Didn't I tell you this word would be used a lot during this chapter?) You shouldn't rebid your clubs because you only have five cards in your clubs suit. A one no trump rebid says that you have a minimum hand and denies four of your partner's suit.

Hand 5: Two clubs. You have a six-card suit and nothing else to rebid. Again, this tells your partner you have opened up a minimum hand.

Look at these hands:

You	Partner
♠ 82	♠ KQ96
♥ AKQJ9	♥ T7
♦ J85	♦ K976
♣ Q54	♣ JT2

How would you bid it as opener and responder? Before looking at how it should be bid, go ahead and bid it, assuming no intervening bids.

Okay, here's how it went. You opened one heart, right? You have 14 points, so you couldn't open one no trump. Responder bid one spade. That's correct. Responder has 9 HCP and four spades, a perfect bid.

So what's your rebid? You could rebid your strong hearts, although you only have five. Your better response is what we've been discussing: one no trump. You have 14 points, but 10 of them are in hearts; therefore, you let your partner know that you're basically a minimum open with a balanced hand. Your partner clearly can't take another call. Her response was minimum. Unless you make a forcing bid, she has to pass whatever you bid. It was passed out at one no trump and that's what it made: exactly one no trump.

Rebidding with Better Than a Minimum Hand

When you open a hand with extra values—a big hand—your rebids must communicate the strength of your hand to your partner. You should make a bid that she can't pass.

As explained at the beginning of the chapter, a reverse is when opener bids a higher-ranking suit at the two level than the suit she opened with at the one level. Example: You open one club. Your partner responds one spade. You bid two diamonds. Diamonds is higher ranking than clubs and you have bid them at the two level, so you have reversed.

To repeat, a reverse promises that you have at least 17 points and is forcing on your partner for one round. In other words, your partner should bid again, no matter how weak her hand, if you reverse.

Generally, a reverse also tells your partner that you have more cards—at least five—in the suit you opened and fewer cards—usually four—in the suit to which you reverse. So in the previous example, you would have five clubs and four diamonds or, rarely, six clubs and five diamonds.

If you play reverses—and most good players do—it causes problems when you have merely an opening hand with a longer, lower-ranking suit. For example, look at this hand:

♠ 98
♥ 75
♦ AK84
♣ KQ983

Normally, from what you've learned so far, this would clearly be a hand that you would open one club, because you have five clubs. But—and this is another rule you've already learned and that you should have ingrained in your head—*when you open the bidding, be sure you have a rebid*. If you don't have a rebid, you shouldn't open the bidding. This hand illustrates the latter rule if you are playing reverses.

Here's why: If you open one club and your partner responds with one heart or one spade—which, due to the perverse nature of the bridge gods, she is almost certain to do—given the shape of your hand, you have no rebid! Why? Because you can't rebid one no trump when you don't have the other major stopped. You can't rebid two diamonds because your hand isn't powerful enough. A rebid in two diamonds after your partner responds one of a major over a one-club open would be a reverse showing at least 17 points. You could rebid two clubs, but it's not a great description of your hand.

So in this instance, you should open this hand one diamond. Then when your partner responds with one heart or one spade, you can rebid two clubs, showing a minimum hand. This is one of the few times when you may open a shorter, higher-ranking suit instead of a longer, lower-ranking suit, and this generally only applies when you have a minimum opener with five clubs and four diamonds.

Let's look at some hands that we examined earlier. When we first looked at these hands you had opened the bidding with a bid of one heart, your partner passed, and your RHO bid two clubs. This time, however, let's say that you still open one heart, but your partner bids two clubs. (Please note that Hand 1 has been altered somewhat.)

1. ♠ K43   2. ♠ AJ75   3. ♠ 86   4. ♠ 98
   ♥ AK763   ♥ QJ872   ♥ AKJ943   ♥ JT9854
   ♦ 64   ♦ A   ♦ K84   ♦ AQ76
   ♣ K63   ♣ 984   ♣ 74   ♣ A

What's your rebid?

Hand 1: Two hearts. You can't bid two no trump because you don't have diamonds stopped. This hand is as weak as it can be and still have enough points to open.

Hand 2: Three clubs. This hand is very weak. You can't bid two spades (your other four-card suit) because that would be a reverse, and you are far too weak to make a reverse. Your action in supporting partner's suit here shows a minimum hand and invites a pass.

Hand 3: Two hearts. You have six hearts and nothing else to bid. Again, this describes a minimum hand.

Hand 4: Two diamonds. Your hearts are terrible, even though you have six of them. You are just asking your partner to take a preference. You're going to pass whatever she does unless she makes a forcing bid.

If you have a minimum hand with a higher-ranking four-card suit over your opening five-card suit, you have four choices when your partner responds by bidding a new suit, and you can't reverse because your hand isn't strong enough:

- Bid a new suit at the one level.

- Raise your partner's suit at the lowest level.

- Rebid your own suit at the lowest level.

- Rebid no trump at the lowest level, but you must have no-trump distribution. You shouldn't rebid no trump if you have a void or singleton.

Strong Rebid Jump to Game

If you open a hand at the one level and your partner responds in a suit you can support and you have 20 points, you should immediately jump to game. Look at the following hand:

♠ AT92
♥ AK8
♦ A
♣ K7632

The bidding goes as follows.

RHO	You	LHO	Partner
Pass	One club	One diamond	One spade
Two diamonds	Four spades		

The point to remember here is that when your partner gives you a minimum response, you jump to game immediately with this hand. Why? Because all you need for game in a major suit is 26 points. Your partner has absolutely promised you two things by her bid:

- She has at least four spades.

- She has at least 6 points.

That's all you need for game in spades. You know that you have at least an eight-card fit in trump and you know you have at least 26 points between you both. (Actually, you know you have at least 27 points, because when you find that you have a trump fit your singleton is reevaluated upward by an extra point.)

When she responds with these promises, you jump to game. This is *not* a *sign-off bid*. With extras, your partner may bid on to slam.

 DEFINITION

A **sign-off bid** is one intended to close the auction.

This bid is a strength-showing bid, asking your partner to continue bidding to explore slam if she has the values. When you make this bid, you're promising your partner that you have at least 20 points.

Opener's Jump to No Trump

If opener jumps to 2 no trump or 3 no trump after partner has bid a new suit at the one level, the requirements are as follows.

Rebid	Requirements
Two no trump	18 to 19 points, all unbid suits stopped
Three no trump	20 to 21 points, all unbid suits stopped

Opener's Jump Shift

If you skip a level of bidding that is available to you and bid a new suit at the same time, you've made a jump shift, and have shown a hand that is between 19 and 22 points. A jump shift that skips a level is forcing to game. Look at the following hand:

♠ A
♥ A8
♦ K76534
♣ AK83

The bidding is as follows.

You	LHO	Partner	RHO
One diamond	Pass	One spade	Pass
?			

You can't jump in no trump because you have a singleton in your partner's suit. You can't reverse into hearts, a two-card suit. A rebid of two clubs would show a minimum hand. You want to make a forcing bid to find out more about your partner's hand. What should you do?

The answer is to make a jump shift to three clubs. It's 100 percent forcing on your partner to bid. She can't support you unless she has at least four cards in the suit. By this bid, you're telling your partner that you have a big hand but are groping for where to play it. You need more information from her.

The difference between a jump shift and a reverse is that when you reverse you don't skip a level of bidding that is available to you. One club — one spade — two hearts is a reverse; it doesn't skip a level available to you. One diamond — one spade — three clubs is a jump shift, because it skips a level available to you: two clubs. It shows a bigger hand than a reverse.

Both a reverse and a jump shift are forcing, and therefore both could be just short of a strong two opening. They are distinguished only because a jump shift must arrive in game, whereas a reverse sequence may stop short, because a reverse is forcing for one round only.

To summarize:

Bid	Points	Result
Reverse	17+	Forcing for one round
Jump shift	19+	Forcing to game

Evaluating Your Partner's Bid over Interference

If your partner has bid over another bid by your LHO (her RHO), it tells you something different than if she bids without interference. If she bids one no trump over your opening one-bid without interference, it tells you, simply, that she doesn't have a four-card major higher ranking than the suit you opened and that she has between 6 to 10 HCP without a singleton or void. If she bids one no trump over an interfering bid by her RHO, however, it also promises that she has a stopper in the interfering bidder's suit.

When you open one diamond and your LHO overcalls one heart, if your partner responds one no trump, it tells you three things: first, she has 8 to 10 HCP; second, she doesn't have four spades; and third, she has hearts stopped at least once.

There is defensive value to straining to support your partner's suit over interference. This is especially true if your opponents are going to be forced up a level if they want to bid their suit again. So if your partner opens one spade and your RHO overcalls two clubs, if you raise to two spades, your LHO will have to go to the three level to bid a suit other than clubs.

You're telling your partner that you are minimum, so you don't have to worry that she'll overevaluate your hand by this bid. Basically you're just competing, and your partner should know this and shut up if your opponents compete to the three level in clubs. Unless she has extra values in her hand, she should let them play at the three level. You will have a better chance of setting them at the three level than you would have playing a three-spade contract with your weak hand.

The Least You Need to Know

- If you have a minimum hand, your rebid should show the values by bidding a lower-ranking suit at the next level—no trump—or supporting your partner's suit.
- You must have four cards in the suit to support your partner's suit.
- A reverse is a bid of a higher-ranking suit at a higher level than the suit you bid at your opening bid and shows a minimum of 17 points.
- A jump shift changes suit and skips a level of bidding available to you and shows a minimum of 19 points.

Rebids by Strong Opener and Responder

Chapter 15

In This Chapter

- Rebids by strong two-diamonds, -hearts, or -spades opener
- Rebids by strong two-clubs opener
- How responder rebids when opener supports her suit
- How responder rebids when opener doesn't support her suit and shows a minimum

This chapter consists of two parts. The first part deals with rebids by a strong two opener. This topic is fairly straightforward, so it doesn't need a lot of space. The second part of the chapter covers responder's first rebid.

As with the first rebid by a one of a suit opener, the first rebid by a strong two opener is very important. And responder's first rebid really completes the first phase of communication between the partners and sets the stage for concluding the final contract.

When someone opens with a strong two, this bid determines how much information the opener can give to responder. Initially, responder only knows that opener has a very strong hand. With the opener's rebid, the auction is moved to the next level. Responder's rebid is extremely important because it determines whether or not you're going to play for a partscore, game, or slam.

Rebids by Strong Two Opener in Diamonds, Hearts, or Spades

If you open with a strong two in diamonds, hearts, or spades and your partner gives you a negative response of two no trump, you let her off the hook if you rebid your opening suit at the three level. If you do rebid your suit, your partner may pass. This is the only time that your partner may pass when you open with a strong two in these three suits until a game bid is made.

It follows, therefore, that if you bid a new suit, it's forcing on your partner to make another response. For example, suppose the bidding goes as follows.

You	Partner
Two spades	Two no trump
Three clubs	Three spades
Four clubs	Four spades
Five diamonds	?

Your partner must bid. Anytime a strong two opener bids a new suit, responder must bid again. This is especially true when, as here, opener made a bid after partner (responder) bid game in her suit.

This bid is called a *two demand*. Unless you rebid your opening suit, you're demanding your partner to keep the bidding open until you reach game.

Following is a hand that shows some of the problems encountered by a strong two opener:

♠ A
♥ AKJ832
♦ A7
♣ AKT8

Here's the bidding:

You	Partner
Two hearts	Three diamonds
?	

The first thing to remember here is that when your partner gives you a positive response, which is any bid other than two no trump or raising your suit a level, she's making a game-forcing bid. You don't need to worry about her passing you out short of game. You can rebid your heart suit here without thinking that you're allowing her to pass. If you go straight to four hearts, you could find your partner with a void. Your heart suit isn't strong enough for this.

TRICKS OF THE TRADE

A bid by opener of four hearts in this situation is weaker than a bid of three hearts. Why? Because after a positive response from your partner, a jump to game by a bid of four hearts would be a sign-off, whereas a bid of three hearts asks your partner for more information.

The better bid here is to bid your four-card club suit. Your partner should know that you may only have four. The problem with this is that it bypasses three no trump. However, you could be very uncomfortable if you were to bid three no trump and find that your partner doesn't have a spade stopper.

Your partner has told you that she has better than a minimum, however, because she bid three diamonds instead of two no trump. This told you two things about her diamond suit:

- She has at least five diamonds.
- She has two of the top four diamond honors with at least the king.

Those two honors could be king–jack, so you don't have total control of any suit. In a contract of three no trump without a spade stopper in dummy, you could be set by more than one with a spade lead.

So you're trying to find a fit. If your partner has two hearts, she should just close out in four hearts.

As it happened, because your partner had four cards in your second suit, she supported it by bidding five clubs. You know by that that your partner has four clubs because she can't support your second suit without at least four cards in it. With the strength of your hand and your partner's initial positive response by bidding a new suit, you should probably bid six clubs and try for the slam.

Here's how the bidding actually went.

You	LHO	Partner	RHO
Two hearts	Pass	Three diamonds	Pass
Four clubs	Pass	Five clubs	Pass
Six clubs	Pass	Pass	Pass

Partner's hand:

♠ Q83
♥ Q
♦ KQ954
♣ J532

Initially, that looks like a pretty weak 10 HCP, with only one king and no aces. But when you have opened with a two demand, your partner's honors become much more powerful. If she has 10 HCP and you open with a two demand, she knows that you must be in game and should be thinking about slam.

Remember, when you bid a new suit—four clubs—your partner is forced to make another bid. If she had only three clubs but had two hearts, she should probably just bid four hearts. But because she had four clubs, she could support your second suit.

ALERT

Slam bidding is covered in Chapter 16.

After she has shown you a positive response with her initial bid of three diamonds, you are well within your rights to make a try for six clubs, a small slam. You have 26 points and she has given you a positive response.

Following is the layout of all the hands and how it was played. Again, I suggest you lay the hands out and play it yourself and see how you do.

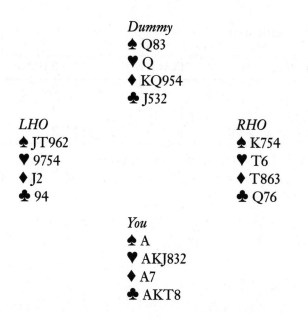

Dummy
♠ Q83
♥ Q
♦ KQ954
♣ J532

LHO
♠ JT962
♥ 9754
♦ J2
♣ 94

RHO
♠ K754
♥ T6
♦ T863
♣ Q76

You
♠ A
♥ AKJ832
♦ A7
♣ AKT8

Here is the play. L means that card led; * means that card won the trick.

	LHO	**Dummy**	**RHO**	**You**
1.	J ♠ L	3 ♠	7 ♠	A ♠*
2.	7 ♥	Q ♥*	6 ♥	2 ♥ L
3.	4 ♣	J ♣ L	Q ♣	K ♣*
4.	9 ♣	2 ♣	6 ♣	A ♣*L
5.	6 ♠	3 ♣	7 ♣	T ♣*L
6.	4 ♥	8 ♠	T ♥	A ♥*L
7.	5 ♥	Q ♠	3 ♦	K ♥*L
8.	9 ♥	4 ♦	6 ♦	J ♥*L
9.	2 ♦	5 ♦	8 ♦	8 ♥*L
10.	J ♦	9 ♦	4 ♠	3 ♥*L
11.	9 ♠	K ♦*	T ♦	7 ♦L
12.	T ♠	Q ♦ L	5 ♠	A ♦*
13.	J ♠	5 ♣	K ♠	8 ♣*L

Because the queen of clubs is favorably positioned and because your partner has the singleton queen of hearts, it makes seven. This is a slam that should be bid, even though you are playing in a 4–4 fit in a minor suit at the six level. You get more points by playing a minor suit slam than a major suit game.

Rebids by Strong Two-Club Opener

There are only a few possibilities for responses you'll get from your strong opening of two clubs. The most common response you'll get—more than 90 percent of the time, actually—is that your partner will bid two diamonds, a waiting bid.

What did two diamonds tell you? Did you say, "Nothing, Idiot, it was a waiting bid"? If so, go to the corner and put on the dunce cap.

Although it's true that two diamonds is a waiting bid in response to a strong opening of two clubs, it most definitely tells you something. One of the great things about bridge is that it teaches you to draw inferences from things. This is a good example. You're saying, "Well, two diamonds is a waiting bid, isn't it? It's just keeping the bidding open and asking partner to describe her hand further; isn't that correct?"

Sure, that's correct. But don't forget that responder has choices. Although two diamonds is the most common response to a strong two-club opening, it is not her *only* bid. Remember I said that if responder has a good five-card suit she should bid it? Well, if she bids two diamonds in response to your two-club open, what does that tell you about her hand? It tells you that she does *not* have a good five-card she wants to bid. Isn't that good information for you? Of course it is.

Further Distribution Description

So the first thing you want to do now is to tell your partner what kind of distribution you have in your hand. Did you open a balanced hand with 22-plus points? Or did you open a hand that has strong clubs? If you opened the former, you rebid two no trump.

Making Sure Your Partner Doesn't Pass Out Too Soon

One thing with which you must concern yourself is the possibility of your partner passing you before you get to your contract. When you open a strong two-club bid, you must prepare yourself for what your partner is going to do when you make a rebid. So this gets to the questions of how you bid your hand, and can you bid anything other than a two-level bid when your partner responds two diamonds.

Allowing Your Partner to Quit at the Right Time

If you have opened up a balanced 22- to 24-point hand, you know that you need *something* from your partner to make game—even in no trump—because your points are just not enough. Although it's rare to hold a Yarborough (4-3-3-3 distribution and no card higher than a 9) when you have at least 22 HCP in your hand, there is a much greater possibility of your partner having a Yarborough than if you open up a hand with 15 HCP or less.

You don't want to be in game if you don't have it. That's the purpose of the two–no trump rebid. It tells your partner that she has the right to pass if she thinks there isn't game between you.

No Trump Rebids

When you rebid two no trump, it's like opening no trump. It means *systems are on*, so your partner can bid Stayman to find out if you have a four card major.

> **DEFINITION**
>
> **Systems on** means that when you make a no trump bid that's not an opening bid, you're still playing the normal responses that come after a no trump opening, like Stayman.

If you open two clubs, your partner responds two diamonds, and you bid two no trump, and your partner bids three clubs, she's asking if you have a four-card major. When you rebid two no trump, you are once again making her the captain of the team and leaving it up to her where you play the contract. You are, in effect, inviting her to bid Stayman, if she can. If she doesn't, that tells you something about her hand. When you rebid two no trump, she must then evaluate her hand as if you had opened two no trump but with a minimum of 22 points instead of 20 to 21 points. This means that systems are on.

Respecting Your Partner's Opinion

When you open up one no trump, you have a good hand: 15 to 17 points. But you've learned that when you do this you appoint your partner captain of your hand. You surrender power to her, even though you probably have the better hand of the two of you.

This isn't so difficult to do with a 15- to 17-point hand. But when you have a hand containing 22 points or more, it's much harder to pay attention to what your partner is telling you. You have more than half the points in the deck. You've got the power. Your partner is sitting over there with virtually nothing. Who is she to tell you what to do?

Ah, but you need her because she could have the few points you desperately need for game. And she could very well have a Yarborough or close to one. You must listen to her and respect what she tells you. If you have a balanced hand and have less than 25 points, you need her advice and opinion. You need her help. So you tell her what you have and listen to what she says she has. If the points she tells you she has in her hand don't total game when added to yours, pass it out at the lowest level possible.

Rebids by Responder

The second part of this chapter focuses on how a responder rebids. When it comes time for you to make your first rebid as responder you have heard your partner bid twice, so you should have a much better idea of how many points she has in her hand and what her suits are. It's up to you to make some decisions.

Partner Opens a Minor, You Bid a Major, and Opener Supports You

The bidding goes, for example, one diamond — one heart — two hearts. What do you do? A very specific series of bids defines your response:

- If you, as responder, have four hearts and 10 points or fewer, pass.

- If you have four hearts and 11 to 12 points, bid two no trump. If your partner is at the top of her bid (at least 14 HCP), she goes to game. If she has 13 or fewer points, she closes out in three hearts. This bid of two no trump is a very limited bid. It tells your partner specifically the hand you hold. It says nothing about playing the hand in no trump. It is inviting one of two bids: either three hearts or four hearts.

- If you have four hearts and 13 to 15 points, bid game (four hearts).

- If you have five hearts and 10 points, bid three hearts.

- If you have five hearts and 11 to 12 points, bid game (four hearts).

This is a standard bid, but my experience is that very few players use it. If you use it you must have a firm understanding with your partner about what the bids mean. But you will find that you will arrive at the correct contract much more often than others who get these types of hands. Look at the following hands when your partner opened one diamond, you responded one spade, and your partner rebid two spades:

1.	♠ AT43	2.	♠ AT432	3.	♠ AT43	4.	♠ AT43
	♥ KQ7		♥ K73		♥ K32		♥ T43
	♦ J87		♦ QT5		♦ K73		♦ KQ7
	♣ 963		♣ T5		♣ JT4		♣ A83

Hand 1: Pass. You have 10 points and four spades. Even if your partner has a maximum hand at 15 points, you don't have enough for game unless you're lucky.

Hand 2: Three spades. This describes your hand specifically. You have 10 points and five spades. It invites your partner to bid four spades if she's at the top of her bid.

Hand 3: Two no trump. This also describes your hand specifically. You have 11 to 12 points and four spades. You are asking your partner to bid three spades if she has 13 points, four spades if she has 14 or more. She can't pass two no trump unless she violated your partnership agreement and supported you with only three spades.

Hand 4: Four spades. Don't get excited and think about slam just because you both have opening hands and a major-suit trump fit. Your partner has told you that she has a minimum hand by her simple raise of your major suit bid. You have a 4–4 fit and probably a maximum of 29 points. Forget slam and be content with a fairly safe game.

Captaincy

When it comes time for you to make a rebid as responder, you have the advantage of having a lot of information at your fingertips. You know much more about the potential of your hands than your partner. Your partner's opening bid, as you remember, just got the ball rolling, and probably described a hand that has between 13 points and 21 points (unless she opened no trump).

Your response, unless it was a limit raise or a jump, just told her that you had at least 6 points and a minimum number of cards in the suit you bid.

By her rebid, she described her hand much more specifically to you. She should have told you whether or not she had a minimum, or more, and given you a good indication of her distribution.

At this point you have so much information that you're in control of the hand. It's up to you to tell her whether you want to play in a partscore, a game, or try for a slam.

Opener Shows a Minimum Without Supporting Your Suit

If you make a bid in response to your partner's opening bid, you will basically have one of several types of hands:

6 to 9 points, a minimum. If you're at the bottom of your range—6 to 7 points— you should pass any response by your partner that doesn't force you to bid again. If you're at the middle or upper range of your bid—8 to 9 points—you can give her another bid if she encourages it. Under no circumstances do you have the flexibility to pass a forcing bid, like a reverse. But if the bidding goes like this …

Partner	*You*
One diamond	One heart
Two clubs	?

… your partner is describing a minimum to medium opening and is telling you to take your pick between diamonds and clubs. If you feel clubs is a better contract, pass. If you like diamonds, then bid two diamonds. Your bid of two diamonds is pretty much a drop-dead bid to your partner, and tells her that you don't have much but that you prefer she play the hand in diamonds rather than clubs. You shouldn't have to worry about her bidding on.

10 to 12 points. This is a good hand with game potential. So you must be certain that your first response is one that doesn't allow your partner to pass. You can't respond one no trump or make a simple one-over-one raise of her suit, because those bids describe minimum hands that invite a pass. Your rebid will be something that tells your partner that you're interested in game and doesn't invite a pass. For instance, if you were to rebid your suit at the two level, you would be telling her that you had a minimum hand, didn't like either of her two suits, and were satisfied playing it in your suit at the two level. A rebid of your suit would not describe a hand of 10 to 12 points, but would, rather, invite your partner to pass.

13 points or more. This is a hand that you know you want to play in game; therefore, you must make a forcing bid on your partner, either by jumping or bidding game yourself, so that she may not pass short of a bid of game. You have to tell her your strength now because it must be decided whether or not you will be satisfied just playing in game or whether you want to try for slam.

With these as guidelines, refer to the chart later in this chapter showing how to respond to opener's second bid after you have a better idea of what opener's hand is like.

Consider the following auction.

Partner	You
One diamond	One heart
Two clubs	?

How do you bid the following hands?

1.	♠ K74	2.	♠ K74	3.	♠ K74	4.	♠ K74	5.	♠ KJ74
	♥ QJ743		♥ KQ8643		♥ KJ86		♥ KJ863		♥ KJ86
	♦ Q74		♦ 74		♦ 87		♦ 87		♦ Q82
	♣ 72		♣ 84		♣ J832		♣ 862		♣ JT

Hand 1: Two diamonds. Your partner has asked you to choose between diamonds and clubs and you like diamonds better because you have three, headed by an honor.

Hand 2: Two hearts. You have a minimum hand with a six-card suit. You don't like diamonds or clubs especially. Because you have six hearts headed by two of the top three honors, you prefer to try playing in the major at the two level. Whatever your partner does next—unless it's a forcing bid, which is unlikely given her minimum rebid in clubs—you're telling her you're going to pass.

Hand 3: Pass. You have minimum, but your clubs are clearly better than your diamonds. Better to play in two clubs. Any other bid would mislead your partner into thinking you are stronger than you are. You shouldn't raise clubs just because you have four of them. Your hand is too minimum.

Hand 4: Two diamonds. Your hand is very minimum. It's possible that your partner is 4–4 in diamonds and clubs (or 5–5, or 5-4), but you should assume that she has five diamonds, anyway; it would be better to play a 5–2 fit in her opening suit than a 4–3 fit in her second suit. When in doubt, when partner gives you a choice between two suits, it's generally preferable to pick her first-bid suit.

Hand 5: Two no trump. You have 11 HCP and good body cards. Two no trump promises your partner that you have the unbid suit—spades—stopped, and tells her that you have more than a minimum. It invites her to bid game if she has anything but a bare minimum.

The following table shows how to respond to opener's second bid after you have a better idea of what opener's hand is like, assuming that opener did not make a forcing second bid.

Opener	Your Hand	Your Rebid
13–15 points	6–9	Pass.
		Support partner's suit at the two level.
		Rebid your good five-card suit or six-card suit at the two level.
	10–12	Two no trump, if balanced.
		Support partner's suit at the three level or bid your suit at the three level.
	13+	Bid game in a suit in which you have a fit or three no trump.
		Bid a new suit, forcing partner to bid.
16–18 points	6–7	Pass as soon as possible!
		Support partner's suit with a simple raise.
	8–9	Rebid your suit if it has six cards in it.
	10+	Bid game in a suit in which you have a fit or three no trump.
		Bid a new suit, forcing partner to bid.
19+ points	6–7	Support partner's suit if possible.
		Rebid a suit in which you have a fit.
		Rebid your own five-card or longer suit.
		Bid no trump at the lowest level available.
	8+	Support partner's suit.
		Rebid a suit in which you have a fit.
		Jump to three no trump.
		Bid a new suit forcing partner to bid.

These bids are based on simple arithmetic. In the bids where your minimum hand and your partner's minimum hand show that you have enough points for game, you must either bid the game or make a bid that forces your partner to bid again. However, when you add your points to your partner's minimum hand and don't get enough for game, you have to let her decide by giving her the information on your hand. At that point you make an invitational bid to her, which tells her that you're above your minimum and if she is also above her minimum you should be in game, but it's up to her to bid it. She knows that if you had a hand that, when added to her minimum hand, would make game, you would either bid game or make a forcing bid. So if you make a bid that allows her to pass, you're telling her that your hand, when added to her minimum hand, will not make game.

Let's look at some hands.

Hand	Bidding	
Hand 1	*Partner*	*You*
♠ T	One heart	Two diamonds
♥ 8	Two spades	?
♦ AQT754		
♣ KT863		
Hand 2	*Partner*	*You*
♠ A9872	One club	One spade
♥ A4	Two spades	?
♦ QJ76		
♣ AQ		
Hand 3	*Partner*	*You*
♠ 8652	One diamond	One heart
♥ KJ73	Two clubs	?
♦ 73		
♣ A43		
Hand 4	*Partner*	*You*
♠ K8	One diamond	One heart
♥ Q9875	One spade	?
♦ Q72		
♣ JT5		

Hand 1: Three clubs. You have 13 points with a very distributional hand. Rather than rebid your six-card diamond suit, it's better to mention your five-card club suit at the three level to show your partner your strength and distribution. Your partner—who has reversed, showing at least 17 points—may not pass a new suit by responder at the three level.

Hand 2: Three diamonds. You've already established a trump fit in a major suit: spades. So your bid of three diamonds is at least game invitational and forcing on your partner to bid again. When you, as responder, rebid a new suit after establishing a fit in a major suit, it means that you have a better than minimum hand and you should consider game, at least. When you have a major suit fit, there's no reason to bid a new minor suit unless it's to tell your partner something about your hand. Here you have 17 points and are sniffing for slam. Your bid of a new suit is absolutely forcing on your partner to bid again.

Hand 3: Pass. You have a minimum. Your partner doesn't have four spades or she would have bid them. She must have a distributional hand or she would have bid one no trump. You have the *ace third* of her second suit. You can't get hurt too much in two clubs and it can't be much worse than two diamonds, even if she is 6–4 in diamonds and clubs. She's basically asking you to take your pick between clubs and diamonds. If you had three little clubs you should take her back to diamonds, because that was her first suit and she probably has at least five of them. But because you have the ace of clubs with two others, I'd leave her in two clubs.

DEFINITION

Ace third means that you have three cards in the suit headed by the bare ace. Any card followed by a number, like third or fourth, means that you have that card plus that number of cards in the suit. So **king fourth** means that you have Kxxx in the suit.

Hand 4: One no trump. Your five-card heart suit is too weak to rebid at the two level and your hand is too weak to go to the two level without a more encouraging bid from your partner. You know that your partner doesn't have five spades or she would have opened one spade, so you don't want to leave her in a 4–2 fit. One no trump describes your hand well here: weak and fairly balanced. This is a bid that says that you might have a little more than the minimum, but not much more, and allows your partner to pass.

The Least You Need to Know

- A two-diamond, two-heart, or two-spade opening bid begins a game-forcing auction if responder doesn't bid two no trump.

- After a two no trump response, the responding hand must continue bidding as long as the opener changes suits. If opener rebids her original suit or bids three no trump, responder may pass.

- Responder's bid of two diamonds after an opening bid of two clubs is a waiting bid and denies a five-card or longer suit headed by at least the king–jack.

- If a two-club opening bidder rebids no trump, she shows a balanced strong hand and does not promise a club suit.

- If your partner's rebid shows that you have enough points between you for game, you should either bid game yourself or make a forcing bid that your partner can't pass.

Going for the Gold: Slam Bidding

Chapter 16

In This Chapter

- Evaluating your hand for slam
- Using Blackwood to indicate the number of aces in your hand
- Fooling your opponents using deceptive bidding

I've alluded to slams before. Essentially, *slam* occurs when you bid a contract to take either all tricks but one, which is a *small slam*, or all tricks, which is a *grand slam*. So to make small slam you must make a contract to take 12 of the 13 tricks, and then actually do so; to make grand slam, you must make a contract to take all 13 tricks, and do so.

This chapter explains how to evaluate your hand for slam and how to bid to slam.

Points Needed for Slam

You look for slam through arithmetic. Basically, the points required for slam are as follows:

Small slam	33 points
Grand slam	37 points

The bonuses involved are wonderful. They are as follows.

Bid	Not Vulnerable	Vulnerable
Small slam	500	750
Grand slam	1,000	1,500

Clearly, these are significant bonuses. The question is, can you make it? This is especially important when you're vulnerable because if you have a vulnerable game that can't be defeated, you're risking at least 600 points to try for the slam.

Two Ways of Looking for Slam

There are two basic ways to explore the specific cards in your hands to see if you can make a slam: One is by the use of Blackwood. A second way to explore for slam is through the use of cue bids. I cover both of these techniques later in this chapter.

The vast majority of rubber bridge players use Blackwood. If you were to try to use a cue bid with the average rubber bridge player, however, you'd feel like a pair of brown shoes at a party for tuxedos.

But before you get to Blackwood, you need to communicate with your partner to see whether the hand has the potential for the use of Blackwood.

Identifying Slam Potential

When you count up the points in your hand and find that you have an opening hand and then you hear your loving partner open the bidding, you will generally think, "Hmmm. I've got an opening hand. She does, too. Maybe we have slam!"

Not so fast. Two opening hands only equal 26 points, just enough for a game in a major suit or no trump. You shouldn't start thinking slam until your partner jumps the bidding.

ALERT

Two opening hands opposite one another do not equal slam.

A jump bid always indicates extra values. So if one partner opens and responder jumps, that's when you start thinking about slam. If one partner opens, the other partner responds, and opener jumps, responder may start thinking about slam if she has an opening hand herself.

This is the theory behind jump responses. They make your partner aware that you not only have most of the points between you and her, but that at least one of you has extra values. This alerts her to the fact that you think that game is well within your reach and that you should explore the possibility of slam.

Analysis by Opener When Responder Jumps

If your partner just makes a standard response showing a minimum hand, like responding two diamonds over your one-spade opening, you aren't thinking slam. It's when she does something other than a standard bid that your gray cells get working.

If your partner jumps the bidding, she's showing you a specific number of points in her hand. So remember what a jump means:

	You	**Partner**	**Meaning**
Hand 1	One heart	Two no trump	13–15 HCP, balanced hand, stoppers in the three unbid suits, denies four spades.
Hand 2	One heart	Three no trump	16–18 HCP, balanced hand, stoppers in the three unbid suits, denies four spades.
Hand 3	One heart	Two spades	16 or more points, five spades, game forcing, looking for slam, does *not* deny three or four hearts, could be totally unbalanced.

Let's say you open a 13- to 15-point hand with a bid of one heart. How should you respond to your partner's jump bids set forth above?

Hand 1: Three no trump. You have a maximum of 30 points between you two. That's not enough for slam, even if you're at the top of your bid.

Hand 2: If you have your minimum, or bottom, of your bid—13 or 14 points—you should pass. However, if you have 15 points (the top of your bid) you should continue, probably with a quantitative bid of four no trump, asking your partner if she's at the top or bottom of her bid. You'll learn about quantitative bids shortly in this chapter.

Hand 3: If you're at the bottom of your bid and have three spades in your hand, bid four spades. This is a minimum response that denies slam interest, but shows three-card support. Your partner's minimum hand is 16 points. She could have more. So you must describe your hand so that she can evaluate slam potential. If you're at the top of your bid, you should either bid three spades or bid a new suit if you have one with some power.

When your partner makes a game-forcing bid at a level where you can bid her suit short of game, if you jump the bidding to bid game directly, it's a weak bid, showing no slam interest. When she makes a jump shift to two spades, your bid of four spades directly shows weakness. If you were to bid three spades, you would be telling her that you have a good hand and it would be an invitation to slam.

Why? Because the bid she makes requires you to keep the bidding open to game. It allows you to communicate with one another without fear of either of you passing short of game. If you make a jump bid to game, you're telling her that you don't have anything further to tell her and you're not much interested in anything she might want to tell you. If you make a bid in her suit short of game, you're telling her that you want to hear more about her hand.

If you have more than a minimum opening and responder jumps to anything other than two no trump or a limit raise, you clearly should explore for slam. Your more than minimum opening would show a hand of 16-plus points. Any other jump by your partner would indicate that you probably have enough points for slam and you should proceed by going to Blackwood (described later in this chapter). Take a look at the following hand you hold in first seat—a minimum hand that you open one club:

♠ 654
♥ A4
♦ K4
♣ KQ6432

Following are your responses to various bids by your partner after you open this hand at one club:

Partner	You	Meaning
Two no trump	Three no trump	Your partner is showing 13–15 HCP; you have 12 HCP, enough for game. Plus you have a nice six-card club suit. Slam shouldn't even enter your mind because your partner has limited her hand.
Three no trump	Pass	Again, your partner has limited her hand to a maximum of 18 HCP. Add your 12 to that and you get 30, not enough for slam.
Two diamonds	Three clubs	You are conveying to her that you have a minimum. She's shown five diamonds and at least 16 points, but you must tell her that your hand is a minimum with a long club suit as its best feature. Now it's up to her to evaluate further.

Following are you and your partner's actual hands:

You	Partner
♠ 654	♠ AT
♥ A4	♥ K2
♦ K4	♦ AQJ86
♣ KQ6432	♣ AJ85

She has 19 HCP and 21 total points. Added to your 14 points, that's 35 points and a club slam is cold. But that's up to your partner to determine after you've told her your hand is minimum and you have a club suit.

Analysis by Responder When Opener Shows Extra Values

The other way you can find slam is when you give your partner a standard response and she reverses or jumps the bidding, showing extra values.

To refresh your memory, your partner opens one of a suit, you respond, and your partner reverses or jumps. Opener's bids mean the following.

Opener's Second Bid	Meaning
Two no trump	18–19 points, all unbid suits stopped.
Three no trump	20–21 points, all unbid suits stopped.
Reverse	17-plus points.
Jump shift	19–22 points.

Again, your responses are based on simple arithmetic. If your response was a minimum 6- to 9-point hand, here's how you should respond:

Opener's Jump Bid	Your Response
Two no trump	Pass if 6 points. For balanced 7-plus points, you should bid three no trump because you should have a game, given your partner's promised minimum of 18 points.
Three no trump	Pass. You don't have slam because your partner has a maximum of 21 and you have a maximum of 9. That's only 30 points, not enough for slam.
Reverse	If the bidding is passed to you by your RHO, you *must* make another bid. A reverse is forcing on you for one round. Either rebid your five-card suit, support the suit of your partner that you can, or bid no trump to deny support for both of your partner's suits and to indicate a weak hand.
Jump shift	A jump shift is forcing to game so you must continue bidding if your RHO passes until you have bid to the game level. If your hand stinks, just make the weakest bid you can, supporting your partner's suit for which you have the best support or rebid your own suit if it's adequate.

Blackwood: The Easiest Convention of All

If both you and your partner have communicated to each other that you have good hands, the thought will start to germinate that maybe you can bid and make slam. So far, however, you've just been communicating how many points each of you has in your hand and how many cards you have in the trump suit.

BRIDGEBIT

Blackwood was devised by Easley Blackwood in 1933 and has been almost universally adopted as the standard for asking for aces and kings.

When you start to consider slam, you start to realize that you need to know exactly what cards each of you has, and, specifically, how many aces and kings in which suits.

This is where Blackwood comes into play.

Blackwood is very simple. When your partner bids four no trump, she's asking one question: How many aces do you have in your hand? You tell her by bidding suits, as follows:

Bid	Number of Aces
Five clubs	0 or 4
Five diamonds	1
Five hearts	2
Five spades	3

Is that easy, or what?

If your partner then bids five no trump, she's telling you that you and she hold all four aces, and she's asking you how many kings you have. Let me elaborate:

- **She's telling you that you and she hold all four aces.** This is an absolute promise. After bidding four no trump asking for aces, she should not bid five no trump asking for kings if your pair is lacking one ace. So if you respond, for example, five diamonds (telling her that you have one ace) and she comes back with five no trump (asking for kings), you should be able to take it to the bank that she has the other three aces in her hand.

- **She's asking you how many kings you have.** You answer in exactly the same manner as you answered for aces, only you're up one level.

Bid	*Number of Kings*
Six clubs	0 or 4
Six diamonds	1
Six hearts	2
Six spades	3

That's Blackwood. When she has your answers to her questions, she places the contract. If she places the contract somewhere, you should accept her decision and pass. For example, if you agreed that trump is spades and she bids four no trump after you bid four spades, let's say you respond five diamonds, showing one ace. She then bids five spades. She's saying, "Okay, partner, you've told me your holding and we don't have enough, so let's just play it in five spades." You should pass. She knows more about your two hands than you do. You should trust her.

When You Shouldn't Use Blackwood

Blackwood is a terrific convention if your slam depends on the location of all the aces. But there are two instances when you shouldn't use Blackwood.

The first is when the bidding has been opened in one or two no trump. Look at the following bidding:

You	Partner
One no trump	Four no trump

A bid of four no trump here would not be ace-asking. When a hand is opened one no trump and you look like you're going to play it in no trump, a bid of four no trump is called a *quantitative bid*.

> **DEFINITION**
>
> A **quantitative bid** is a bid that is natural, limited, and nonforcing.

In this instance, four no trump is quantitative because it isn't conventional; that is, it doesn't ask for aces. What, you may be inquiring, is it asking? Good question. Obviously there must be some meaning to it, because three no trump is game and bidder has bypassed three no trump. What it's asking is simple. In this bidding sequence—or any sequence when the bidder goes from any no trump bid directly to four no trump—bidder is asking partner to go to slam (six no trump) if she's at the top of her bid, and to pass if she's not at the top of her bid.

In this situation, you've shown your partner that you have a balanced 15- to 17-HCP hand. She probably has 16 HCP herself. So she's asking you whether you opened a 15-point hand or a 17-point hand. Because 32 HCP should be very close to making a small slam, she's just saying to you, "If you have 17 HCP or a good 16-HCP hand, go to six no trump. If you have 15 HCP or a bad 16-HCP hand, pass and we'll play it in four no trump." Again, it's just arithmetic.

The second situation in which you shouldn't use Blackwood is if you have a void in your hand and don't need that ace for slam. If you have two aces and a void in your hand, what good does it do to discover that your partner has one ace? If it's the ace in which you have a void, it won't do you any good at all. So if you have a distributional hand with a singleton or void, you should examine slam potential through the use of cue bids, which I discuss later in this chapter.

How to Get Out of Blackwood

Sometimes you get in Blackwood and discover that you don't want to be in slam but you want to play the contract in five no trump. Look at the following bidding sequence where your partner has only one spade and two aces:

You	LHO	Partner	RHO
One club	Pass	Two hearts	Pass
Three clubs	Pass	Three hearts	Pass
Four clubs	Pass	Four no trump	Pass
Five diamonds	Pass	?	

After your five-diamond bid she wants to play it in five no trump. But if she bids five no trump directly you will think she's telling you that you have all the aces between you and is asking for kings. How can she get it so you can play in five no trump?

The answer is to bid the unbid suit. In this situation she would bid five spades. This says nothing about spades. It merely asks you to bid five no trump, which she will pass.

So the rule is this: If you're in Blackwood and want to play the contract in five no trump, bid the unbid suit, asking your partner to bid five no trump. This is obviously a tactic that can only be used by the player who first bid four no trump.

Cue Bids

The Official Encyclopedia of Bridge (Truscott, Executive Editor, 1994) defines a cue bid as "a forcing bid in a suit in which the bidder cannot wish to play." The most easily understood cue bid is a bid of opponent's suit. Very few rubber bridge players use cue bids. If you were to throw one into your bidding, probably everybody at the table would think you had lost it. In this section, I explain how cue bidding can be used as a substitute for Blackwood to find out what specific cards partner may hold or to tell partner specific cards you hold.

After trump is established, many people use the convention that a bid of another suit indicates that you have first round control of that suit, with either an ace or a void in your hand. This doesn't require that you bid opponents' suit. Look at the following bidding:

Partner	RHO	You	LHO
One spade	Pass	Three spades	Pass
Four clubs	Pass	Four diamonds	

You have already agreed on trump. Your partner's bid of four clubs is a slam try, probably telling you that she has a good club suit and asking you to describe your hand further. Your four-diamonds bid tells her that you either have first round control of diamonds—either the ace of diamonds or a void in diamonds—or a diamonds unbid suit after you have agreed upon a trump suit. Clearly you aren't going to introduce diamonds as a possible trump suit after you've agreed that spades—a major—is going to be trump; so a cue bid doesn't necessarily have to be a bid of opponents' suit.

There are other types of cue bids. One of their big advantages is that they force your partner to bid, because she can't pass you out in a bid of opponents' suit or a previously unbid suit after an agreement on another suit as trump. But it can be dangerous unless you have a firm partnership agreement and an understanding about what your cue bid means.

Making Responder Captain

Now I'm going to focus on a hand I discussed previously in Chapter 14. Look at your hand:

♠ QJ643
♥ 95
♦ 9
♣ AQJ85

Here's how the bidding went:

LHO	Partner	RHO	You
Pass	One club	One diamond	One spade
Two diamonds	Four spades	Pass	?

By this time you should know what your partner's bid means. Do you remember? Is it a sign-off, or something else?

If you remember what you learned in Chapter 14, you know that this bid by your partner shows a 20-point hand. Why? Because you are only promising her 6 points with your bid. If you have a four-card spades suit and 6 points, you can bid one spade to show that you have at least 6 points and at least four spades. But your partner jumps to game! She can only do that if she adds up all the points and determines that from your minimum bid she can make game. And the only way she could make that determination is if she has enough points in her hand to make game. You showed at least 6. So she must have 20 points in her hand to make this bid. What do you do?

What you do *not* do with this hand is meekly pass. You have 13 points. She has 20 points. 13 + 20 = 33. How many points do you need for a small slam? 33. How many points do you have? 33. Should you pass your partner's four-spades bid?

You have two alternatives: One is just to bid six spades. The other is to bid Blackwood. Blackwood is the best option because you might be missing at least two aces, in which case you don't want to bid six. You need to find out how many aces your partner has. If she only has one, you don't want to be in slam. Following is your partner's hand:

♠ AT92
♥ AK8
♦ A
♣ K7632

If you passed four spades and laid down your hand, which is cold for six (it makes seven because the king of spades is *onside*), you won't be able to find a closet far enough away to hide.

DEFINITION

Onside means that a card is placed so that if you take a *finesse*, the finesse will be successful. A **finesse** occurs when you take advantage of a higher-ranking card in your opponents' hand (see Chapter 20 for details).

Following is a layout of all four hands:

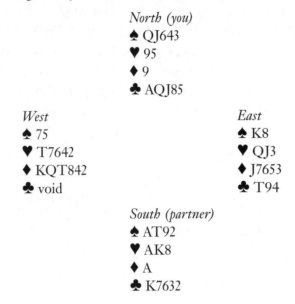

North (you)
- ♠ QJ643
- ♥ 95
- ♦ 9
- ♣ AQJ85

West
- ♠ 75
- ♥ T7642
- ♦ KQT842
- ♣ void

East
- ♠ K8
- ♥ QJ3
- ♦ J7653
- ♣ T94

South (partner)
- ♠ AT92
- ♥ AK8
- ♦ A
- ♣ K7632

So when your partner makes a bid like this, jumping to game after you've made a minimum response, she's not saying, "Pass, partner, I want to play this in game and that's why I bid game." No, she's saying, "I've got a big hand. I want to be sure we play in game because with your minimum bid I have enough in my hand to make game. If you have more than your minimum bid, bid on. Maybe we have slam."

In essence, she's making you the captain of the team again, because you know a lot more about her hand than she knows about yours.

A Slam Try When Your Partner Preempts

What if you look at a huge hand and hear your partner open a preemptive bid? Look at the following hand after you hear your partner open up with a bid of four spades:

- ♠ A
- ♥ KT32
- ♦ KQ965
- ♣ K54

Wow! You were getting ready to open one diamond and then reverse into two hearts. And you hear your loving partner open the bidding with four spades! Are you sniffing slam? You bet you are.

But hold on a minute. What's your partner telling you when she opens the bidding with four spades? She's virtually yelling at you, "Partner, my hand is *weak!*" She's got *less* than a minimum opening hand. Does that change your orientation? It should.

Clearly, your bid here is pass. Sure, you have 15 HCP and 17 points if you count your singleton ace. But the singleton ace is in your partner's trump suit. So even though it's nice that you have the ace of trump, the fact that it's a singleton doesn't make your hand any better at all. In fact, it makes it worse.

Furthermore, your heart suit is pretty weak. If your LHO has the ace, your king isn't worth much. And your club suit only has one trick.

Even if the vulnerability is unfavorable—which would mean that your partner was overbidding her hand by only two tricks—you only have three quick tricks in your hand: the ace of spades, the king–queen of diamonds, and Kxxx and Kxx in hearts and clubs (each is a half quick trick). If that's the case, you might make one overtrick. Pass.

As it was, you were wise to pass. Here's your partner's hand, followed by your hand:

Partner
♠ KT876532
♥ 94
♦ A7
♣ 9

You
♠ A
♥ KT32
♦ KQ965
♣ K54

You lose a club and a heart, maybe two depending on the location of the ace, even with a 2–2 trump split (where each of your opponents holds two trump), which is only a 40 percent chance. Never forget: When your partner preempts, she has a weak hand, even if she's preempting in game.

Investigating for the Correct Slam

When your partner opens and you have a huge hand, you're going to be tempted to jump the bidding immediately to tell your partner and the world that you have a terrific hand. You don't need to do this.

If you know you have a preponderance of the points in the hand, it's much better to proceed slowly so that you can communicate with each other to determine the correct contract. Jumping the bidding squeezes you and takes away bidding space you might need. Look at the following hand after your partner opens the bidding with one club:

♠ AK65
♥ AK96
♦ AQ6
♣ KJ

That's a 24-HCP hand, and your partner has opened? You're going to have to be tied down to keep from jumping—nay, leaping! But you don't need to leap or even jump. Your correct bid is one heart!

You might be thinking, "One heart? Are you kidding? I've got 24 HCP, my partner opens the bidding, and I just show her a minimum 6-point hand? Are you nuts?"

No, I'm not nuts. Remember that your one heart bid is 100 percent forcing on your partner to bid again. You want to find out what she has. Does she have four hearts? Does she have four spades? What does she have? If you jump to something like three no trump, for example, how is she going to respond? As long as you make a bid that forces her to bid again, you've done what you want to do. You want to find out about her hand at the lowest level so you know whether you're going to play this hand in clubs, hearts, spades, or no trump. A jump to three no trump does *not* force your partner to bid again.

TRICKS OF THE TRADE

Keep in mind that any bid of a new suit by responder is 100 percent forcing on opener to bid again for one round.

So you bid one heart and your partner responds one no trump. What do you do?

Now you know what you want to know. Your partner doesn't have four hearts or she would have supported you. Your partner doesn't have four spades or she would have bid one spade. Your partner has a balanced hand with no voids or singletons. She has shown 13 points and you have 24 HCP. That's 37 points, enough for a grand slam. You should bid seven no trump immediately. There's nothing more you need to know.

Maybe you won't make seven no trump every time with this hand, but you've got the points for it and should bid it. The key to the hand is that you kept your head and didn't jump. You made a forcing bid at the lowest level possible, then determined the correct contract and bid it.

Just remember this rule: *A one-over-one bid* by responder to partner's opening bid is 100 percent forcing on partner to bid again.

> **DEFINITION**
>
> A **one-over-one** bid is when you bid a suit at the one level after your partner has bid a different suit at the one level.

Knowing When Not to Bid Slam

Just as important as finding the proper slam is knowing when you shouldn't bid slam. Staying out of improper slams is probably more difficult than finding the right slam and bidding it. Look at this hand after your partner opens one club:

♠ AQ75
♥ KQ73
♦ AQ62
♣ 8

That's 17 HCP. What do you bid? Again, you want to make the lowest bid you can make that forces your partner to bid again. So you bid the lowest ranking of your three four-card suits: one diamond. Your partner responds one no trump. What now? Do you have slam?

Your partner has told you that she has a balanced hand that is no more than minimum. Her maximum holding is 14 points. You have 17 HCP. In no trump your singleton isn't worth anything. Your partner doesn't have four hearts or four spades or she would have bid them. That's the end of the story. You have a maximum of 32 points and that's not enough for slam. Bid three no trump, a bid that is a sign-off, and play it there.

> **TRICKS OF THE TRADE**
>
> Frank Stewart, one of the best bridge writers and players around, gives a good rule that you should follow for any bidding, but especially when considering slams: If you are considering a contract and partner must have just the right cards, forget it!

Sometimes your partner will have a hand that results in your taking all but one trick. But you must trust your arithmetic. If your points don't add up, don't try to project something into your partner's hand that you don't know is there. Don't bid speculative slams.

Deceptive Bidding

Sometimes you lie to everybody. When you really trust your partner, you can fool your opponents and lure them into a foolish double or a foolish act. But it requires total confidence in your partner. Look at the following bidding.

You	LHO	Partner	RHO
Two spades (1)	Pass	Two no trump (2)	Pass
Three hearts (3)	Pass	Three spades (4)	Pass
Four clubs (5)	Pass	Four spades (6)	Pass
Five diamonds (7)	Pass	Five hearts (8)	Pass
Six diamonds (9)	Pass	Six spades (10)	Pass
Seven no trump	Double	Pass	Pass
Redouble			

Here's what it means:

(1) I have a huge hand. Keep the bidding open.

(2) My hand stinks. Please let me pass.

(3) I have a huge hand. Do you prefer hearts or spades? Please bid again.

(4) Spades. Please, please, let me pass.

(5) Not yet. We have now agreed that spades will be trump. However, I also have the ace of clubs. Do you have any aces you want to bid? Please bid again.

(6) No, all I have is minimal support in spades. Please. Let's play this here. My hand is awful.

(7) Not yet. I also have the ace of diamonds, at least a first-round stopper. How do you like them apples? Please bid again.

(8) I got plenty of nothin'! I hope this will put an end to this foolishness! My hand is terrible. However, I do have minimal support in hearts. Because I have to bid, and because you already know about my spades, I thought I might as well mention it here.

(9) Thanks. That's nice to know. Not so fast; I not only have the ace of diamonds, I also have the king of diamonds. Because we've agreed that spades is going to be trump and I'm bidding diamonds, I want you to bid again. I want to hear more.

(10) Okay, my spades are better than my hearts and my whole hand stinks. Stop while we have the chance.

Responder's hand was the following:

♠ 8642
♥ Q83
♦ 7632
♣ 64

Seven no trump? Look at declarer's hand:

♠ A
♥ AK
♦ AK
♣ AKQ98754

Declarer never bid clubs as a suit, which was his real suit. He knew he had seven no trump cold from the start. But he went through the bidding process hoping he could get a double of seven no trump. If he had just opened at seven no trump it would have been passed out. But from the bidding, where it looked like his two suits were spades and hearts, he whetted the appetite of his opponents and sucked them into a double of a cold, cold seven–no trump contract.

BRIDGEBIT

Just because a contract is doubled, doesn't mean that the bidding is ended. If you are so confident that you can make the contract, you can redouble. Redoubling doubles the bonus points you get if you make it. But it also doubles the bonus points for your opponents if you don't make it!

The point of this exercise isn't that it's okay to lie to your partner. On the contrary, you should *not* lie to your partner. The point of this exercise is that both partners had such wonderful trust in one another that they complied with their agreements and continued to bid.

Declarer could bid all these false suits in the sublime confidence that he was in total control of the hand because he trusted his partner to continue bidding and not take some unilateral action to pass him out in one of his one- or two-card suits. He didn't care what his partner had. All the bidding was to create a false impression on opponents. He knew he was in control, that his partner would keep bidding so long as he demanded another bid, and that the final contract was going to be seven no trump; regardless of the cards held by his partner and regardless of his partner's responses.

And his partner trusted declarer to know what he was doing and continued to bid despite the abysmal cards he held. The result was an awful lot of points. Seven no trump doubled and redoubled is the most you can make offensively in bridge if you are vulnerable.

The Least You Need to Know

- You need 33 points for a small slam, 37 points for a grand slam.
- In Blackwood, a bid of four no trump asks partner to respond with the number of aces in her hand.
- Partner responds to Blackwood by bidding five clubs with zero or four aces, five diamonds with one ace, five hearts with two aces, and five spades with three aces.
- Don't bid slam if your partner must have specific cards for you to make it.
- After trump is established, a bid of a new suit may be a cue bid showing first-round control of that suit, either an ace or a void.

Not So Fast! Overcalls and Takeout Doubles

In This Chapter

- Requirements for making an overcall
- Takeout doubles
- Balancing-seat overcalls
- Overcalling preemptive bids

Up until now we've been talking about how you open the bidding or respond when your partner opens the bidding. But half the time your opponents open the bidding, and you're in the position of overcalling your opponents' opening bid. An overcall is a bid by either partner after an opponent has opened the bidding. This chapter discusses what you need to overcall and how you do it. It also explains what a takeout double is and how you do that.

Why Overcall?

When opponents open the bidding, you know that at least one person at the table is sitting there with a pretty good hand, and it's not your loving partner. So when should you overcall, and, a better question, why?

Because we know that you need 13 points to open the bidding and there are 40 total HCP in the hand, that leaves a maximum of 27 points, plus some distribution points, spread among the three other players. If you subtract the points in your hand from that 27, it tells you approximately how many points you can expect from the other two players.

If you have 12 points, that's 25 total points accounted for. This means that there are approximately 15 points left to be distributed between your LHO and your partner. To make game in no trump you need 25 points. You have 12. That means that your partner must have 13 of the 15 remaining points for you to make game.

All this leads up to the question, why overcall? If you can't make game, why say anything?

There are four reasons:

- **You might make game.** You have to tell your partner what you have. You know what the possibilities and the probabilities are. What you don't know are the *facts*. Tell her what you have and let her tell you what she has. The way to do that is to make an overcall within the parameters upon which you and your partner have agreed.

- **You might make a partscore.** Don't just roll over and play dead because you think your opponents might have better hands than you and your partner. If you have a bid, make it. You and your partner might be able to make three diamonds, for instance. If your opponents can make two hearts, but not three hearts, you should bid to three diamonds. If they bid to three hearts and you set them, you score points that you wouldn't have made had you not overcalled.

- **You tell your partner something about your hand to help her defend the contract if your opponents win the auction.** Without your bid, she has no clue as to what's in your hand and she will probably assume you don't have much. With an overcall at the one level you tell her what your preferred suit is and that you have at least 8 points.

- **You crowd the bidding a little for your opponents.** If they open one club and you can overcall one spade with an 8-point hand and five spades, it means that they will have to go to the two level to communicate, and that might be difficult.

With those reasons in mind, if you have a hand to overcall you turn the auction into a *competitive auction*, and that makes it more unlikely that your opponents will bid to game than if you were not competing with them.

DEFINITION

A **competitive auction** is one where both pairs are bidding and competing to get the contract.

Suit-Length Requirements

Back when I was on the beginning side of the learning curve, my RHO opened one heart and I overcalled two clubs with a 10-point hand and a five-card suit. We were vulnerable and the bidding went pass — pass — double — pass-pass — pass. I was down two for a terrible result.

After the hand, my LHO, Arlen O'Hara (who has since become one of my partners), knew that I was relatively new to the game, so she gave me some advice. "I never," she said, "overcall at the two level unless I have an opening hand or a six-card suit."

Her strategy sounded good to me, so I adopted it. I called it *Arlen's Rule*. I played by Arlen's Rule for a while, until I learned more specific point and suit-length requirements for overcalls, which you'll learn shortly. It kept me out of a lot of trouble.

The first question you ask yourself is: how long must my suit be to overcall, regardless of how many points I have in my hand? Answer: *You must have at least a five-card suit to make an overcall.* Look at the following hand, when your RHO opens one club:

    ♠ KQ86
    ♥ K8
    ♦ KQ98
    ♣ 873

Not a bad hand. You have 13 HCP, 14 total points. This is a hand you would clearly open one diamond. But your RHO opened one club. Can you overcall one diamond or one spade? Not in this lifetime, you shouldn't. When you overcall, you *promise* your partner you have five cards in the suit you bid. It doesn't matter that you're only bidding at the one level. Overcalling isn't like responding to your partner's opening bid. It's more like making an opening bid. But you don't have the luxury of being able to open a three-card minor when you only have a four-card major. So when you make an overcall you must have five cards, at least, in the suit you bid.

This is a very instructive hand because it illustrates a principle that you should never forget. When your LHO opens the bidding, just because your partner passes doesn't say that she has a bad hand. She just might not be able to bid what she has. In such an event, she will be counting on you to balance, which I explain later in this chapter.

So your partner's failure to overcall by passing doesn't make her a *passed hand*.

> **DEFINITION**
>
> A **passed hand** is one that is below the requirements to open the bidding. If you fail to open you are a passed hand. If you fail to overcall, you're not a passed hand because you might have a hand you could have opened, but not one that you could overcall.

Point Requirements

The point requirements for overcalling are straightforward. You may overcall in accordance with the following rules.

To overcall at the one level …

- You should have no less than 8 points and no more than 15 points. This is flexible and varies according to your partnership agreement. For example, some people play 7 to 17.

To overcall at the two level …

- With a five-card suit, you must have no less than 11 points and no more than 16 points.

- With a six-card suit, you may overcall at the two level if you have at least 10 points.

If you overcall at the one level with an 8-point hand, however, you should have a very good suit. It would not be wise to bid a poor five-card suit with only 8 points. Look at the following two hands:

1.	♠ JT984	**2.**	♠ AKT84
	♥ A87		♥ J98
	♦ K83		♦ 873
	♣ 73		♣ 73

Hand 1: What's the point of overcalling one spade? You have 9 points, but your spade suit is terrible. If your partner is on lead, she's going to trust you and lead a spade, even though she might have a better lead in her hand (Maybe she has the KQx of hearts and would normally lead the king of hearts). You would be misleading your partner and making a big mistake.

Hand 2: You have a wonderful spade suit. So even if your partner doesn't have spade support and the opponents get the contract, you want your partner to lead spades so you can cash your two-spade tricks. Further, if your partner has a doubleton, you might get your two-spade tricks plus allowing your partner to ruff the third spade. So in Hand 2 you have every right to overcall one spade.

Let's look at some more hands after your RHO opened the bidding at one heart as dealer:

1.	♠ AT964	**2.**	♠ A863	**3.**	♠ K983	**4.**	♠ QJ976	**5.**	♠ K983
	♥ Q4		♥ KQ5		♥ 7		♥ J6		♥ 7
	♦ AQ93		♦ 83		♦ T74		♦ T97		♦ Q74
	♣ 32		♣ A873		♣ KQJ52		♣ AJ4		♣ KJ752

Hand 1: One spade. This is a clear hand. You would open it. It's got a five-card major. You have 14 points. No problem.

Hand 2: Pass. You shouldn't make a takeout double this hand because, as you will learn later in this chapter, a double promises tolerance for all unbid suits. You can't tolerate a diamond bid.

Hand 3: Two clubs. This is a minimum hand to overcall at the two level. You have 11 points and five clubs. Your club suit is good enough to serve as a *lead directing call* if your partner is on lead. If vulnerable you should probably pass.

> **DEFINITION**
>
> A **lead directing call** or bid is one made for the main purpose of telling partner what suit to lead if you're defending and she has the opening lead.

Hand 4: Pass. You have 10 points, but a weak spade suit. Really the only trick you have in your hand is the ace of clubs. Forget it. At equal or unfavorable vulnerability, pass and let your partner carry the ball. With favorable vulnerability, overcall one spade.

Hand 5: Pass. This hand is identical to Hand 3 except that your club suit lacks the queen and your diamond suit has the queen; the points are identical. But you should pass this because your club suit isn't strong enough and isn't good enough to serve as lead directing for your partner.

Now look at the following hand after RHO opened the bidding at one spade as dealer, and you are vulnerable:

♠
♥ KT9873
♦ J98
♣ KJ84

What do you do?

Pass. Remember, on this hand, RHO opened one spade. This is a shot in the dark. Against good players the bidding could go as follows.

RHO	**You**	**LHO**	**Partner**
One spade	Two hearts	Pass	Pass
Double	Pass	Pass	Pass

Result? Down two for 500 points above the line for the bad guys. Even though you have 11 points and six hearts, your heart suit is far too weak to overcall at the two-level vulnerable (or even nonvulnerable, unless your opponents are vulnerable). Based on the bidding you're going to get the sinking suspicion that the hearts are sitting behind you (in other words, in the hands of the opponent who plays immediately after you) and that you're going to get killed. This is a hand that mediocre players often rush in where good players fear to tread. In the *direct seat* you must always take into consideration the possibility of this type of bidding, to which we have referred earlier, the reopening double. To overcall at the two level without opening-hand values, you must have control of your trump suit.

DEFINITION

The **direct seat** is the seat immediately to the left of the opening bidder.

Bridge authority Charles Goren gives a very good rule: *Don't overcall at the two level unless you can promise you will not lose more than two trump tricks.* You should adopt that rule. This hand doesn't promise that, even though it has six trump, including two honors.

Second-Position Overcalls

If dealer opens and you're in second position, your overcalls should be disciplined. The reason is that your partner's hand is undefined. If you overcall with a weak hand—8 points—and she's sitting there looking at a 12-point hand, she's going to be thinking game. So in second seat you shouldn't overcall, even at the one level, unless you have at least 10 points. Look at the following hand after dealer, your RHO, opens one spade:

♠ 3
♥ AK9863
♦ J96
♣ 832

Like your hearts? You have six of them. And a singleton spade. Are you tempted to overcall two hearts? I don't blame you. I know a lot of people who would. Now take a look at your LHO's hand:

♠ J74
♥ QJT74
♦ Q85
♣ 97

Your RHO opened one spade so you know that he has an opening hand. How do you think you're going to fare in two hearts with all those hearts sitting behind you? If you're up against savvy opponents, this is how the bidding will go.

RHO	You	LHO	Partner
One spade	Two hearts	Pass	Pass
Double	Pass	Pass	Pass

You'll probably be set two or three and your partner will be seething. This is the danger of overcalling on a good long suit with nothing else. The two hands behind you are unknown. If you're lucky, your partner will have the holding shown above in your LHO's hand. But there's at least as good a chance that it will be your opponent and you'll be in for a long, long hand.

However, look at the next hand after your RHO opens one club as dealer:

♠ 73
♥ QJT6543
♦ A
♣ T52

What do you think? This is a seven-card suit, but it's not as good a suit as the six-card suit led by the ace–king. The answer is that you have 10 points and long, long suit, and you should overcall one heart.

Third-Position Overcalls

You can be more aggressive when you're in third position. You've already heard from your partner and she's passed, telling you that she doesn't have an opening hand. (Remember, when you're in third seat, your partner is the dealer and opening bidder.) You need have no fear that if you bid, her eyes will light up and immediately think of game. It's here that you can bid your 8-point hand with the good suit. This bid tells her, "Partner, I have a nice suit. If you can support it, let me know and we will compete. If you can't support it, this is the suit you should lead if you are on lead."

Additionally, in third position you're in a perfect spot to try to foul up your opponents' communication. So you have three incentives to make an overcall in third position:

- Tell your partner you have a good hand, good suit, or both.
- Give your partner a lead direction.
- Interfere with opponents' communication.

Fourth-Position Overcalls

You can be aggressive here, too. In fourth position both your partner and one of your opponents have passed. However, it matters who opened the bidding. If dealer opened and your partner passed, she could have a good hand that she couldn't overcall. So she will be relying on you to make a bid. I'll talk about this shortly when I discuss balancing.

If your RHO opened the bidding in third seat, you know that both your LHO and your partner don't have opening hands. If you bid, you'll be interfering with your LHO's ability to respond to his partner's opening bid. This is another situation where you have an incentive to interfere even though you have a weak hand. This is especially true if you can elevate the level of bidding so that your LHO will be forced to respond at the two level. For instance, if your RHO opens one diamond and you can overcall one spade, it makes it difficult for your RHO to tell his partner he has four hearts with a minimum 6-point hand. If you can overcall two clubs it's even better, because that eliminates your LHO's ability to communicate any four-card major he might have to his partner at the one level.

No Trump Overcalls

If your RHO opens the bidding and you overcall one no trump, it's the same as opening the bidding with one no trump. A one no trump overcall shows 15 to 17 HCP, no voids or singletons, and no more than two doubletons. This is only true if you are in the direct seat (immediately to the left of the opening bidder).

Balancing Calls

A *balancing call*, also called a *balancing bid*, is a bid or takeout double made to keep the bidding open after opponents have opened. It is only made in the *passout seat*, which is the seat immediately to the right of the opening bidder after two passes. So an overcall in the balancing seat could be a bid to keep the bidding open for one of two reasons:

- You don't want to let opponents play the hand at a low level.

- You're protecting your partner in the event she was forced to pass what might be an opening hand because her RHO opened before she could bid.

Determining When to Make a Balancing Call

Look at your partner's hand:

♠ KQ8
♥ K85
♦ KQ98
♣ 873

This is your partner's hand (referred to earlier in this chapter) when her RHO opened the bidding with one club. She shouldn't bid, but she has 13 points. She is relying on you to balance if the bidding is passed around to you. If you don't have a five-card suit to bid yourself then you can make a takeout double, which I explain later in this chapter. This doesn't say much about your hand. But you know that your RHO (opener's partner) can't have more than 5 points in his hand or he would have been forced to respond when your partner passed. So you count the points in your hand, add 5 to it, add 14 to that, subtract that from 40, and you come up with a reasonable expectation of what your partner has in her hand. Take a look at your hand:

♠ A9532
♥ 763
♦ J3
♣ K92

The bidding has gone one club — pass — pass to you. What do you do? Following is the way you can fairly reliably determine where the points are in this hand:

You	8 points. You know this for sure because you can see them and count them.
RHO	A maximum of 5 points. He passed after your partner passed. If he had 6 points he would have bid.
LHO	Probably 14 points. He opened the bidding at one of a suit. It's possible he's got a big hand—17 points or more—and is just waiting to jump or reverse, but that occurs less frequently. You can feel fairly certain that he's got a maximum of 14.
Total	8 + 5 + 14 = 27
Partner	40 – 27 = 13

That's 13 points in your partner's hand. What does that mean? That means you and your partner have the preponderance of the points. You shouldn't let opponents play this in one club unless your partner is sitting there with a lot of clubs.

So what you do is bid your five-card suit, even though your hand is minimal and your suit isn't great. You know that your partner's hand is going to be a source of some tricks for you, even if she only has two spades, so you aren't taking much risk in bidding a weak five-card suit when you know your RHO has garbage. You aren't selling out at the one level when you and your partner have 22 points between you. Moreover, you're protecting your partner. When you bid with this kind of hand in the passout seat, you give your partner the confidence to pass her 14-point hand without a five-card suit when her RHO opens the bidding because she knows she can rely on you to balance to protect her.

 BRIDGEBIT

Balancing is called *protection* in England, which is probably a more descriptive term for what you're doing.

Balancing No Trump Overcalls

When your LHO is dealer and opens the bidding and it's passed around to you in fourth seat, your no trump overcall is different than if you make it in the direct seat. As you remember, if you make a one–no trump overcall in the direct seat, you're promising a standard 15- to 17-point hand that you would have opened one no trump had you been the opening bidder.

But when you're in the passout seat, your no trump overcall can be made with three less HCP in your hand. In the passout seat, your bid of one no trump promises 12 to 14 HCP, not 15 to 17.

Overcalling Opponents' Opening Bid of One No Trump

If your RHO opens one no trump, you know that at least 15 HCP are in his hand. But if you have an opening hand, too, and a good five-card suit, there's no reason why his one–no trump open should intimidate you and keep you from bidding. The fact that you're sitting behind him makes your hand valuable because you're in a good position to take his high cards with your high cards.

You can overcall an opponent's opening bid of one no trump if you have an opening hand and a good five-card suit. If your RHO's hand is a balanced 15 HCP and his partner has a Yarborough, you and your partner have 25 HCP between you and probably some distribution points, too; you could have game. You should bid your hand, even if your opponents open with one no trump.

ALERT

You must be absolutely certain that you and your partner are on the same wavelength on the meaning of a one–no trump overcall in the passout seat. If she thinks you're showing 15 to 17 HCP when you only have 12 HCP in your hand, you could find yourself in a three–no trump contract real fast, down two.

Overcalling Preemptive Bids

When your opponents make a preemptive bid and it's your turn to bid in the direct seat, you shouldn't bid unless you have extra values. This means that if you have a mere opening hand—13 or 14 points without a good five-card suit—and your RHO opens three diamonds, you pass. You will be relying on your partner to make a balancing bid in the passout seat if it's passed around to her with a subminimum hand of 11 points.

Look at the following hands after a three-diamonds opening by your RHO:

1.	♠ AK73	2.	♠ AK732	3.	♠ KQ4	4.	♠ KQJ732
	♥ KQ83		♥ KQ8		♥ JT98		♥ 94
	♦ 87		♦ 87		♦ 87		♦ 9
	♣ 943		♣ JT3		♣ AK86		♣ KQ84

Hand 1: Pass. You have a minimum opening hand with no five-card major. You'd ordinarily open this one club. If your partner doesn't have enough to make a balancing bid or double, you'll be in trouble in three of anything.

Hand 2: Pass. You have a nice five-card spade suit, but what if your LHO has a lot of spades? Do you want to start off at the three level with this hand? I don't. Again, it's a minimum opening hand; you don't want to start bidding with a minimum opening hand at the three level. Also, you can support your partner on anything she bids, if she bids. Two hands are unknown, your LHO's and your partner's. If the remaining points are evenly distributed between the two hands, it's a crapshoot whether anybody can make a three bid. In that event, I'd rather defend. Wait until you know the lay of the land, which will be after your LHO bids. If he passes, your partner will have the opportunity to bid or make a balancing double. Then you'll be able to bid more confidently.

Hand 3: Pass. This is another minimum opening hand that can support your partner if she bids. Don't go searching for a fit with minimum points unless your partner asks you to do so.

Hand 4: Three spades. Finally, a bid! This is a good hand with which to overcall a preemptive bid. You've got a nice six-card spade suit, and nice distribution with a singleton and a doubleton. Plus, your clubs will give you at least one trick.

When you're in the passout seat, the rules change. If the bidding has gone three diamonds — pass — pass to you, you must protect your partner in the event that she has passed with one of the opening hands above. So in the passout seat, you should bid with a subminimum opening hand. If you have 11 points, or 10 points with a six-card suit, you should make some sort of call; either bid a suit or double if you can support all the unbid suits. The rules in the passout seat are that you should bid with the following minimum holdings:

- At least 10 points and a fair six-card suit (two of the top four honors), bid your suit.

- At least 11 points and a good five-card suit (two of the top three honors), bid the suit if you can bid it at the 3 level.

- At least 11 points and 4–4–4–1 distribution with the singleton in the pre-empted suit, double. Your partner will either bid her longest suit or, if she has a good hand and at least four cards in the preemptive suit, will leave the double in for penalty.

- At least 11 points and 4–4–3–2 distribution with the doubleton in the preemptive suit, you can double because you can support your partner in anything she bids. If she bids your three-card suit, you can pass.

I go into more detail about how you and your partner interact in this type of situation in Chapter 18.

Overcalls by a Passed Hand

What if you are dealer and the bidding goes pass — pass — pass — one diamond. You're a passed hand. What should you do? Obviously you don't have at least 13 points or you would have made a bid.

An overcall by a passed hand shows between 8 to 12 points and a five-card suit. If you're doing it with 8 points, it should be a very good five-card suit. And if you're doing it at the two level, you should have a six-card suit and no less than 11 points.

Don't forget, you don't have many values in this hand because you know your partner doesn't have an opening hand, either. Making an overcall when you are both passed hands can be risky business, indeed.

Jump Overcalls

A jump overcall (like one club–two hearts) shows a very big hand, more distributional than for you to overcall one no trump. It promises at least six cards in the suit and at least 16 points. Following is an example of a typical hand where you would want to make a jump overcall:

♠ AKT964
♥ AK6
♦ 864
♣ 7

This is a hand that is close to game with no help. If trump splits favorably and your partner has trump support, you have eight tricks.

A jump overcall requests help from your partner in outside suits. You're telling her, "Don't worry too much about my trump suit. If you have help in other suits, let's keep bidding."

If your partner has two quick tricks in outside suits, she should jump to game, even without much trump support. She can jump to game even if she only has a singleton honor in your suit. It's the cards in her hand that are outside your trump suit that you're interested in.

By now, you should be aware that rules change when you're in the balancing seat, and that's true for jump overcalls, too. If you are in the direct seat, a jump overcall is very strong. But in the balancing seat, you should have 14 to 15 points and a six-card suit in order to make a jump overcall.

Defensive Value of an Overcall

To show how valuable an overcall can be in defending a hand, look at the following, which I played recently. My RHO opened one heart and I held the following:

♠ 832
♥ K43
♦ AQ983
♣ A4

This is a no-sweat two-diamonds overcall, so that's what I did. The auction went like this.

RHO	Me	LHO	Partner
One heart	Two diamonds	Two spades	Pass
Three hearts	Pass	Three no trump	Pass
Pass	Pass		

My partner, the aforementioned Arlen O'Hara, was on lead, so she led the 10 of diamonds. Dummy came down with the following hand:

♠ Q4
♥ AQJ953
♦ J5
♣ K63

What a terrific lead by her! I had a strong suspicion that declarer had the king of diamonds with three small diamonds. He was in a terrible position because Arlen's lead—which she would have never found had it not been for my overcall—set up my hand totally. My 9 of diamonds became very powerful because she led the 10 and the jack was on the *board* in dummy's hand.

DEFINITION

The **board** is another name for the hand in dummy, which is exposed.

Declarer played low from the board. I ducked (played low, avoiding getting the lead). I was in terrific shape. He had no hope of making this hand solely because of Arlen's lead. We had four cold diamond tricks because all he was going to get was his king. I had two sure entries, the ace of clubs and the king of hearts. He held up on taking his king, so Arlen led her other diamond, the 6. Dummy played the jack. I covered with my queen and he was forced to take his king. I now had the two top diamonds out: the ace and the 9. (The king, queen, jack, and 10 had all been played.) He had two diamonds left, but they would fall on my ace and 9, setting up my fifth diamond. That's four diamond tricks plus the ace of clubs and the king of hearts.

The only reason we set this hand was because my two-diamond overcall told Arlen what to lead, and she led her top diamond. The point here is to show the value of an overcall on defending the hand. Arlen actually had a Yarborough, so they had 27 HCP between them. We set them because of the overcall. With any other lead they make three no trump easy.

Downside of Overcalling

As with anything you do in bridge, there's a downside to overcalling. You give information to your opponents that they otherwise would not have. For example, if you overcall two hearts over a one-spade opening, it gives your opponents a pretty good hint as to where the hearts honors are if they play the hand. If you overcall and your partner remains silent, the honors will be marked (meaning that your opponents will know you have it) in your hand for the missing power. It will make it easier for them to play the hand.

So while you're giving your partner information, you're giving your opponents the same information. However, it's generally worth the risk to give your partner information she can use on defense.

Takeout Doubles

Previously I have referred to a bid called a takeout double. It occurs, under partnership agreement, when one partner doubles an opponent's bid, asking partner to bid. Your partner has the option of bidding or leaving the double in for penalty if your LHO passes. You are not doubling for penalty. You are doubling to tell your partner that you have values and to ask her to describe her hand. She can't leave the double in for penalty unless she has a lot of cards in the opponents' suit.

Distribution Is More Important Than Points

Generally speaking, a takeout double at the one level is telling your partner that you have some values and are short in opponent's bid suit, but that you don't have the requirements to make a bid on your own. For example, you might only have a four-card major, but have an opening hand. You can't overcall on a four-card major, so if the opponents have bid the other major, you can double to tell your partner that you not only have opening or near-opening values, but you also have four cards in the unbid major.

For a normal takeout double, you must be able to support any suit your partner bids. What is *support?* Ideally it is at least four cards, but this is impractical. Sometimes you will have a 4–4–4–1 hand and your RHO will bid your one-card suit, but more often you have two four-card suits and a three-card suit. If you have sufficient HCP, you can make a takeout double with 4–4–3 in the unbid suits because if your partner bids the suit in which you have three cards you can pass and you'll only be at the two level. So playing in a 4–3 fit won't be a disaster.

BRIDGEBIT

A 4–3 fit is called a *Moysian fit,* named after Alphonse Moyse Jr., who argued in favor of opening four-card majors and raising with three-card support.

You shouldn't double for takeout if you can only support two of the unbid suits. For example, if you hold the following ...

♠ AK43
♥ 872
♦ 94
♣ KQ87

and your RHO opens one heart, you have an opening hand but cannot overcall one spade because you only have four spades. It might appear to you that this is a good takeout double, but it's not because you cannot support your partner if she bids diamonds—you only have two diamonds.

Remember, your partner is forced to bid if your LHO passes your double. She must bid even if it's only a four-card suit. Sometimes, in rare but very uncomfortable circumstances, you find yourself having to bid a three-card suit in response to your partner's takeout double. Look at the following hand:

♠ 984
♥ 943
♦ JT83
♣ 543

In the prior bidding sequence your RHO opened one heart; if you were to double with your four spades and four clubs but only two diamonds, if your RHO passes, your partner might bid two diamonds with this hand. What would you do? You'd have to pass. So you could easily be in a terrible contract with no hope of making it. If you were against good opponents you would probably be doubled and have nowhere to run. So remember this rule: *In order to make a takeout double you must be able to support all unbid suits.*

Following are requirements for a takeout double:

- Shortness (no more than two cards) in suit bid by opponent
- Support for all unbid suits
- Minimum of 10 HCP

Doubling and Then Bidding Your Own Suit

Another use of the takeout double is to show a big hand. If you have a hand that's too big for an overcall with a good suit, the way you show it is to double whatever your opponents bid; then, regardless of what happens, you bid your suit at your second opportunity. This shows a hand bigger than the maximum hand you need for an overcall. Generally you need at least 17 points and a good five-card suit to employ this strategy.

In a nutshell, the requirements for bidding your own suit after doubling are as follows:

- At least 17 points
- A good five-card suit headed by three of the top five honors

Shortness in the suit bid by opponents is not a requirement for this bid.

The reason you double and then bid your suit is so that you have a way to tell your partner the size of your hand, which you can't do with an overcall. Look at the following hand:

♠ AKJ76
♥ 54
♦ A7
♣ KQ54

If your RHO bids one club, what are you going to do? Overcall one spade? Okay, but what does that tell your partner? You can overcall in this auction with a good five-card spade suit and 8 points. How does your partner know whether you're overcalling a minimum hand or a huge hand?

The answer is that there's no way she can know this unless you have a way to bid big hands in a manner different from an overcall. And that way is to double the one-club bid first. Then bid your spade suit at your next opportunity, regardless of what your partner bid or what your opponents bid. Your hand is strong enough to bid your spades up to the three level. You could have game if your partner has the following minimum hand and if the spades are properly positioned:

♠ 432
♥ 862
♦ T983
♣ A76

If you were to overcall one spade, your partner would undoubtedly pass. Whereas if you've told her that you had a hand that contains at least 17 points, she might make a bid here after you bid your spades. And if the spades split 3–2 and your RHO has the queen of spades, you can make four spades, even with your partner's dismal hand. And it's a hand with which she'd never respond if you just overcalled one spade.

Let's look at some hands. Your RHO opens one diamond. What's your bid with the following?

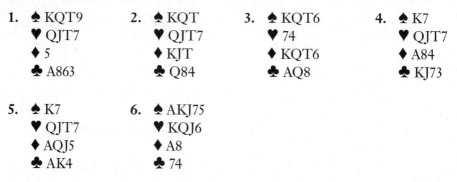

Hand 1: Double. You can support all the unbid suits, plus you have an opening hand.

Hand 2: Pass. You have an opening hand but you shouldn't make a takeout double for a couple of reasons: First, you have too many cards in opponents' suit. Second, you have minimal support in two of the unbid suits. With these deficiencies, the fact that you have a minimum hand suggests that you pass.

Hand 3: One no trump. You have enough points for a no trump opener. You have the opponents' suit stopped. You have a balanced hand. A one no trump overcall in any seat other than the balancing seat guarantees no trump opening values and a stopper in opponents' suit.

Hand 4: Pass. You have too many diamonds and not enough spades. With a minimum hand you must have support for every unbid suit to make a takeout double.

Hand 5: Double. It is okay to make a takeout double without support for every suit as long as you have more than 16 points. If your partner bids spades (remember, she must bid something!), you will then bid no trump at the lowest possible level. This will tell your partner that you have 18 to 20 HCP, a balanced hand, and opponents' suit well stopped.

Hand 6: Double. This is a classic hand for doubling and bidding your own suit. If your partner responds to your double with a bid of two clubs—which is likely because you're short in that suit—you can freely bid two spades to show her that you have at least 17 points and a good spade suit.

Doubling RHO's Opening Bid of One No Trump

A double of your RHO's opening bid of one no trump promises your partner that you have a hand that you could have opened one no trump yourself: 15 to 17 HCP, no voids or singletons, and no more than two doubletons.

The Least You Need to Know

- To overcall at the one level, you must have at least five cards in the suit and between 8 and 15 points.
- To overcall at the two level, you must have at least five cards in the suit and between 11 and 15 points; with six cards in the suit you need only 10 points.
- To make a takeout double, you must have support in all unbid suits and at least 10 points.
- To double and bid your own suit, you must have at least 17 points, a five-card suit, and three of the top five honors.

Responses to Overcalls and Takeout Doubles

In This Chapter

- Responding to an overcall by your partner
- Responding to a takeout double by your partner
- Responding when RHO bids

When your partner overcalls, you're in a relatively ticklish position because of the large disparity between her minimum and her maximum. As you learned in Chapter 17, when she overcalls, her upper maximum is 15 points, but her minimum is just 8 points. That's a lot less than the minimum for an opening one bid. This chapter discusses how you respond when your partner makes an overcall.

What Do You Know?

When you're the partner of an overcaller, you have a lot of information at your fingertips. First, you know where at least half the points in the hand are located. Opener—one of your opponents—has at least 13. Your partner has at least 8. That's 21 points at minimum. So you can look at your hand and evaluate it with much more confidence than if there had been no bidding.

Furthermore, you know that if your partner bid a suit, she has at least five cards in it. That's very valuable because it means that if you have three cards in her suit, you have at least an eight-card fit.

Responding to Major-Suit Overcall with Support

If your partner made a major-suit overcall and you have three-card support, here's how you should respond based on the number of points in your hand:

6 to 10 points	Make a one-level raise.
11 to 13 points	Make a jump (limit) raise.
14 to 17 points	Jump to game.

Look at some hands after the bidding has gone as follows:

LHO	Partner	RHO	You
One club	One heart	Pass	?

Here are the hands to evaluate:

1. ♠ KJ7
   ♥ 9832
   ♦ A87
   ♣ K84

2. ♠ JT98
   ♥ A82
   ♦ 943
   ♣ J83

3. ♠ A98
   ♥ 32
   ♦ K832
   ♣ KJ43

4. ♠ AQ973
   ♥ 8632
   ♦ KQJ
   ♣ 9

5. ♠ J973
   ♥ 3
   ♦ KQJ4
   ♣ T965

Hand 1: Three hearts. You make the same bid you'd make if she opened one heart, a limit raise showing 11 to 13 points and at least three hearts.

Hand 2: Two hearts. Don't mess around showing a weak four-card spade suit. You only have one bid, and your first obligation should be to tell your partner that you have a trump fit. The advantage you have in an overcall situation is that you know at least one of your opponents is sitting there with an opening hand—at least 13 points. You want to get to your trump fit as quickly as possible. If you respond with one spade and partner has a minimum overcall, she won't rebid her hearts and you'll miss your fit. Your hand is too weak to bid spades and then bid hearts later. A simple raise to an overcall supporting your partner's suit shows 6 to 10 points. You really have no hope for game here, but you want to bid for two reasons:

- You have safety because of your trump fit, so you can't be hurt too badly if you get the contract.

- You make it a little more difficult for your opponents to bid because you're raising the level for opener to bid if he has a fairly big hand.

Hand 3: One no trump. You have 11 HCP and opponents bid clubs. You can't support her hearts with only two. And you have their clubs stopped twice. A one–no trump response to an overcall shows 8 to 11 HCP.

Hand 4: Four hearts. You have a five-card trump support with 14 points. Again, you don't want to mess around with a one-spade bid. Get to game without any further communication between your opponents.

Hand 5: Pass. Just because you have diamonds well stopped, that's no reason to bid without a fit. Your partner is limited to 15 points and it is unlikely that there is a game here. Don't bid to "save" your partner.

Responding by Bidding a New Suit

When you're responding to an opening bid, a new suit bid by you is forcing on opener. However, when responding to an overcall, a new suit bid by you is *not* forcing. Before I give you some examples, you should know the reasoning behind this.

When you respond to an opening bid, you're looking to make game, and doing so is a real possibility because you know your partner has at least 13 points. However, when responding to an overcall, making game is much more unlikely because you know that one of your opponents has an opening bid in his hand. While game may be possible, it's not probable.

So your goal in responding to an overcall is to quickly find an area where you can compete. The requirements for responding to an overcall are similar to responding to an opening bid. And it's very important that, if you're going to bid a new suit at all, you do so at your first opportunity.

The requirements for responding to an overcall with a new suit follow:

- If you're at the one level, you should have at least 8 points and a good five-card suit.

- If you're at the two level and have only 8 points, you should have a six-card suit.

- If you have three-card support for your partner's major suit overcall, you shouldn't bid a new suit unless you have opening-hand values or a good six-card suit. The idea is to quickly find a fit in which to compete. If you have a fit in your partner's major suit you should tell her immediately, because a new suit by you isn't forcing. Otherwise, she might pass your bid of a different suit and you could find yourself in a terrible fit when you could have had an eight-card fit had you just supported her at your first opportunity.

Points to consider in responding to your partner's overcall with a new suit include the following:

- Your partner may pass your bid, so you must be certain that you will be willing to play the hand in your suit if your partner can't support you.

- You partner is going to consider leading your suit if she's on lead. So it's not a good idea to bid a new suit unless it's a good suit that could give you some defensive tricks if you're on defense.

- Beware of introducing a new suit if opponents have shown power. If opener's partner has bid a new suit over your partner's overcall, for example, they probably have the majority of the points in their hands. If you were to bid the fourth suit here, you could be getting into a world of hurt.

- Don't respond to your partner's overcall by bidding a new suit at the three level unless you have a good six-card or longer suit and at least 11 points. A "good" suit is one with three of the top five honors with at least the king.

Responding to Your Partner's Two-Level Overcall

When your partner makes an overcall at the two level, you know that she either has at least 11 points with a five-card suit or a six-card suit with at least 10 points. Therefore, you know that she's stronger than if she overcalled at the one level.

Let's take a look at some hands when partner overcalls at the two level. The bidding has gone as follows:

RHO	You	LHO	Partner
		One spade	Two diamonds
Pass	?		

Here are the hands to evaluate:

	1.	2.	3.	4.	5.
♠	K4	KQT	86	7	7
♥	9863	T974	AQJT7	AK	AJ5
♦	QJ86	K843	96	T8763	Q954
♣	964	KJ	T642	JT974	JT974

Hand 1: Pass. Even with support, there is little hope of game. Because of the one-spade bid, your king of spades rates to be of little use.

Hand 2: Three no trump. Because this hand is balanced and you have spades well stopped, three no trump is more likely to make than five diamonds.

Hand 3: Two hearts. You have minimal values but a good suit. It is possible you have game in hearts.

Hand 4: Five diamonds. Your extra trump, spade shortness, and long club suit should make this a good game.

Hand 5: Four diamonds. A limit raise based on your singleton spade and 5-card trump suit, which means that opponents will only be able to take a maximum of one trick in their strongest suit. Remember that when you have a trump fit, a singleton is worth 3 points. To make this bid you must have not less than four trumps and not a lot of HCP. Remember, also, that a two-level overcall by your partner promises a stronger hand than a one-level overcall. So this 11-point hand is game invitational if your partner is at the top of her bid.

Responding to an Overcall After a Raise by RHO

When your RHO makes a simple raise of opener's suit over your partner's overcall, he's showing weakness, so you can be more assertive. If you have a good six-card major suit, you can even bid it at the three level in this situation. But you must either have length or shortness in the opponents' suit.

Why? Because length would strongly indicate that your partner has shortness. If you're bidding at the three level, you can only lose four tricks. You don't want to start right off with two losers in opponents' suit, which is what might happen if you have a doubleton. If you have three or four, it's highly likely that your partner has no more than a singleton.

Look at the following hands and determine how you are going to respond to your partner's overcall. The bidding has gone as follows:

RHO	You	LHO	Partner
		One club	One spade
Two clubs	?		

Here are the hands to evaluate:

	1.		2.		3.		4.
	♠ 7		♠ 843		♠ 74		♠ QJ
	♥ KJ53		♥ A74		♥ KQ532		♥ KJ9
	♦ QJ73		♦ QJ73		♦ A64		♦ AQT986
	♣ K873		♣ J98		♣ JT3		♣ 74

Hand 1: Pass. You can't support your partner with only one spade. Even though you have all the other suits stopped, you can't bid two no trump because you have a singleton in your partner's suit. If your opponents get the contract, you have a good defensive hand.

Hand 2: Two spades. You have three-card support, even though the rest of your hand isn't too good. But you do have scattered values. You should assume your partner had opening-hand values (even though she might not) and make the bid you'd make if she opened—which is two spades.

Hand 3: Two hearts. Your partner might have three hearts. You're telling her that you have a good five-card or longer hearts suit and some values. But remember that the bid of a new suit by an overcaller's partner is not forcing on overcaller to bid again. So you might end up playing the hand in 2 hearts and she might not have very good support for you.

Hand 4: Two diamonds. You only have two cards in spades, but they're both honors. But you have a terrific diamonds suit, and this might be the only opportunity to tell your partner about it in the event she is on lead. If she rebids spades, you have support for her with your two honors. If she passes, you shouldn't be in too much trouble in two diamonds because you have a six-card suit and three of the top five honors.

Responding to Minor-Suit Overcalls

This is a good time to tell you that there are five basic game contracts (meaning that the final contract is a bid to make game) into which you can enter. They are as follows:

- Three no trump

- Four hearts or four spades

- Five diamonds or five clubs

Two of these contracts are not favored. Can you guess which two? It's five diamonds and five clubs, and the reason is that minor-suit games require you to take all but two tricks, which can be extremely difficult. Furthermore, three no trump, four hearts, and four spades give you more points despite having to take fewer tricks.

So, if possible, you should exert every effort to play contracts in hearts, spades, or no trump.

With that as a prologue, your responses to a minor-suit overcall are the same when you have support for your partner's suit and your hand is the minimum 6 to 10 or 11 to 13. That is, with the former you give a simple raise, and with the latter you give a limit raise by jumping a level.

It's good to point out here the difference between responding to a minor-suit overcall and a minor-suit open—and it's a big difference. When responding to a minor-suit open by your partner you don't know how many cards she has in the suit. She could have as little as three cards in the suit. So you can't respond by raising her suit with minimum support.

But when your partner overcalls in a minor suit, she is promising you that she has at least five cards in the suit. So you can confidently raise with three-card support.

However, when you have the big hand—14-plus points—instead of jumping to a minor-suit game at the five level, you should try to bid three no trump if you have stoppers in the other suits.

Responding in No Trump

You have a similar obligation to keep the bidding open for your partner's overcall as you do when your partner opens the bidding, if you have the point-count and suit-length requirements set forth previously. However, if your partner has overcalled at the two level, you may pass if your hand is 6 to 9 points without support. You should only bid without support if your hand contains 10 or more points.

Responding to a Takeout Double

If your partner makes a takeout double and there is no intervening bid by your RHO, you should bid your longest suit—unless you have a four-card major—regardless of the number of points in your hand. When responding to a takeout double, you should prefer a four-card major to a longer five-card minor. In case there is a game in the hand, it's easier in a major than in a minor. Your partner's takeout double strongly implies four cards in unbid majors. Even if you have a Yarborough, you must bid. Remember, your partner will not make a takeout double unless she can support anything you bid. So you can rely on her to have at least three cards in all of the unbid suits.

If you have at least 10 points, you should make a jump response. This shows her that you have at least 10 points and at least four cards in the suit you bid. There are two exceptions to this requirement of bidding in response to your partner's takeout double:

- If you have a lot of cards in opponents' suit and you think you can set them, you can pass. This tells your partner that you're willing to defend the hand for penalty.

- If your RHO makes an intervening bid and you have less than 10 points and no five-card suit or no four-card major, your pass tells your partner that your hand is nothing to get excited about.

Look at the following hands after your partner has made a takeout double over her RHO's opening bid of one diamond:

1.	♠ A873	2.	♠ K9873	3.	♠ A98	4.	♠ 986
	♥ QT83		♥ K83		♥ K73		♥ 8975
	♦ 8		♦ 87		♦ 87		♦ 963
	♣ JT63		♣ A73		♣ JT873		♣ 742

Hand 1: One heart. You bid your four-card suits up the line. You have less than 10 points, so you just bid your cheapest long suit, which is hearts.

Hand 2: Two spades. You have more than 10 points and a five-card suit, so you make a jump response to show your points.

Hand 3: Two clubs. You must bid your longest suit. You're not jumping to go to the two level because the only way you can bid clubs over diamonds is to go up a level. This bid, not being a jump, shows that you have less than 10 points and that clubs is your longest suit.

Hand 4: One heart. You are forced to bid this stinkeroo hand. The best you can tell your partner is that you have less than 10 points. You're going to pass anything she does unless she makes another forcing bid, like two diamonds, which is opponents' opening bid.

The Least You Need to Know

- In responding to partner's overcall, with support for your partner's suit you make a one-level raise with 6 to 10 points, a limit raise with 11 to 13 points, and jump to game with 14-plus points

- To bid a new suit at the one level, you must have a five-card suit and at least 8 points; to bid a new suit at the two level, you should have a six-card suit.

- If you have three-card support for your partner's suit, you should not bid a new suit unless it is a good six-card suit.

- You must bid if your partner makes a takeout double and your RHO passes, unless you have a lot of cards in opponents' suit and want to leave the double in for penalty.

- Make a jump bid in response to your partner's takeout double if you have at least 10 points.

Doubles, Defensive Bidding, and Etiquette

In This Chapter

- Penalty doubles
- Negative doubles
- Etiquette

In its pure form, a double is a defensive bid. It says to your opponents, "I don't think you can make your contract, and I'm so confident of that I'm going to double you."

In this chapter, you find out about penalty doubles and negative doubles and how to distinguish one from the other. I also help you figure out how to deal with a partner who irritates you or whom you irritated, and how to avoid such confrontations.

Penalty Doubles and Redoubles

A penalty double is like a double or nothing bet. If you double for penalty and your opponents don't make their contract, you get twice the penalty bonus for setting them and more than twice the penalty bonus if you set them more than one trick. If they're not vulnerable and they go down one, you'd ordinarily get 50 points above the line. If you double them and they go down one, however, you get 100 points above the line. On the other hand, if you don't set the contract, your opponents get a bonus for making a contract doubled.

If a declarer is really confident, he can redouble. That means, "So you don't think I can make it? Oh, yeah? Well, I'm so confident I can make it that I'm going to redouble," which causes the *doubled* score to be doubled!

Lots and lots of points result from doubles and redoubles. The following table shows how much you can make (or lose!). (Recall that an *undertrick* means that declarer didn't make her contract, and each undertrick is the amount by which she did not make it.)

Penalties

Not Vulnerable

Undertricks	Not Doubled	Doubled	Redoubled
1	50	100	200
2	100	300	600
3	150	500	1,000
4	200	800	1,600
5	250	1,100	2,200
6	300	1,400	2,800

Vulnerable

Undertricks	Not Doubled	Doubled	Redoubled
1	100	200	400
2	200	500	1,000
3	300	800	1,600
4	400	1,100	2,200
5	500	1,400	2,800
6	600	1,700	3,400

The following table lists the points given for overtricks, or how many tricks declarer took over her contracted amount.

Overtrick Points

Not Vulnerable

Not Doubled	Doubled	Redoubled
Trick value	100 per trick	200 per trick

Vulnerable

Not Doubled	Doubled	Redoubled
Trick value	200 per trick	400 per trick

Trusting Your Partner's Bidding

I've emphasized that you must not mislead your partner. Time and again I've told you how important it is that you be consistent in your bidding and refrain from making unilateral bids that are inconsistent with your partnership's understandings, just because you might *like* your hand.

Now you'll learn one of the reasons why this is so important. When you or your partner make a penalty double, you are generally doing it as a result of the auction and what you've learned about your partner's hand, as well as the hands of your opponents. Let's say the auction went like this:

RHO	You	LHO	Partner
One club	One heart	One spade	Two diamonds
Two spades	Pass	Three spades	Pass
Four spades	?		

Your partner has made a bid that has told you that she has at least 10 points in her hand, and you have 10 points in your hand, and your opponents have bid a major-suit game. You would be entitled to think to yourself, "Well, I have 10 points, and my partner has made a free bid at the two level, and we've agreed that she can't do this without 10 points. They need at least 26 points to make game. If we have 20 points between us, there aren't enough points in the deck for them to have 26 between them; so there's a very good chance they won't make this contract." Therefore, you say with confidence, "Double."

Now, what if during the play of the hand you discover that your partner doesn't have the 10 points she indicated she had in the bidding, and your opponents make four spades doubled for a big score? You're not going to be very happy, are you? After the hand your conversation will probably go something like this:

You: I thought you had 10 points.

Partner: Well, I had such a nice diamonds suit.

You: How many points did you have?

Partner: I had such a nice diamonds suit.

You: How many points did you have?

Partner: Uh, er, my diamonds were real nice.

You: How many points did you have?

Partner: Uh, well, I had the ace and queen of diamonds and they were nice.

You: You had 6 points?

Partner: Yes, but my diamonds were so nice; I thought you'd want to know about them.

You: I doubled on your having 10 points, which is what your bid said you had.

Partner: (embarrassed silence)

You need feel no guilt about being annoyed. Your opponents received a big bonus for making the contract doubled. You were absolutely correct to take the chance on doubling the contract based on your partner's bid. But your partner didn't have her bid. *Don't lie to your partner!*

Listening to Your Opponents' Bidding

Doubling is a real art. It requires deductive reasoning and strict attention to the auction. If your opponents have made a preemptive bid (showing a weak hand but a lot of trumps) you have to take into consideration the possibility that one of them will be short in the suit in which you have your power.

If you're sitting there with ace–king–queen of clubs and the ace of hearts, for example, and your LHO opens the bidding at one spade; your partner overcalls two clubs and your RHO makes a preemptive jump to game, should you double? You look at your hand and think you have four cold tricks. But your RHO has five spades in his hand. It's very likely that his short suit is clubs, because you and your partner have at least eight of them between you both. You might only get one club trick. For sure you won't get three club tricks because the best the suit could split for you is 3–2 in your opponents' hands. This is not a hand to double on because you know that it's distributional, and if they have long spades, they're short in some suits.

They Won't Be as Aggressive the Next Time

Another advantage of doubling, and of getting the reputation that you're not afraid to double, is that it can inhibit opponents' bidding. If you double them successfully, it hurts them, and they'll remember.

When you're playing people who you know won't double you, you feel freer to take chances and bid to questionable games, knowing that the penalty will be minimal if you don't make your bid. But if you're playing someone who has no fear of doubling and will *hit* you if you make a chancy bid, you're more reluctant to take the chance. So doubling has the added benefit of making your opponents more cautious in their bidding.

DEFINITION

The term **hit** is synonymous with *double*. So if someone says, "I was just waiting for you to bid four spades because I was going to hit it," it means he was going to double you if you bid four spades.

Negative Doubles

A negative double is a double by you when your partner has opened the bidding, and RHO has overcalled, to tell your partner that you have exactly four cards in the unbid major and a certain number of points. So let's say that you're in third seat and the bidding has gone one diamond by your partner, one heart by your RHO, and you hold the following:

♠ KQ75
♥ T9
♦ J76
♣ 8732

Not wonderful, is it? But you do have four spades and you do have 6 points. From what you've learned so far, you would just bid one spade and let it go at that. But how does your partner know how many spades you have? You could have five spades, or you could have four spades.

The negative double takes care of this problem for you. If you have at least five spades and this hand, you bid one spade. However, if you have four spades, you double!

ALERT

The negative double is another bid that many rubber bridge players don't play. If you want to play negative doubles, you must be absolutely positive that your partner is playing them, too, or you could end up with weeping and gnashing of teeth.

This is another conventional bid that doesn't mean what it says. In other words, it's not a *penalty double*. You aren't saying to your partner, "Hey, pard, we got 'em. We can set this baby, so I'm doubling!"

No, it doesn't say that at all. Instead, it says, "Partner, I have at least 6 points and exactly four spades in my hand. Not five spades. Not six spades. Not three spades. Exactly four spades."

Negative Doubles at the One Level

The requirements for a one-level negative double—that is, a negative double that allows your partner to make a bid and stay at the one level—are as follows:

- At least 6 points
- Exactly four cards in the unbid major

Negative Doubles at the Two Level

The requirements become more stringent as you force your partner to higher levels of bidding. Look at the following hand:

♠ T97
♥ KQ85
♦ 73
♣ KT64

Bidding goes like this:

Partner	RHO	You
One diamond	One spade	?

Now from what you've learned, you know that you can't bid a new suit at the two level without at least 10 points. If you were to bid this hand at the two level, you would be lying to your partner. And you don't want to have one of those conversations when she takes action on your promised strength only to find out you lied, do you? Of course not.

So what are you to do? Your hand isn't bad, and you do have four hearts, which your partner might like to know about.

TRICKS OF THE TRADE

You might have more than 6 points when you make a negative double at the one level and more than 8 points when you make it at the two level, but you are promising that you have at least 6 points at the one level and at least 8 points at the two level.

Ah, you're probably way ahead of me. Negative double? Absolutely. In this hand you have four hearts and 8 points, exactly what you need to make a negative double, which forces your partner to bid at the two level. The negative double is a terrific way to tell your partner what you have without lying to her.

Again, I am going to stress that you cannot lie to your partner. If, instead of the hand I just described, you had the following hand and the bidding went the same (one diamond by your partner and one spade by your RHO), what do you do?

♠ T97
♥ KJ85
♦ 73
♣ QT64

Well, one thing you don't want to do is make a negative double, because if you did you would be forcing your partner to bid at the two level, and you don't have 8 points. Your bid here would be to pass. Your partner has another bid, so you have no obligation to keep the bidding open. You can't bid your suit at the two level because you don't have 10 points, and you can't bid one no trump because you don't have spades—your RHO's bid—stopped. So all you can do is pass.

I know a lot of players who would be tempted to make a negative double with this hand, even though they don't have enough points. But I hope you're not one of these people. Don't lie to your partner. Have I said that before?

Two-Level Negative Doubles with a Five-Card Major

There is one exception to the 8-point minimum for negative doubles at the two level: if you have five cards in an unbid major but not enough points to make a suit bid at the two level, you can use the negative double. Look at the following hand:

♠ T97
♥ KJ852
♦ 73
♣ QT6

Bidding is as follows.

Partner	RHO	You
One diamond	One spade	?

You can't bid two hearts because you only have 7 points. But you do have five hearts. What to do?

In this situation, I make a negative double. You don't have 8 points, but you do have five hearts. So you can amend the rule a little to say that you can make a negative double, which forces your partner to bid your suit at the two level in either of the following circumstances:

- Four cards in the unbid major and at least 8 points
- Five cards in the unbid major and at least 7 points

Upper Limit for Making Negative Doubles

You can play negative doubles through any level you and your partner wish. I generally play them through three hearts. I recommend that you start playing negative doubles through bids of two spades. If you choose to do this, any double of a bid over two spades would then be for penalty. So look at the following hand you hold:

♠ 86
♥ KQJT
♦ A763
♣ 874

The auction goes as follows.

Partner	RHO	You
One spade	Three clubs	?

If you are only playing negative doubles through two spades, you can't double the three clubs bid here to show that you have four hearts. If you double three clubs, your partner will leave it in as a penalty double, probably. (Remember, when playing negative doubles only through two spades, if you double any bid over two spades, you're doubling for penalty.)

ALERT

Negative doubles through two spades is by partnership agreement. That's the way you should play it while you're learning. Many advanced players play them through three spades. One of my partners plays them through four diamonds.

Negative Doubles and Five-Card Majors at the One Level

If you have a five-card major and sufficient points, you must bid the suit. If you have a four-card major and a five-card major, don't use a negative double to describe this hand; instead, bid the five-card major. Your partner will be relying on you to bid a five-card major at the one level if you have it. If you're using negative doubles, bidding the suit at the one level over an intervening bid promises five cards. A double promises four cards.

Only One Four-Card Major

If your partner and your RHO have both bid minor suits and you only have one four-card major, you shouldn't use a negative double to describe your hand, because a negative double promises four cards in each unbid major suit. Look at the following hand:

♠ KQ75
♥ Q73
♦ 872
♣ 983

Your partner opens one club and RHO bids one diamond. You shouldn't make a negative double. Your only bid is one spade. If you made a negative double you'd be promising four spades *and* four hearts. Because you don't have four hearts, you shouldn't make a negative double.

On the other hand, if your RHO had overcalled one heart instead of one diamond, then you could make a negative double because the only unbid major suit would then be spades—and you have four of 'em, and at least 6 points.

Remember that a negative double promises four cards in the unbid major. So if the bidding goes one club by your partner, one-diamond overcall by your RHO, you must have *two four-card majors* to make a negative double.

Recap: Point Requirements for Negative Doubles

The following chart shows point requirements for negative doubles:

Level	Points
1	6
2	8
3	10

To recap:

- If your negative double will enable your partner to bid your suit at the one level, you can make a negative double with 6 points in your hand.

- If your negative double forces your partner to bid your suit at the two level, you must have 8 points in your hand.

- If your negative double forces your partner to bid your suit at the three level, you must have 10 points in your hand.

Reopening Doubles

Even a lot of experienced players aren't aware of the fact that the reopening double is an integral part of the negative double system. A *reopening double* is a bid by opener when opener's LHO has bid a suit and partner and RHO pass the hand back to opener. If opener passes, the bidding ceases. If she doubles, she's "reopening" the bidding.

What if you're in third seat and the bidding goes one heart by your partner, and two diamonds by your RHO? It's now your bid and you hold the following cards:

♠ A86
♥ 95
♦ AKJ86
♣ K42

You could bid two no trump, but wouldn't you like to hit two diamonds? Alas, you can't double it because that would be a negative double, wouldn't it? It won't do you any good to make a negative double for two reasons: First, you don't have the bid.

You don't have four spades. Second, you want it to be a penalty double, not a negative double. So how can you defend two diamonds doubled in this hand? Clearly you cannot double because your partner will respond as she has to in the negative-double system.

The answer is that if your partner opens the bidding followed by a bid at the two level by your RHO, and you pass, and your LHO passes, your partner should double with shortness in the suit bid by opponents and tolerance (at least three cards) for the unbid suits. *Shortness*, in this context, means no more than a doubleton. So if your partner has two or less of your RHO's suit, she should double. To be specific, here's how the bidding goes.

Partner	RHO	You	LHO
One spade	Two diamonds	Pass	Pass
?			

In the previous situation, your partner should protect you by doubling when it's her turn. Then you can either let it sit for penalty—which you would do with the above hand—or pull it by either bidding your partner's suit at the 2 level (if you can) or making the best bid you have under the circumstances.

This is called a *reopening double* because it's made by the opening bidder and she's reopening the bidding by doubling since, with two passes to her, if she passes, the bidding will stop. If she doesn't bid or double, the auction is over.

Of course, you might have a legitimate pass, too. You might *not* be passing because you have opponents' suit. You might have the following:

♠ 862
♥ 75
♦ T96
♣ QT873

If you have this holding and your partner makes a reopening double, you should just pull the double and support your partner's opening suit, in which she'll have at least a 5–2 fit. Your partner anticipates this. Her double is just inviting you to let it stand for penalty if you have a lot of opponents' suit. If you don't, just retreat to the best contract. If you retreat, your partner will know you passed because you don't have much.

Requirements for a reopening double are as follows:

- Only opening bidder can make a reopening double, and only after LHO has overcalled and there are two passes by your partner and your RHO.

- Opening bidder has no more than two cards in overcalled suit.

- Opening bidder must have tolerance (at least three cards) for all unbid suits.

- Opening bidder's hand cannot be distributional, meaning that she doesn't have any doubletons or singletons in the unbid suits. If opener has a long suit, six cards or more, or is 5–5–2–1, she should either rebid her six-card suit, in the former, or bid her second suit in the latter.

Look at the following two hands:

1. ♠ J5
   ♥ AQT864
   ♦ 8
   ♣ AQT8

2. ♠ J75
   ♥ AKT864
   ♦ 8
   ♣ AK9

Bidding is as follows.

You	LHO	Partner	RHO
One heart	Two diamonds	Pass	Pass
?			

How do you, as opening bidder, respond with each?

Hand 1: Two hearts. This is not a hand with which you should use a reopening double. True, you have a singleton in your LHO's suit and, true, your partner is almost certainly sitting behind your LHO with a lot of diamonds. But your hand has two shortcomings that make it inappropriate for a reopening double:

- You don't have tolerance for all unbid suits. Your spade doubleton is insufficient for support if your partner responds to your double with a bid of two spades. Remember, your partner might be short in your suit. So if you double and your partner doesn't want to sit for the penalty double at the two level, she has to either support your suit if she has two cards in it, or bid her longest suit. If she has five diamonds but not enough to sit for the double, her longest suit might be spades. She could be 4–1–4–4, so she would be forced to bid spades, and you can't support her.

- Your hand isn't strong enough. You really only have two fairly certain tricks: your two aces. Remember, you have to take six tricks to set them. Otherwise, they're going to get a terrific score, making two or more, doubled!

Hand 2: Double. This is a very good hand with which to make a reopening double for two reasons:

- You have tolerance for both unbid suits, so if your partner can't support your heart bid you have at least three cards in the unbid suits. The worst that can happen is that your partner will be playing in a 4–3 fit at the two level, which isn't a disaster.

- You have a good hand, with two ace–king combinations. If you are defending, you have good trick-taking capability.

Remember this: Just because you have an opening hand and shortness in LHO's suit, you don't automatically make a reopening double. Your hand must fit the requirements, in addition to shortness and the appropriate bidding, after your open.

Trust Your Partner: Partnership Etiquette

Bridge can be a difficult game on relationships; whether you're playing with a friend, a spouse, a significant other, or someone who doesn't fit any of those categories, bridge tests the limits of a relationship. Why? Because it goes to the essence of your being—the way you think and reason. When someone questions something you did, that person is questioning your intelligence, and the questioning can become destructive.

My experience has been that the area of penalty doubles is where many emotional problems arise. That's why I'm digressing a little here to discuss etiquette and to make some suggestions for getting along.

When you don't trust your partner to know what she's doing and you take some unilateral action inconsistent with what she has done, you are communicating a lack of respect that can, in its most virulent form, destroy a relationship. The following story illustrates what can go wrong.

I was playing in a club championship with one of my best partners. We were good enough to have won a regional championship together. When we first played together, we had a problem because she continually *pulled* my penalty doubles. She, unilaterally, didn't think we could set our opponents; she didn't trust my doubles. I asked her to respect my penalty doubles.

> **DEFINITION**
>
> To **pull** means to make a bid that is inconsistent with what partner clearly intended. So if partner doubles for penalty and you bid another suit when it's your turn, you have "pulled" her penalty double, saying, in essence, "You might think we can set this contract, but I don't."

We stopped playing for quite a while, and when we started again she exhibited more respect for my game. The first test of this was in a game where I doubled someone who had balanced. The bidding went as follows.

Me	LHO	Partner	RHO
One diamond	Pass	One heart	Pass
Two hearts	Pass	Pass	Three clubs
Double	Pass		

My partner thought for a while and finally passed. We set them two for a score of 300. I thanked her for not pulling my double and felt more confident about our partnership.

We continued to play and did well, winning championships. Then we came to a club championship and, with us vulnerable and our opponents nonvulnerable, the bidding went as follows.

RHO	Me	LHO	Partner
One club	One diamond	One heart	Pass
Four hearts	Double	Pass	

This was my hand:

♠ Q5
♥ KQJT
♦ KT876
♣ A8

I had three certain trump tricks and the ace of clubs. The only way I could be kept from setting them at least one was if the game were terminated by an earthquake.

My partner started thinking and I started getting worried. Finally, after long thought, she bid four spades! My RHO doubled her 4 spade bid. I could do nothing but pass. As my partner played the hand, I saw that she was missing the ace and king of spades, as well as the queen I had in my hand. She was down three. Doubled. Vulnerable. So she took what was going to be a very nice hand for us, setting them at least one for a score for us of 100, and turned it into a fantastic hand for them, down three doubled and vulnerable for 800 above the line for them.

While she was playing the hand, I was talking to myself, "Don't say a word, Tony. Just start the next hand and go on." But when the hand was over our opponents started talking and the devil got control of me. I asked, "Why did you pull my double?"

She leaned over the table and castigated me in a voice loud enough for everyone in the room to hear. Although I hadn't been abusive or abrasive, I felt bad because I had embarrassed her.

Now I'll stop the story and lay down some rules:

You must trust your partner. If you can't trust your partner's bid, you shouldn't play with her. My double was clearly penalty. She knew that I was a good enough player and that I wasn't going to double unless I had a very good chance of setting them. And, from the bidding, I had to have it in my hand. I couldn't rely on anything in her hand because she hadn't bid!

Sometimes you might pull a penalty double of your partner's if you have bid and you feel that you've made a mistake and your partner has misinterpreted the strength of your hand—especially if you are nonvulnerable and your opponents are vulnerable (commonly called "nonvulnerable against vulnerable"). You have a logical argument if you misrepresented your hand and can say that you pulled it because you felt your partner was relying on something you didn't have.

But here she hadn't bid. She had to trust that I knew what I was doing. Furthermore, we were vulnerable and they weren't. The worst that could happen was that they'd make it, doubled, and would get a bonus of 170 points. But if she pulled it (which she did) and went down three (which she did) because we were vulnerable, they got 210 points more than they would have if she had left my double in and they made it. From a bridge point of view, there was no logic or reason to her pulling the double. As it was, they would have been set at least one, so it was a difference in the score of 900 points.

Don't discuss hands or bids at the table. When you question someone, it challenges their intelligence and ability to reason in front of others, which can be embarrassing and demeaning. I should have waited until the game was over and talked about it on the way home.

Don't be abusive. Don't call your partner names. If you do discuss the hand, limit it to bridge and try to discuss it calmly and logically with the purpose being to avoid misunderstandings in the future. Don't make the purpose of the discussion to put the person down.

Remember that your partner is trying to do the best she can. If she makes a mistake or a bad play, it wasn't because she is trying to do something personally harmful to you—that would harm the partnership. If she makes a mistake, realize that she probably feels worse about it than you do, so try to minimize it at the time. You can talk about it later if it's important enough to the partnership. The best way to strengthen a partnership is to be supportive when your partner makes a mistake. Instead of criticizing, give her a pat on the back and say, "Don't worry about it."

If your partner criticizes you, realize that bridge is competitive and your partner is competitive. Partners are human. When they see you do something they think is incorrect or—let's face it—stupid, they can react emotionally on the spur of the moment. There are very few saints, and most saints don't play bridge. The Pope might have reacted emotionally to his partner pulling a penalty double in that situation. So I reacted, even though I tried not to do so. When your partner reacts to something like that and asks, "Why did you trump my ace?" try to realize that it's just a human reaction of the moment and that she'll get over it. Turn the other cheek and let her get it out of her system by verbalizing her frustration. If you felt it was offensive or embarrassing, talk with her about it later and express your feelings then by saying something like, "Please don't criticize me during the game. What you said embarrassed me. I'm sorry for what I did, but that wasn't the time to talk about it." Something as simple as that will bring it out in the open and keep it from festering. If your partner doesn't react with compassion and understanding toward you, it may be time to consider taking a vacation from one another—which is what my partner and I did.

Take responsibility! If you do something stupid or wrong or inconsistent with your partnership understanding, take responsibility as soon as possible. I was once playing with Mike Shuman, one of the giants of the game. I opened the bidding and he finally passed me out at three diamonds. When he laid down the dummy he said, "I apologize if we have game, partner." Well, that completely disarmed me. What could

I say? If we had missed game he had taken all the responsibility, so I didn't have to say, "Why did you pass three diamonds?" There was nothing to criticize. If my partner had said, "I'm sorry," after she saw my dummy and realized that she had pulled a perfectly good penalty double, it would have instantly relieved me of the anxiety I felt at having my wonderful double pulled. There's really not much you can say when your partner assumes full responsibility for a glitch and apologizes. Any partner who doesn't graciously accept such an apology is someone with whom I wouldn't want to play. Taking responsibility is the number one way to make sure a partnership runs smoothly and for a long time. And it's the best way to avoid contentious conversations and arguments at the table.

We made up and continued to play. So another thing to remember is to forgive and forget.

The Least You Need to Know

- You double for penalty when you think you can set opponents' contract provided it is not a takeout double.
- A negative double promises four cards in the unbid major and 6 points if your partner can bid your suit at the one level, 8 points at the two level, and 10 points at the three level.
- A reopening double occurs when opener's LHO makes an overcall followed by two passes. Opener may reopen the bidding with a double if she has shortness in the overcalled suit and has at least three cards in both unbid suits.
- Be considerate of your partners. Treat them as you would like to be treated.

Defense and Play of the Hand

Bidding is one thing, but when it comes down to actually playing a hand, you may feel like a real dunce. Don't let this happen to you! Make sure you read this part carefully.

This part teaches you how to play or defend the hand once the bidding is completed. You'll find out how to play the hand as declarer, along with how to play some basic card combinations that arise again and again.

If your opponents win the contract, you're on defense. You'll learn how to begin your defense of the hand by your opening lead and some common techniques to use after the opening lead. You'll also get some pointers for communicating with your partner by the card you play, without even uttering a sound.

Put Up or Shut Up: Declarer Play in No Trump

In This Chapter

- Counting winners
- Setting up a long suit
- Entries
- The finesse and the hold up
- Ducking

If bidding is a team effort, playing the hand as declarer is entirely unilateral. It's up to you to play this hand by yourself. Your partner is dummy and can only sit and watch. Feel the pressure?

Your goal in any contract depends on the final contract you make. If you have contracted to make a one bid, you must take seven tricks, which means that you can afford to lose six tricks. If you have contracted to make a four bid, you must take ten tricks, which means that you can afford to lose three tricks.

The first thing you do is set your goal and realize what your objective is. If you're playing in a one contract, your objective is to take seven tricks. It might be nice if you could take eight, or nine, or more, but you don't want to risk your ability to take seven by trying to take eight. Many times good players will try for the overtrick and fail to make their contract as a result. Always keep in mind that your goal is to make the contract. Overtricks are just bonuses. Don't risk your contract to try to make a bonus.

Playing a No Trump Contract

Playing no trump is probably the most challenging task for a declarer, but it's also probably the most fun. In no trump, all suits are equal and high cards dominate. Because all suits are equal, having the lead is all-important in no trump.

Take a look at the following two opposing hands for which you are declarer in a no trump contract:

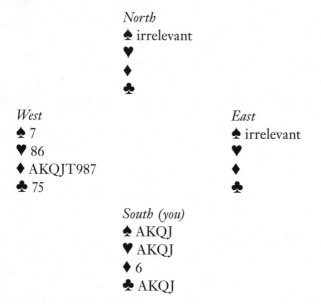

You look at your hand and think you should take twelve tricks. West, your LHO, looks at his hand and thinks he should take eight tricks. Who's correct?

He is! He is correct because he is on lead. And in no trump, whoever has the lead is the monarch so long as he retains the lead. He runs his eight diamonds tricks and you must throw off seven of your winning tricks until he runs out of diamonds and has to lead something besides diamonds. Since you have all the winners in all the other suits, you will take the rest of the tricks.

This also points out the fact that a long suit is a strong suit in no trump.

BRIDGEBIT

Your strategy for winning differs depending on the type of contract you are playing. When you're playing a no trump contract, you count your winners. When you're playing a suit contract, you count your losers (as discussed in Chapter 21). When your partner lays down her dummy, the first thing you do is to put your two hands together in your mind's eye and count either your winners or losers, depending on the contract.

How to Count Your Winners

In no trump, having the lead is everything. If you have 13 spades, you can't count them as 13 tricks unless you are on lead. If you are not on lead, you have 13 definite losers. Because you have all of the spades and you don't have cards in any other suit, there's no way you can get the lead.

Your opponents could *run* one of their long suits and defeat your contract before you can take your winners.

If your RHO is declarer in no trump and you have 13 spades, however, you have 13 definite winners because you are on lead.

DEFINITION

To **run** a suit means to take the rest of the tricks in that suit without opponents having any way to stop you. This can occur either in No Trump when all the stoppers are gone or in a suit contract when opponents don't have any trump left to stop you.

Look at the following terrific hand between you and your partner:

Dummy
♠ 87
♥ T987
♦ KQT65
♣ AK

Declarer
♠ A6
♥ KQJ
♦ A87
♣ QJT98

You have winners galore. You have seven of the top eight hearts. If you get a spade lead and they take out your ace and you then try to *set up* your hearts by driving out their ace, however, they will run their spade winners and you'll be set before you get the lead back. You can't count any of your hearts as winners because you don't have the ace. They are *potential* winners, but they aren't sure winners, and that's what you have to count.

> **DEFINITION**
>
> To **set up** a suit means to establish it.

In this hand you have nine sure winners: five clubs, three diamonds, and one spade. You should take them before surrendering the lead to the ace of hearts.

The rule for counting winners is *you only count winners that you can take without surrendering the lead*. So you can't count any card in any suit as a sure winner if you or your partner don't have the ace of that suit.

Setting Up a Long Suit

One way to play a no trump contract is to try to set up, or establish, your long suit. In analyzing the cards you control, one of the first things you do is count the number of cards you have in each suit and determine your longest suit. For example, you have two suits in which you have seven cards each, if one of them is divided 4–3 and the other 5–2, the 5–2 suit is the one you should choose to develop, assuming equal strength and entries into the hand with the five-card suit. The five-card suit will give you more tricks than a four-card suit.

Tricks in No Trump

When you're playing a contract in no trump, there are two kinds of tricks you can make: high-card tricks and long-suit tricks. The following sections take a closer look at each.

High-Card Tricks

The first is tricks obtained through your high cards. It doesn't take a nuclear physicist to look at a hand with ace–king–queen in one suit to calculate that you'll probably be able to count on three tricks in that suit.

Long-Suit Tricks

One place where skill and fun come into play in no trump contracts is when you have to take tricks by establishing a long suit. When playing in a suit contract, you can usually count on ruffing power for tricks. But in a no trump contract, all suits are of equal power. If you don't have enough high cards to make your contract, you have to set up a long suit so you can take the rest of your tricks with low cards in that suit. Let's take a look at a hand to illustrate:

North
♠ K87
♥ 872
♦ QJT86
♣ 65

South
♠ AQ3
♥ AQ4
♦ 543
♣ KQ43

Even though you only have 23 HCP between you and your partner, you somehow ended up playing in three no trump and you are South, which is declarer. How are you going to make this contract? Count your winners. You've got three spade tricks, one or two heart tricks, and one or two club tricks. Even at a maximum, that's only seven tricks and you need nine.

To make this contract, you will need to set up your long suit—which is diamonds—and establish your two needed tricks there. Looking at the hand in a vacuum, diamonds appears to be your weakest suit; but actually, because you have eight total cards in it and five in dummy, it's your strongest. Remember: *In no trump, your longest suit is your strongest suit!*

With the above hands, you're lucky enough to get a spades lead. You take it in South and immediately lead a diamond from South's hand to North's queen–jack–10. If they take it, it doesn't really matter because you're counting on a 3–2 split. No matter what they return, you lead a diamond again. You might win or lose. Again, it doesn't matter, because you're going to keep leading diamonds until your 8 of diamonds and 6 of diamonds are established, or set up, and become winners because they're the only remaining cards left in the suit.

Entries

When playing no trump, it is essential that you keep entries into the weak hand if it has the long suit. An *entry* is simply a card that allows you to get the lead in that hand. In the referenced hand with the long diamond suit, you had two sources of entries:

- You had three diamonds in your hand to continue leading up to the dummy

- Dummy's king of spades

But let's change that hand a little:

North
♠ K4
♥ 872
♦ QJT96
♣ 652

South
♠ AQ32
♥ AQ4
♦ 54
♣ KQ43

Now you take the opening spade lead in your hand and then lead a diamond, which they take. They return a spade and you are forced to take it in dummy with your king. You lead a second diamond, which they take. Now how are you going to get back to dummy to cash your winning diamonds? Here's how the hand looks after these plays:

North
♠
♥ 872
♦ T96
♣ 652

South
♠ Q3
♥ AQ4
♦
♣ KQ43

You have no entry into dummy! Your diamonds are good because your 10 and 9 will take the two outstanding diamonds and then your 6 is the only remaining diamond, but you can't get there to cash them. You have admirably established your diamonds, but you lost your entry to cash them.

The rule to remember from all this is: Establish your suit *before* you lose your entries.

Choosing Which Suit to Establish

Sometimes you have suits of equal lengths and have to decide which one to establish. You should attempt to establish the suit in which you could take the most tricks. For example, if you have two suits in which you hold eight cards, but one is divided 4–4 between declarer and dummy and the other 5–3, the suit in which you will probably take the most tricks is the one that is divided 5–3. That is if defenders' cards in those suits both split 3–2 and assuming relatively comparable high-card strength in both suits.

Timing

When you plan your play you not only determine your longest suit, but you know in which suits your opponents have more cards than you do. In those suits, your short suits, you should protect your stoppers. Don't lead those suits yourself because you'll just be helping your opponents establish their suits.

It's essential that you establish your suit before your opponents establish theirs. When playing no trump, it often comes down to a race. Who can establish their suit first: declarer or opponents?

Often it comes down to who is on lead. If you have their long suit stopped twice but you need two leads to establish your long suit, you're going to lose the race. Look at the following hand.

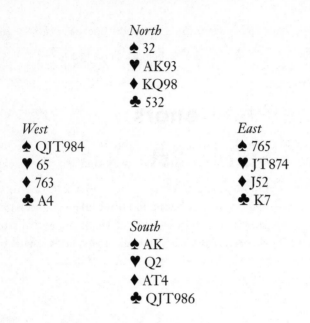

North
- ♠ 32
- ♥ AK93
- ♦ KQ98
- ♣ 532

West
- ♠ QJT984
- ♥ 65
- ♦ 763
- ♣ A4

East
- ♠ 765
- ♥ JT874
- ♦ J52
- ♣ K7

South
- ♠ AK
- ♥ Q2
- ♦ AT4
- ♣ QJT986

Opening lead: Queen of spades

If you try to establish your six-card clubs suit, you're going to lose this battle of timing. You take the queen of spades led and immediately lead the queen of clubs. East takes it and returns a spade, which you take with your last spade stopper in South. You lead the jack of clubs, which West takes with the ace of clubs and runs his four remaining spade winners. He has established his six-card spades suit before you could establish your six-card clubs suit because you only had two stoppers in his suit and you needed to drive out two losers in clubs. The timing is against you in this hand.

The point is that you should see this after the opening lead and abandon all hope of establishing clubs. You should look to see if there's any other way to make this hand in three no trump, and there is. If defenders' diamonds split 3–3, or if the jack is a singleton or doubleton, you can make three no trump *off the top* by taking the following cold tricks:

Two spades

Three hearts

Four diamonds (because they split 3–3 or the jack is a singleton or doubleton and falls, setting up the rest of your diamonds)

DEFINITION

Off the top means that you take all your tricks before losing a trick to opponents.

How to Play and Win Honors

Honors in a suit consist of the ace, king, queen, jack, and 10. They are the most powerful cards in the suit. Generally, honors are the cards that win the tricks. But an honor, unless it's an ace, is not a sure trick.

If the king is in the hand sitting to the right of the hand with the ace (called "sitting in front of the ace"), the king probably won't win a trick. If the queen is sitting in front of the ace or the king, it probably won't win a trick. Look at the following holdings in spades, for example:

North
♠ AT76

West   *East*
♠ K95   ♠ J82

South
♠ Q43

The only winner in this hand is North's ace, because North will play after West and North can take West's king when he plays it if he waits for it to be played. West's king is not a winner because it's sitting in front of North's ace. Similarly, South's queen is not a winner because it's sitting in front of West's king. It's the same with East's jack.

Now let's reverse East and West's holdings:

North
♠ AT76

West   *East*
♠ J82   ♠ K95

South
♠ Q43

Now the situation is a horse of a different color. East's king will be a winner because it sits behind North's ace. Unless East leads his king (which would certainly be foolhardy) he shouldn't lose it because if North is dummy, East can see where the ace is and play the king on a trick where the ace has not been played. Similarly, if South knows the location of the king, her Queen is a winner because it is sitting behind East's king.

The bottom line is that you can't count on these cards being winners until you know the location of the missing honors. This leads us into the discussion of how to play honors so they win tricks.

When you don't know the location of the honors that are higher than your honor, you must lead up that honor. To *lead up* to a card means to lead a lower-ranking card in your partner's hand, or in the case of declarer, to lead a low card to a higher-ranking card in your other hand. For example, in the hand just displayed, if you wanted to try to win the queen, you would lead a low spade from North to South's queen. If East has the king, you should win the queen. Because if East plays low, you play the queen, hoping that East has the king. Here, East did have the king so the queen wins. But if East *goes up* (plays a high card when he has a choice of playing high or low because he's not on lead) with the king when you lead low from North, you play a low spade from South. Although East has won the trick, you have set up the queen as a definite winner because you hold the ace and two additional spades in North and the queen and one additional spade in South. You can play the ace and play low from South, then lead a low spade to the queen, which is a definite winner because the king has already been played.

Playing Sequential Honors

If all your cards in a suit consist of honors in a sequence, it doesn't matter whether you lead from the hand that contains the sequence or if you lead up to them because you don't have any other low card to play. If you hold the king–queen–jack *tight* (meaning that those are the only three cards in that suit), even if you lead up to them and your LHO goes up with the ace, you still have to play one of your honors on the ace.

DEFINITION

To hold a card or cards **tight** means that you don't have any other cards in the suit but that card or those cards. Holding the ace tight means that you have a singleton ace. Holding the king–queen–jack tight means that those are the only three cards in the suit in your hand.

Furthermore, it doesn't matter how or where you hold the sequential honors. Look at the following holding:

North
♠ KJ3

West   *East*
♠ ?   ♠ ?

South
♠ Q65

Unless you have an entry problem in one of your hands, it doesn't matter how you play these honors (king-queen-jack) or how you lead. You're going to take two tricks and lose one to the ace. It doesn't matter if you lead the queen from South, or if you lead low. If you lead low and West goes up with the ace, you will discard low and will still take two tricks.

Leading Up

However, what if you hold KQxx in a suit? How should you play it to maximize your trick-taking power? You can count on this holding for one sure trick because if you lead the king or the queen, it will lose to the ace, but then the remaining card will be the top card out in the suit, a definite winner. But if you lead up to the king–queen holding, you have a chance to win both cards if the king–queen sit behind the ace. Look at the following:

North
♠ KQ84

West   *East*
♠ A97   ♠ JT6

South
♠ 532

If you lead from South's hand up to North's hand and West ducks (loses the trick on purpose when she could have won it; more on this strategy later in this chapter), you will win with either the king or the queen. You then get back into South's hand and lead up to North again. If West ducks, you win with the remaining honor. If West goes up with the ace, you play low and your king and queen become sure winners.

However, if you were to lead the king from North's hand, it would lose to the ace. Then the queen would be the only winner you would get in the suit because after you play the queen, East will win the next spades trick with the jack. So leading up to North gets you an extra trick.

Playing Single Honors

Leading up is especially important when you hold a single, nonsequential honor. Look at the following:

North
♠ K4

West　　　　　　　　　　　　　　　　　　　　*East*
♠ ?　　　　　　　　　　　　　　　　　　　　♠ ?

South
♠ 53

If you lead the king or the 4 from North, you aren't going to take a trick with the king. If you lead the 4 and East goes low, West will win with his lowest spade. Then, any lead that produces the ace will win your king. Obviously, if, instead of leading your 4 you lead the king from North, opponent's ace will win it.

The only way you can hope to win the king is to lead low from South to the king. If West produces the ace, your king will win the next trick. If West goes low, you must play the king, hoping that West had the ace. If he did, you'll win. If East has the ace, you'll lose. When you have this holding you can count on the king as a half trick because you have a 50 percent chance that West has the ace and you'll win the king, and a 50 percent chance that East has the ace and you'll lose the king. (Assuming your opponents have not bid, so you have learned nothing about their hands during the bidding.)

This holding also shows why you shouldn't do two things on opening lead unless you have an awfully good reason for them:

- You should not underlead an ace.

- You should not lead an ace.

You shouldn't *underlead* an ace because you make the king good. If either opponent underleads the ace, your king will win if you play it. If you lead your ace, especially if you are East, you just give up the chance of winning the king with it. Remember this axiom: *Aces were created to take kings and queens.* If you lead an ace, it won't take either unless the king or queen happens to be a singleton.

DEFINITION

To **underlead** means to lead a lower card in a suit instead of leading your highest card in that suit. To underlead an ace means you have the ace in your hand, but you lead a lower-ranking card of the same suit.

The Finesse

The Official Encyclopedia of Bridge (Truscott, Executive Editor, 1994) defines a *finesse* as "the attempt to gain power for lower-ranking cards by taking advantage of the favorable position of higher-ranking cards held by the opposition." Say, what? If you know what a finesse is, I guess that's as good a definition as any. But if you don't know what a finesse is, that won't help you much.

An easier definition might be this: A *finesse* is any play that depends on finding a specific card in a specific place. You can play a finesse with both no trump and in a suit.

So if you're South and you make a play that depends on the king of spades being in West's hand, that's a finesse. The best way to define a finesse is to show you one. Look at the following holdings:

North
♠ AQ

West   *East*
♠ K8   ♠ 65

South
♠ 97

You are declarer and playing the South hand, and South has the lead. You play West for the king of spades. So you lead the 7 of spades. If West plays the king you take it with the ace, obviously. If West plays the 8 of spades, however, you play the queen, hoping that West has the king. If he does, as he does here, you win the trick with the queen. That's a finesse. In this instance, it works. If the East and West holdings were reversed and East held the king, the finesse wouldn't work. You'd play the queen and East would take it with the king.

The lead must be up to the cards where you'll work the finesse. If the lead were in North, there would be no way for you to win both the ace and the queen, because if you lead the ace, West will go low and then win your queen with his king. If you lead the queen, West will take it with his king. Either way, you only win one trick. But if you have the lead in the hand with the weak cards leading up to the hand with the strong cards, you can work the finesse.

> **BRIDGEBIT**
>
> The ace–queen holding is called a *tenace* (pronounced like "tennis"), which is a holding of two cards, one of which is two levels below the other. Examples are ace–queen, king–jack, 10–8. If cards in between two cards have been played, the cards are said to be in a tenace position. So if the king, queen, and jack have been played, the ace–9 is a tenace (because the only remaining card between them is the 10).

The Double Finesse

If you have alternating cards, like the ace, queen, and ten, you should usually finesse twice, no matter what happens the first time. Look at the following:

North
♠ AQT86

South
♠ 432

If you haven't learned anything from the bidding or the play of the hand, you should first lead low from South and if West ducks (plays low), play the 10 of spades. If that forces out the king from East, you'll be okay because both the ace and the queen will be good. That would mean that West has the jack. If East had the jack, he'd win the trick with the jack, not the king. Because East won with the king, he doesn't have the jack. If he doesn't have it and you don't have it in either of your hands, West must have it. But it doesn't matter because the ace and queen are now good.

If East wins your 10 with the jack, however, the next time you get the lead you should finesse the queen. The reasoning is that the odds favor the honors being split. Of course they won't be split all the time. But with no clue from the bidding you should try the finesse twice.

The Eight- and Nine-Card Finesse

It's often the case that when you're playing a contract—generally a suit contract—you and your partner have eight or nine trump between you. This means that there are either four trump out against you or five trump out against you. You have the ace, king, jack, and 10 between you and your partner's hands. You need to find the queen.

One axiom to remember is that *an odd number of cards tend to split evenly and an even number of cards tend to split oddly.* This means that the odds are in favor of five cards splitting 3–2. And the odds are in favor of four cards splitting 3–1, not 2–2. Surprised? Actually four cards will split 2–2 only about 40 percent of the time, whereas they'll split 3–1 about 49 percent of the time.

So if your ace and your king are in different hands, and your jack and your 10 are in different hands, and you have no clue from the bidding, you should pull a round of trump, leading low to the high honor and then back again. The advantage of this is that it gives you three plays from your opponents. One of them may be forced to drop the queen because it's a singleton or doubleton. If not, then you have to decide whether or not to take the finesse. Look at the following layout.

> *North*
> ♠ AJ98
>
> *South*
> ♠ KT652

You have to find the queen, and there are four cards out against you. If you're in South, you lead the deuce. If West plays the queen (because it's a singleton), you're home free. If West plays low, you play the ace. If East plays the queen (because it's a singleton), you're home free. If East plays low, you've won the trick with the ace.

Now you lead the jack back to South's hand. If East drops the queen (either because it was a doubleton or because he's covering your honor to protect his partner because—not knowing the exact lay of the cards—he might think his partner had 3 to the 10), you're home free. If East shows out and discards another suit, then you've lost this round because West has the Queen protected by 3. If East plays low, then you have to decide whether the cards split 2–2 (in which event you should play the king and watch the queen fall) or 3–1 (in which event you should play low and let the jack win the trick).

Playing for the Drop

Instead of finessing, another way to find the queen is to play for the *drop*. To play for the drop means to lead high-ranking cards hoping that a missing high card, lower-ranking than the cards you led, will have to be played because holder is short in the suit.

> **TRICKS OF THE TRADE**
>
> Whichever way you want to go—finessing or playing for the drop—I think you should be consistent. Don't play for the drop once and then take the finesse the next time. Decide which way is best for you and do it every time. If you vacillate between positions, the odds won't work in your favor. If you do it the same way all the time, you'll at least have the odds working for you.

Eight ever, nine never is a famous bridge axiom. It means that if you're missing the queen and you have nine cards in the suit, you should play for the drop. If you have eight cards in the suit, you should take the finesse.

Bridge expert Charles Goren advises to play for the drop when there are four out against the queen, but he doesn't advise you to play for the drop when there are three out against the king. And he has good reason.

Three cards will split 3–0 22 percent of the time, which means that they will be divided 2–1 78 percent of the time. This means that two thirds of the time they divide 2–1, and the king will be protected. Look at the possible divisions you could face in a 2–1 split of three cards:

| 1. Kx | 2. x | 3. xx |
| x | Kx | K |

So Goren is correct. Two thirds of the time that the cards split 2–1, you're going to be looking at a protected king, and your lead of the ace playing for the drop is not going to work.

How to Play the Opening Lead

When you're declarer playing a no trump contract, how you play the opening lead often sets up whether or not you make the contract. Following are common holdings with which you will find yourself faced time and again:

1. Dummy	**2.** Dummy	**3.** Dummy
♠ Q4	♠ QT4	♠ Q74
Declarer	Declarer	Declarer
♠ A93	♠ A73	♠ A93

LHO leads a low spade. What do you play? Your problem is to find who has the king: your LHO or your RHO.

Holding 1: You must play the queen. If you play low—whether or not you win the trick with the ace—your queen will be sitting there unprotected. Opponents will play the king at their first opportunity. Furthermore, your RHO, if he has any smarts at all, won't play the king even if he has it, knowing that playing it will give you an extra trick if you hold the ace. The only chance you'll ever have to make this queen good is now, hoping that your LHO underled the king (a standard play that you will learn about in Chapter 22).

Holding 2: Play the 10. The hope is that your RHO holds king empty. If so, playing the 10 here will force out the king and you'll get two tricks in this hand. If your RHO does play the king, you take it with the ace and your queen is good. If the 10 forces the jack from RHO, win the ace and later lead up toward the queen. If LHO had the king, your queen will be a winner.

Holding 3: Play low. If RHO's opening lead was from JTxx, RHO will have to play the king or you'll win with the 9. If RHO doesn't play the king, but plays the jack or 10, you can win with the ace. You still have your queen protected by a second card and can lead up to it. If your LHO has the king, your queen will then win. If he doesn't, you're going to lose it anyway.

The Holdup

When your LHO leads your weakest suit on opening lead, a suit in which you only have one stopper, often you need to hold up taking your trick. This occurs when your LHO leads a suit in which you have Axx, for instance. You have two or three in dummy. You guess that your LHO has at least five, maybe six cards in the suit, and you hope he has no other entries in his hand. Instead of taking the trick immediately with your ace, you play low and allow him to win the trick. He continues and you allow him to win the second trick. Only when he forces you to play your ace with a third lead of the suit do you take the lead. The reason for all this is that you want to be sure that your RHO is out of his partner's suit. That way, if he gets the lead, he can't return the suit to your LHO for him to run his remaining winning tricks in the suit. Look at the following hand:

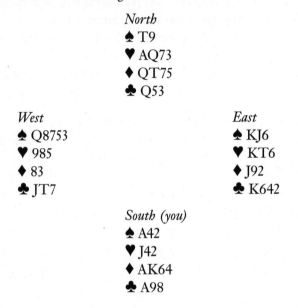

North
♠ T9
♥ AQ73
♦ QT75
♣ Q53

West
♠ Q8753
♥ 985
♦ 83
♣ JT7

East
♠ KJ6
♥ KT6
♦ J92
♣ K642

South (you)
♠ A42
♥ J42
♦ AK64
♣ A98

Bidding is as follows:

South	West	North	East
One no trump	Pass	Two clubs	Pass
Two diamonds	Pass	Three no trump	Pass
Pass	Pass		

West's Opening Lead: 5 of spades

West leads the 5 of spades. East plays the king. What do you do? If you take the ace, you're doomed to being set. You can't take nine tricks off the top. You can take four diamond tricks and your three aces. That's only seven tricks. You need to develop one or two hearts tricks or a club trick. That means that you might have to surrender the lead twice. But if even one of your finesses fails, you're dead. Because you only had spades stopped once, as soon as your opponents get in they'll run off four spade tricks, which will set you one trick. As the cards lay, you'll lose your heart finesse and East will return the jack of spades, which wins. Then he returns a low spade to West's queen, and the hand is history as West plays his two remaining low spades—both of which are good because they're the only two remaining cards in the suit.

So you must hold up taking your ace of spades and plan on taking your heart finesse into East. The idea is to surrender two spade tricks at the outset. This loses two tricks, but what you want to do is drive East out of spades so he can't get back to West to run his good spades. So, after holding up on two rounds of spades and then taking your ace of spades when East leads them a third time, this is what the hands look like:

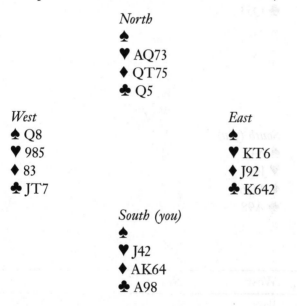

North
♠
♥ AQ73
♦ QT75
♣ Q5

West
♠ Q8
♥ 985
♦ 83
♣ JT7

East
♠
♥ KT6
♦ J92
♣ K642

South (you)
♠
♥ J42
♦ AK64
♣ A98

Now things look a little better. There's no way for West to get the lead again. You take your four diamond tricks and then try the heart finesse, which loses to East. Under no circumstances do you want to take a finesse into West. The heart finesse is safe because if West has the king you can always cover with the ace. When West plays low, you go low and East shows up with the king and wins the trick. But what's East going to lead? He can't get back to West's hand. If he underleads his king of clubs—which is about all that he can do—you won't know where the king is, so you'll go up and take it in your hand with the ace. You'll then take your three remaining heart tricks, and that's nine tricks—one spade, one club, four diamonds, and three hearts. You've made your contract, but only because you held up on the first two rounds of spades!

Ducking

It goes against your grain, but sometimes you have to lose a trick intentionally. This often occurs when you're playing a no trump contract and you have a long suit in dummy with the only entries being in the long suit. Look at the following hand where you are South playing in three no trump:

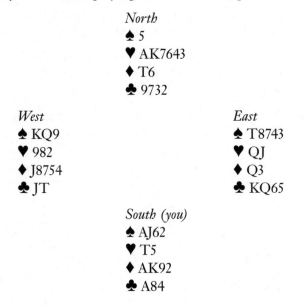

North
♠ 5
♥ AK7643
♦ T6
♣ 9732

West
♠ KQ9
♥ 982
♦ J8754
♣ JT

East
♠ T8743
♥ QJ
♦ Q3
♣ KQ65

South (you)
♠ AJ62
♥ T5
♦ AK92
♣ A84

Opening lead: 5 of diamonds

Count your winners. You have six, the ace–king of hearts, the ace–king of diamonds, the ace of clubs, and the ace of spades. But that leaves you three tricks short of your contract. How are you going to make this?

Your only chance is to set up your heart suit in dummy. But you've got a serious entry problem, because you only have two hearts in your hand and no other entry on the board. How do you play it?

This is where you *duck*, which means to lose a trick intentionally, to set up the heart suit. You must lose the first heart trick. So you take the opening lead in your hand with the king of diamonds. Now you lead a low heart to the board. West plays the deuce. You play the 6, allowing East to take the trick! You are hoping for a 3–2 split in hearts. East returns a diamond, which you take with your ace. You then lead your last heart to the ace–king on the board. Hearts split 3–2 as you had hoped, and you can run your five heart tricks.

The only way you could make this hand was to lose the first heart trick by ducking. That took out two of opponents' hearts and allowed you to pull the remaining hearts with your ace and king when you got back in the lead. If you don't duck, you have no way to get back to dummy without losing the lead when you try to take out the last heart. If you lead to the ace on your first lead of hearts and then play the king, you're out of hearts and North still has the 9 of hearts, which will take the next heart lead. Then there's no way for you to get back to dummy to cash your remaining good hearts.

Furthermore, if you lead to the ace and then lead a low heart, you still can't get back because you only have two hearts in your hand and the second heart will go on your second lead. So you must lose the *first* heart trick.

Here's the layout of the hands after the first three tricks if you immediately play the ace and king of hearts:

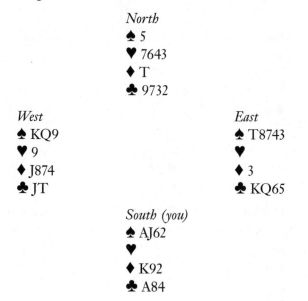

```
                        North
                        ♠ 5
                        ♥ 7643
                        ♦ T
                        ♣ 9732

West                                          East
♠ KQ9                                         ♠ T8743
♥ 9                                           ♥
♦ J874                                        ♦ 3
♣ JT                                          ♣ KQ65

                        South (you)
                        ♠ AJ62
                        ♥
                        ♦ K92
                        ♣ A84
```

Now what? You lead a heart and West takes it with his 9. You have no way to get back to the board to cash your three winning hearts. This is what the hands look like:

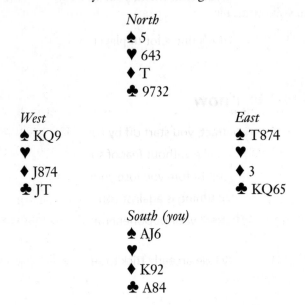

North
♠ 5
♥ 643
♦ T
♣ 9732

West
♠ KQ9
♥
♦ J874
♣ JT

East
♠ T874
♥
♦ 3
♣ KQ65

South (you)
♠ AJ6
♥
♦ K92
♣ A84

Sure you can get the lead again, no matter what West leads, but you can't get back to cash your three little hearts. Now look at the holding after you lose the first heart trick instead of taking it:

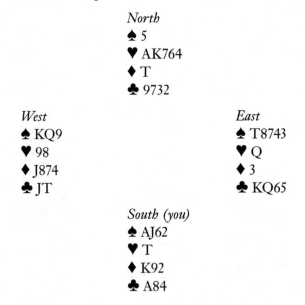

North
♠ 5
♥ AK764
♦ T
♣ 9732

West
♠ KQ9
♥ 98
♦ J874
♣ JT

East
♠ T8743
♥ Q
♦ 3
♣ KQ65

South (you)
♠ AJ62
♥ T
♦ K92
♣ A84

Now you're in great shape. No matter what East leads, you win in your hand and lead to the ace–king of hearts. When you cash them, your three remaining hearts are good and you have made your contract.

This is a fairly common situation, and it's one a lot of players misplay.

The Least You Need to Know

- When playing a no trump contract, you start off by counting your sure winners.
- A sure winner is a trick you can take without fear of surrendering the lead.
- You must establish your long suit before you lose your entries.
- You can't establish a long suit if timing is against you.
- You can hold up to protect against your opponents' ability to establish their long suit.
- You can duck and intentionally lose an early trick to set up a long suit in your weak hand with few entries.

Declarer Play in Suit Contracts

In This Chapter

- Counting losers
- Drawing trump
- Setting up a long secondary suit
- Playing the crossruff

When you're playing in a suit contract, you have a huge basic difference between playing in a no trump contract. That difference is that you have one suit that is all-powerful: the trump suit.

Having a trump suit enables you to take high cards in nontrump suits with low cards in the trump suit if you're void in the suit led. This makes playing a suit contract substantially different from playing in a no trump contract, where an ace that is led will *always* take the trick, and where having the lead is so important.

How to Count Your Losers

If you're playing in a suit contract, you immediately count your losers. How? You must combine your hand and dummy's hand in your mind's eye. Then you gather the high cards in each and see if they will eliminate losers in the other. For example, look at the following spades holding in the two hands:

Dummy
♠ Q65

Declarer
♠ AK43

Declarer has two losers, the 4 and the 3. Dummy has three losers: the unprotected queen, the 6, and the 5. But when you put the two hands together you see that the queen is not a loser at all, but a winner, because declarer has both the ace and the king.

Then you look at the other losers. You see that one of the losers in declarer's hand is protected by the Queen in dummy. So that reduces the number of losers in declarer's hand from two to one.

Dummy still has two losers, the 6 and the 5. But you see that they're protected by the ace and the king in declarer's hand. So dummy has no losers when you combine the hands, and declarer has only one potential loser, which may not be a loser if the suit splits 4–3–3–3 and trumps are drawn (meaning that declarer has played enough trump tricks so that neither opponent holds any trump).

You count losers in the combined hands by two methods:

- Shortness in declarer's hand
- Missing high cards in both hands

Shortness in Declarer's Hand

Shortness in declarer's hand makes up for dummy's losers in a suit.

Here are examples of counting shortness losers:

> *Dummy*
> ♠ 6543
>
> *Declarer*
> ♠ 87

You would have two losers because declarer can ruff dummy's extra losers after losing her 8 and 7.

However, look at the following holding:

> *Dummy*
> ♠ 43
>
> *Declarer*
> ♠ 8765

In this holding, you would have to count four losers because shortness should only count in declarer's hand, unless dummy has at least the same number of trump as declarer. This rule is alleviated if dummy only has a singleton. Why? Because dummy should have at least three cards in your trump suit if you have bid the hand properly, so you should be able to trump losers quickly if dummy has only a singleton. However, you must be leery of being too sanguine about dummy's singleton, especially if you do not have the ace of the suit and you're up against savvy players.

Any defender of quality, who feels he and his partner have the bulk of the high cards in a suit, when seeing a singleton in dummy will immediately attack trump by leading it. He does this to lessen dummy's ruffing power. So if you don't have the ace, you'll have to lose a trick to get rid of your singleton. This will allow your opponents to lead trump to get rid of at least one trump in dummy.

Another disadvantage in counting shortness in dummy is that dummy's trump might consist of high cards you will need in pulling trump. Look at the following hand:

North (Dummy)
♠ T
♥ AQT4
♦ AKQ
♣ T7632

South (Declarer)
♠ J95
♥ 86
♦ 987652
♣ AK

Bidding is as follows:

North	East	South	West
One club	Pass	One diamond	Pass
One heart	One spade	Two diamonds	Two spades
Five diamonds	Pass	Pass	Pass

North liked your diamond bid, because she had the ace, king, and queen, so she jumped to a very questionable game. You'd like to use your spade shortness in dummy to ruff your losers in your hand, but each time you ruff in dummy, you're taking away a high card that can win a trick on its own. If you were to ruff three spades in dummy with the ace, king, and queen, you'd have two trump losers out against you: the jack and the 10. Clearly, the shortness in dummy doesn't help you much with your spade losers because your trumps in dummy consist of high cards you're going to need to take tricks when you pull trump.

If you pull trump, and it takes three rounds because they're split 3–1, and you find that your clubs don't set up, and you then lose the heart finesse, opponents will switch back to spades and you'll lose at least two more tricks because you're out of trump in dummy.

Moral: Shortness in dummy doesn't help you if you need all or most of dummy's trump to draw trump.

Missing High Cards

When you combine the two hands, the number of high cards that are missing is usually the number of losers you have in the suit.

Look at the following hands and see if you can count the losers:

1. *Dummy*
   ♠ Q32

   Declarer
   ♠ KJ8

2. *Dummy*
   ♠ 542

   Declarer
   ♠ AQT3

3. *Dummy*
   ♠ 432

   Declarer
   ♠ KJ8

4. *Dummy*
   ♠ 432

   Declarer
   ♠ AQJ

5. *Dummy*
   ♠ T987

   Declarer
   ♠ J43

6. *Dummy*
   ♠ 32

   Declarer
   ♠ K8

7. *Dummy*
   ♠ Q2

   Declarer
   ♠ K8

Hand 1: One loser. Combined, you have three cards in each hand and they include the king, queen, and jack. The ace is the only loser.

Hand 2: Three losers. The ace is the only winner. You could lose the others. You can't count shortness in dummy unless dummy is loaded with trump, which it usually isn't.

Hand 3: Three losers. The ace and queen could be sitting behind declarer. You could very easily lose all three tricks.

Hand 4: One loser, the king.

Hand 5: Three losers. You're missing the ace, the king, and the queen, and you have three cards in the suit in declarer's hand.

Hand 6: Two losers. The king is not supported by anything.

Hand 7: One loser. You have the king and the queen and only two cards in the suit in each hand. You'll lose the ace, but will win the next trick.

Trump

Trump is what distinguishes suit contracts from no trump. In no trump contracts, each suit has equal power. In suit contracts, the trump suit is all powerful. The deuce of trump can take the ace in any other nontrump suit. Therefore, how you manage your trumps is important.

However, what you've learned in playing the cards in the preceding chapter on no trump contracts still applies. You must be aware of the position of honors, and you'll still have to finesse occasionally. The difference is that you must manage your trumps.

Drawing Trump

Generally—and there are exceptions to this rule—the first thing you try to do in playing a suit contract is to establish your trump suit, sort of like you established a long suit in the preceding chapter. You're not necessarily going to take all the trump tricks, but you want to get rid of all the trump cards in your opponents' hands so they can't ruff any of your good nontrump tricks with their small trump. Look at the following hand.

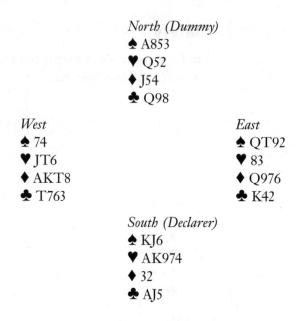

North (Dummy)
♠ A853
♥ Q52
♦ J54
♣ Q98

West
♠ 74
♥ JT6
♦ AKT8
♣ T763

East
♠ QT92
♥ 83
♦ Q976
♣ K42

South (Declarer)
♠ KJ6
♥ AK974
♦ 32
♣ AJ5

You're in a contract of four hearts. West leads the ace of diamonds, which he wins. He follows with the king of diamonds, which he wins. He follows that with the 8 of diamonds, and East covers North's jack with the queen. You, however, can win this trick because you are out of diamonds by now, so you can ruff. This shows you the basic difference between a suit contract and a no trump contract. In a no trump contract, you're helpless when an opponent runs a long suit. But in a suit contract, you can put an end to it by ruffing and taking the trick.

As soon as you get the lead, you should rid the opponents' hands of trump; therefore, you should play the ace and the king of hearts from your hand and then go to dummy to win opponents' last trump with the queen. You can then finesse East's king of clubs and queen of spades, and your contract is safely made. But the important thing is that you don't have to worry about losing one of your club or spade tricks through the opponents' trumping when they run out of the respective suit. That's why you play trump first, and arrange it so you are the only one who holds any remaining trump.

When you bid a contract, you should make sure that you have more combined trump than your opponents. Generally you will have eight or more trump between you and dummy, although occasionally you will find yourself playing a hand with only seven (or fewer) trump between you and dummy.

When Not to Pull Trump Immediately

Sometimes your losers are in your own hand and you're short in that suit in dummy. Let's change the previous hand a little, but you're still in a four-hearts contract, meaning you have to take 10 tricks:

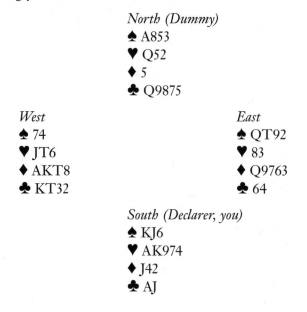

North (Dummy)
♠ A853
♥ Q52
♦ 5
♣ Q9875

West
♠ 74
♥ JT6
♦ AKT8
♣ KT32

East
♠ QT92
♥ 83
♦ Q9763
♣ 64

South (Declarer, you)
♠ KJ6
♥ AK974
♦ J42
♣ AJ

You have problems because you have three diamond losers. Neither your club nor your spade suit is going to set up. If you pull trump, how are you going to avoid losing two diamonds? The only way to make four hearts in this hand is for the play to go as follows:

> West leads and takes the ace of diamonds. Seeing that the dummy is now void in diamonds, he switches to a spade, and you take East's queen with your king.

If you were to draw trump now, you would be making a fatal error. Instead of drawing trump, you lead a diamond from your hand and ruff it in dummy. You return to your hand by leading a low spade from dummy and take it with the jack of spades in your hand. You then lead your last diamond from your hand and ruff it in dummy. Voilà! You have rid yourself of your two diamond losers and have made two small trumps in dummy into winners. Now you can pull trump. Instead of taking five trump tricks, you've taken seven. Add to this your three spades tricks and the ace of clubs, and you make five (Your contract was four hearts, but since you took 11 tricks, you made one trick over contract for an overtrick).

But if you pulled trump immediately after getting the lead with the king of spades, your hand would look like this:

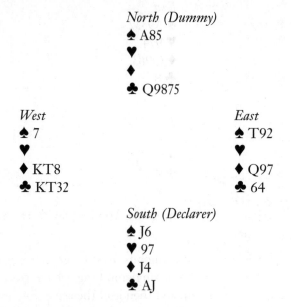

North (Dummy)
♠ A85
♥
♦
♣ Q9875

West
♠ 7
♥
♦ KT8
♣ KT32

East
♠ T92
♥
♦ Q97
♣ 64

South (Declarer)
♠ J6
♥ 97
♦ J4
♣ AJ

Now, what? How do you avoid losing two diamonds, along with the king of clubs, which you have to lose? Sometimes you have to ruff losers *before* you pull opponents' trump. This is the advantage of counting losers in a suit contract. You must know immediately where your losers are and how you're going to handle them before you start your play.

Discarding Losers on Winners

Another way to get rid of losers is to discard them on winners in a longer suit. Look at the following hand, in which you hold the South hand and the contract is six hearts:

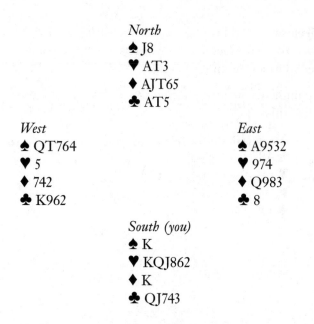

North
- ♠ J8
- ♥ AT3
- ♦ AJT65
- ♣ AT5

West
- ♠ QT764
- ♥ 5
- ♦ 742
- ♣ K962

East
- ♠ A9532
- ♥ 974
- ♦ Q983
- ♣ 8

South (you)
- ♠ K
- ♥ KQJ862
- ♦ K
- ♣ QJ743

Count your losers. For sure you should lose one spade. You lose no hearts, and maybe the queen of diamonds—a risky slam.

But you're lucky because West leads the 7 of diamonds. East is very coy and plays low, but you have to go up and take it with your singleton king, which gives you a diamond void in your hand. You draw trump and then lead the ace of diamonds from dummy. You discard your losing king of spades, and you make the contract because the club finesse is on.

Why can East play low on West's lead of the 7 of diamonds? He can see that he has the diamond 8, 9, and queen, and dummy has the jack and 10. So the only card that can take the 7 of diamonds is the king of diamonds. Playing the diamond 8, 9, or queen avails East nothing, so he plays low.

Ruffing Finesse

There's another finesse in the preceding hand. Can you see it? You can see the club finesse, but where's the other one?

You have what's called a *ruffing finesse* in diamonds, which is when you trump to cover an honor instead of a higher card of the same suit. It's not relevant to making this hand, but because it does appear in this hand I'm going to explain it to you because it's a tool you can use to make some contracts. After you draw trump and get rid of the king of spades, the hands look like this:

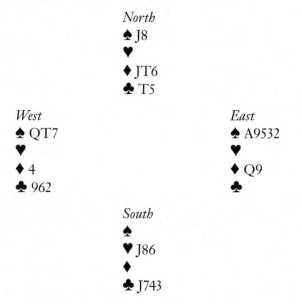

North
♠ J8
♥
♦ JT6
♣ T5

West
♠ QT7
♥
♦ 4
♣ 962

East
♠ A9532
♥
♦ Q9
♣

South
♠
♥ J86
♦
♣ J743

Look at your diamond holding. Three honors are still out: the queen, jack, and 10. You hold the jack and 10 in dummy, opposite a void in your hand. So you lead the jack. If East covers, you ruff it. If East plays low, you let it ride, discarding a club, playing East for the queen. If he has the queen, you win the trick. If West has it, you lose the trick.

Again, there's no reason to use the ruffing finesse in this hand because it doesn't get you anything. But sometimes using a ruffing finesse is the only way you will have to make your contract. I mention it here so you'll recognize it when it arises.

Setting Up a Long Suit to Discard Losers

Another way to get rid of losers is to set up a long secondary suit. Look at this hand:

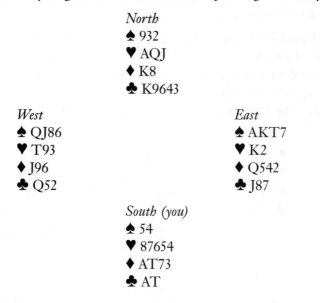

North
♠ 932
♥ AQJ
♦ K8
♣ K9643

West
♠ QJ86
♥ T93
♦ J96
♣ Q52

East
♠ AKT7
♥ K2
♦ Q542
♣ J87

South (you)
♠ 54
♥ 87654
♦ AT73
♣ AT

You ended up in an extremely optimistic contract of four hearts, playing South. You get a spade lead and lose two spades before ruffing the third spade in your hand. You immediately lose a heart finesse. Now your hand looks like this and you can't lose any more tricks:

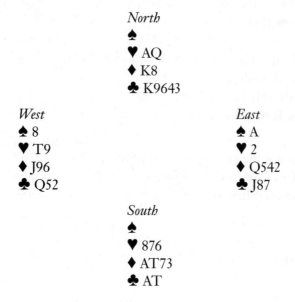

North
♠
♥ AQ
♦ K8
♣ K9643

West
♠ 8
♥ T9
♦ J96
♣ Q52

East
♠ A
♥ 2
♦ Q542
♣ J87

South
♠
♥ 876
♦ AT73
♣ AT

East returns a diamond, which you should take with your ace. Now what? You have diamond and club losers, even though you have the ace–king of clubs and the king of diamonds. Your only chance is to set up the clubs and hope they split 3–3. So you take out trump (lead and take trump tricks until the opponents have none), leaving you one in your hand. Then you lead the ace of clubs and the 10 of clubs to the king. Now your hand looks like this:

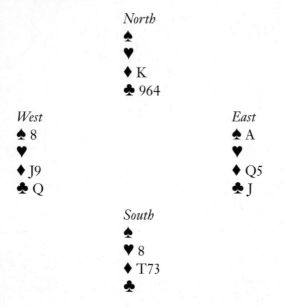

North
♠
♥
♦ K
♣ 964

West
♠ 8
♥
♦ J9
♣ Q

East
♠ A
♥
♦ Q5
♣ J

South
♠
♥ 8
♦ T73
♣

You lead the 4 of clubs and ruff it in your hand. You breathe much easier when you see both East and West discard clubs. Now the only two clubs left are on the board in North's hand, and you have a lead to the king of diamonds on the board. You have made a very difficult contract by setting up your 6 and 4 of clubs as the winning tricks, discarding your losing diamonds on them.

TRICKS OF THE TRADE

Remember the entry problem I mentioned in Chapter 20? You have it here, too. You have to retain an entry to the board to get back there to make your two little clubs good. That's why you took East's diamonds lead in your hand with the ace, preserving the king of diamonds as your entry to the board.

An even better example of a hand where you set up a long suit to make your contract occurred in the 1995 World Wide Bridge Contest. This hand has the added value of also showing the importance of the duck by declarer. Following are the hands:

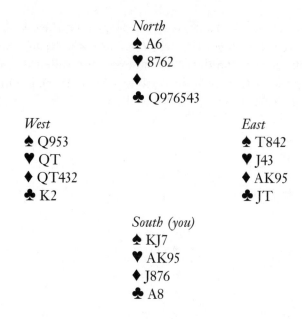

North
♠ A6
♥ 8762
♦
♣ Q976543

West
♠ Q953
♥ QT
♦ QT432
♣ K2

East
♠ T842
♥ J43
♦ AK95
♣ JT

South (you)
♠ KJ7
♥ AK95
♦ J876
♣ A8

Bidding:

West	North	East	South
		Pass	One no trump
Pass	Two clubs	Pass	Two hearts
Pass	Four hearts	Pass	Pass
Pass			

Opening lead: 3 of diamonds

Your partner has a tough decision to make when you open one no trump. With only 6 HCP but seven clubs, four hearts, and a diamonds void, she should do something. She decided to bid two clubs because she had a four-card major. If you responded in two diamonds or two spades, she would bid three clubs as a sign-off bid and you'd play in her seven-card suit. When you responded with a fit in hearts, she jumped to game because her void now became worth 5 points and her hand reevaluates to 11 points. But it doesn't look easy, does it?

The only way to make this hand is to ruff the diamond in dummy. You then play the ace of clubs and another club, losing to West's king, and breathe a little easier when clubs split 2–2. You now have five good clubs tricks on the board if you can get to them and get the trump out.

West chose to lead another diamond, forcing you to ruff again on the board, leaving you with only two trump there. Now, what do you do? If you lead to the ace and king of trump, opponents are left with the high trump. You will be out of trump on the board and the ace of spades is your only entry, which you will have to use now to get there. Here's the hand at this stage:

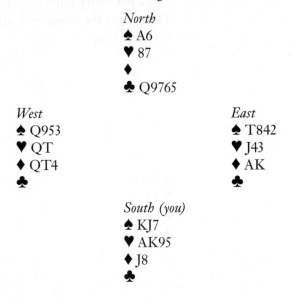

North
♠ A6
♥ 87
♦
♣ Q9765

West
♠ Q953
♥ QT
♦ QT4
♣

East
♠ T842
♥ J43
♦ AK
♣

South (you)
♠ KJ7
♥ AK95
♦ J8
♣

Lead is in North (dummy). If you play the ace and king of hearts, East will be left with the jack. Here's the layout of the hand if you lead a low heart to your ace and then play the king:

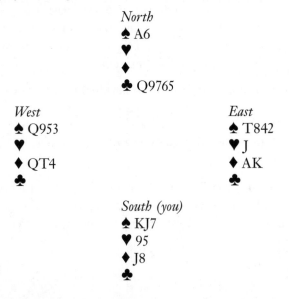

North
♠ A6
♥
♦
♣ Q9765

West
♠ Q953
♥
♦ QT4
♣

East
♠ T842
♥ J
♦ AK
♣

South (you)
♠ KJ7
♥ 95
♦ J8
♣

Now, what? Your only hope in this hand is to make all the clubs good, but you can't lead over to the ace of spades and run the clubs because East will ruff in and then play the ace and king of diamonds and you'll be set. Furthermore, your ace of spades is your only entry to the board.

Instead of leading the ace and king of hearts, lead a low heart and duck, allowing your opponents to win. Now your contract is cold. Here's how the hands look after leading the low heart and ducking, retaining the heart ace and king:

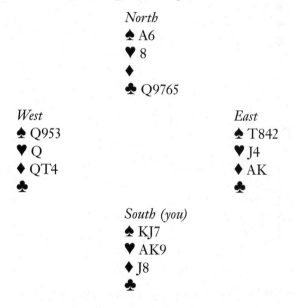

North
♠ A6
♥ 8
♦
♣ Q9765

West
♠ Q953
♥ Q
♦ QT4
♣

East
♠ T842
♥ J4
♦ AK
♣

South (you)
♠ KJ7
♥ AK9
♦ J8
♣

West leads another diamond, which you have to ruff with your last trump on the board. But you get back to your hand by leading a low spade to your king and then pull the remaining trump by leading your ace and king of hearts. You then go back to the board with a lead to the ace of spades and all your clubs are good, making five!

This hand is a very good example of two things you have learned:

- How to set up a long suit in a trump contract

- How to use the duck to make a difficult contract

The Crossruff

I don't think there's anything more enjoyable in bridge than to make a hand by crossruffing. What's a *crossruff*? Simply, it's when you have a short suit in dummy and a different short suit in your hand and you ruff back and forth. Look at the following hand:

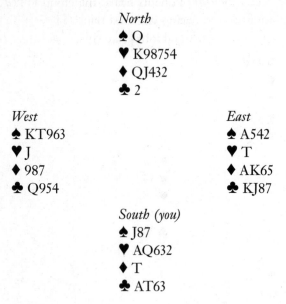

North
♠ Q
♥ K98754
♦ QJ432
♣ 2

West
♠ KT963
♥ J
♦ 987
♣ Q954

East
♠ A542
♥ T
♦ AK65
♣ KJ87

South (you)
♠ J87
♥ AQ632
♦ T
♣ AT63

East–West is vulnerable, you're not. You are South, and the bidding went as follows:

You	West	North	East
One heart	Pass	Four hearts	Pass
Pass	Pass		

BRIDGEBIT

Ruff was a game that preceded whist. The primary feature of ruff was the ability to win a trick by playing a trump. The term *ruff* came to be used as a verb to denote taking a trick with a trump. The concept of no trump was unknown in ruff and whist. It's peculiar to contract bridge.

You've gotten to a major-suit game with only 20 HCP between you and your partner. How are you going to make this? South has three spade losers, three club losers, and a diamond loser. North has a club loser, a bunch of diamond losers, and a spade loser.

You're going to crossruff. Let's say that your opponents lead a spade, which they win with the ace. East switches to a heart, which you win in your hand, and find that you have drawn trump because each of your opponents has a singleton trump. You immediately lead your 10 of diamonds, surrendering your last trick. They switch to a club, which you take with your ace. Now your hand looks like this:

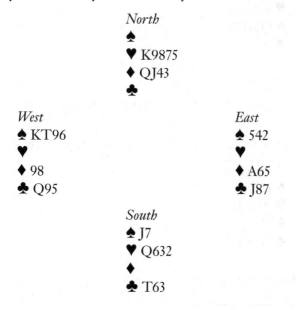

North
♠
♥ K9875
♦ QJ43
♣

West
♠ KT96
♥
♦ 98
♣ Q95

East
♠ 542
♥
♦ A65
♣ J87

South
♠ J7
♥ Q632
♦
♣ T63

You have five losers in South—two spades and three clubs. But you are void in both those suits in dummy and have five trump in dummy! Similarly, you have four losing diamonds in dummy, but you are void in diamonds and have four trump in your hand. It's a simple matter to just keep leading a nontrump suit from one hand and trumping it in the other. What a terrific feeling to take all those high honors with small little trump. With only 20 HCP, this hand makes five hearts, solely through the use of the crossruff!

You should have a compelling reason for making this play, which requires two cards well placed rather than just one for a simple finesse of the jack. Perhaps, by the bidding, West is marked with the queen of spades, which would justify this.

The Least You Need to Know

- When playing a suit contract, you should count losers in your combined hands after you see dummy.
- If you have too many losers, see if it's possible to ruff some losers in your partner's hand.
- If you don't need to ruff losers, generally when you get the lead you draw trump before doing anything else.
- Look for a way to establish one of the nontrump suits in either hand. Then you can discard losers on that suit.
- If you have losers in both hands, sometimes you can crossruff, or take tricks with individual trump in both hands.

Defense of the Hand: Opening Leads

In This Chapter

- Fourth from longest and strongest
- Top connecting honors
- Standard leads
- Leading suits with aces
- Leads against slams

After an auction concludes, the declarer's LHO makes the first lead. This is called the *opening lead*. Entire books are devoted to strategies for making an opening lead. In this chapter, you learn the basics of how to make this important move.

Opening Leads Against No Trump Contracts

The opening lead is made by declarer's LHO. So if declarer is on your right, you will make the opening lead.

The opening lead is the most important aspect of defense. There is a lot to consider. Therefore, before you just throw down a card to get the hand started, you should pause and think about how you're going to defend.

TRICKS OF THE TRADE

In defending no trump, your longest suit is generally your strongest suit. Keep that in mind throughout the following discussion.

Now forget about your hand for a moment. In defending no trump, often you must try to determine what's in your partner's hand and play to her hand.

The first thing you should take into consideration is what you've learned from the bidding. Following are some questions you should consider before making your lead:

- Has your partner bid a suit?
- Has she made a double?
- Have your opponents bid any suits?
- Did the dummy bid a suit?

Let's take these questions in order.

When Your Partner Has Bid a Suit

If your partner bid a suit freely, you know that she has at least five cards in it. How many cards do you have in that suit? If you have three or more, that suit is probably your strongest asset in defending this hand because you have at least eight cards between you and your partner.

If your partner has bid a suit, you must determine which card in her suit you want to lead. Here are the rules:

- If you have at least three cards including an honor (commonly called "three to an honor") lead your lowest card.
- If you have exactly three cards in her suit but no honor, lead the highest card in her suit.
- If you have two in her suit, lead the higher card.
- If you have *connecting honors*, lead the top connecting honor, no matter how many cards you have in her suit.

DEFINITION

A **connecting honor** is a holding of two consecutive honor cards in the same suit, like the king–queen or jack–10.

What if you have a five-card suit yourself? Should you lead your suit or your partner's? Answer: If you don't have a very strong suit, such as a five-card suit with only one honor, *lead your partner's suit!* Here's why:

- Make your partner happy. If you lead your suit and it's the wrong lead, your partner's first question will be, "Why didn't you lead my suit?" If you lead her suit and it's wrong, she can't criticize you. It might sound selfish, but it's the best way to keep your partnership on an even keel.

- From a bridge point of view (yes, we do still think about bridge in our partnerships!), it's better to lead *to* a suit than to lead *from* a suit. So if you lead to your partner's suit it will force your opponents to lead to your suit, or will allow your partner to lead to your suit. Furthermore, you know that she has a suit, so you know that leading her suit will help her. Leading your suit could work to your disadvantage because you're telling declarer where the power is in your suit. Keep that a secret for a while. Because your partner has given you a lead, take it.

TRICKS OF THE TRADE

Interestingly, the selfish lead would appear to be to lead your own suit. In actuality, however, the selfish lead is your partner's suit because you don't want to be criticized. Listen, if you think this sounds silly, even the best players in the world think this way. Nobody likes to have their partner yell at them.

Another thing to consider is when no trump was first bid. Did declarer bid no trump after your partner bid her suit, after their pair had been bidding suits? If so, it's a clear indication that declarer has stoppers in your partner's suit. If you lead the suit, one of the downsides you must consider is that you'll be leading right through her into the power in her suit. Let's say that the bidding went like this:

RHO	You	LHO	Partner
One heart	Pass	One spade	Two diamonds
Two no trump	Pass	Three clubs	Pass
Three no trump	Pass	Pass	Pass

Declarer is telling his partner (and you) that he has no fear of your partner's diamonds suit. But what else do you know about this hand from the bidding? You can glean the following information:

- RHO has five hearts—no more. If he had six hearts he would have rebid them. Because he opened one heart, he must have five, but not six.

- LHO has at least four spades.

- LHO doesn't have three hearts. If he had three hearts, because he knows his partner has five hearts, he would have placed the contract in four hearts because of the eight-card major fit. Because he never supported hearts, he has a maximum of two hearts in his hand.

- Your partner has at least five diamonds and close to an opening hand because she bid at the two level after opponents had bid two suits.

- RHO has diamonds stopped, at least twice probably.

- LHO has at least four clubs, maybe five.

- RHO doesn't have four spades. If he had four spades, because he knows partner has at least four spades, he would have supported spades or placed the contract in four spades after his partner bid three no trump.

- LHO has at least 10 points, probably more.

Knowing this, you should have a pretty good picture of the structure of each of your opponents' hands:

LHO	*RHO (declarer)*
♠ xxxxx	♠ xx
♥ xx	♥ xxxxx
♦ x	♦ xxxx
♣ xxxxx	♣ xx

Your partner might have the following diamonds holding:

♦ KJT875

Your hand looks like this:

♠ J74
♥ 9642
♦ 94
♣ QJ62

What should you lead? Your partner bid diamonds, so that should be your first choice. However, declarer said he had no fear of diamonds. Despite this, you must trust your partner. She has at least five, maybe six. This is why the opening lead is so important. If declarer only has diamonds stopped twice, he could be using his first stopper on the first lead. So let's look at declarer's diamonds holding:

♦ AQ32

Anybody would be willing to bid no trump over his RHO's diamonds bid with the ace and the queen behind the probable king. But if you start out leading the 9 of diamonds, it starts to set up your partner's hand. So with all this thought, you lead the 9 of diamonds. (Remember: if you have two cards in your partner's suit, lead the higher card.) But you can only make this determination by thinking about what you know about the hands from the bidding and, finally, trusting your partner.

When You Can Lead Something Other Than Your Partner's Suit

Sometimes you don't lead your partner's suit. Two such instances follow:

If you have a strong, self-establishing suit of your own to lead. Let's say your partner bid diamonds and your hand looks like the following:

♠ 974
♥ KQJ95
♦ 84
♣ K83

With this holding you should lead your king of hearts because you'll probably be able to take four hearts tricks here, and you have another possible entry with the king of clubs. With this hand you have a good answer when your partner asks, "Why didn't you lead my suit?" But she probably won't ask that. She'll probably say, "Nice lead, Partner!"

If you have a singleton in her suit and you have a suit you might be able to develop in your hand. If you have a basically worthless hand, however, you should lead the singleton because your partner's hand is your best line of defense, and that's her best suit.

When Your Partner Doubles the Final Three–No Trump Contract

If your partner doubles the final three–no trump contract for penalty, it's not just for penalty. *A double of a three–no trump contract asks partner to make a specific lead.* The rules for the specific leads requested by a double follow:

- If your partner (who doubled) has bid a suit, lead her suit.

- If you have bid a suit, lead your suit.

- If neither of you has bid, you should lead dummy's first-bid suit *unless you have a better lead in your hand.* You can use your own judgment here. If you have a holding like the heart holding referred to above, KQJ94, you should lead the king of hearts. But if you don't have a good lead from your hand, your partner's double asks you to lead the dummy's first-bid suit.

- If you have both bid, you should use your own judgment. But if you don't have a terrific suit, lead your partner's suit.

- If no suit has been bid by opponents and neither of you has bid. Look at the following bidding:

LHO	Partner	RHO	You
One no trump	Pass	Three no trump	Pass
Pass	Double	Pass	Pass
Pass			

By doubling, your partner is asking for an unusual lead—like a singleton—from your hand. She's saying that she has a long suit that, if you find it, will set the contract. In this instance, you forget all the standard leads and lead your singleton or the shortest suit in your hand.

When Opponents Have Bid a Suit

If the opponents bid suits, you want to stay away from leading any suit bid by declarer for your opening lead unless it's a very good suit and you're pretty confident that your holding is longer than declarer's. Leading declarer's suit—even if it's your best suit— means that you are *leading into strength*. Declarer will have the last play on the trick and will generally be able to take it with a card that allows an extra trick. If you don't have cards in the suit bid by declarer, there's a fair chance that your partner will. And if she does, you'll be leading right through her into declarer's strength.

Generally, you try to lead a suit that hasn't been bid. If your opponents are bidding their suits and end up in no trump, the longest suit you and your partner have is usually the unbid suit.

When Dummy Bid a Suit

Often it's a good lead to *lead through strength*. This means that if dummy has bid a suit, it's sometimes a good lead to lead through that suit. This is especially true if you don't hold an honor in that suit. The reason is that dummy may have a suit with broken honors, like AQxx or KJxx. There is a possibility that your partner holds the missing honors. This is especially true if dummy was not the opening bidder and responded in a major that was not supported by opener. If you're short in that suit, there's a good chance that's your partner's suit.

Leading with Fourth from Longest and Strongest

The standard lead against a no trump contract is to lead the fourth highest card in your longest suit. Look at the following hand:

♠ AQ4
♥ 84
♦ 98642
♣ KT9

When you're on defense against a no trump contract, your strongest suit is your longest suit. In this hand, the strongest suit is diamonds, and the fourth highest card in your diamonds suit is the 4. So you should lead the 4 of diamonds.

There's sound reasoning behind this lead, even though both your clubs and spades look like better suits. You want to set up one or two diamond tricks. Diamonds may be split evenly. If so, the other three hands hold 3–3–2 in diamonds. That leaves you with two good diamonds if you get in after they've been led three times. And you have three possible entries into your hand, the ace and queen of spades, and the king or 10 of clubs. This is not counting the possibility that your partner might get lucky and take a trick then lead a diamond. Even if opponents hold all the diamond honors, if they're split as anticipated, when you finally get in you'll set three no trump because you'll get two diamond tricks. You have a good chance of getting two spade tricks and a club trick as well. And this isn't counting on partner for anything.

Counting the Points in Your Partner's Hand

How many points do you think your partner has if you're defending three no trump in this hand? The answer: not many. You have 9 HCP in your hand, and your opponents probably have at least 25 HCP. That only leaves 6 HCP for your partner. But that might be enough for her to get in once and lead a diamond.

You must rely on your partner to trust you and lead a diamond when she gets in, regardless of the holding in her hand. She might have five hearts and want to set up her hearts. But she must trust you and return a diamond if you led a low diamond. If she were to switch to a heart, it would destroy your defense and render your good diamond lead valueless. You're probably getting sick of hearing this, but *partners must trust one another.* Following is the entire hand:

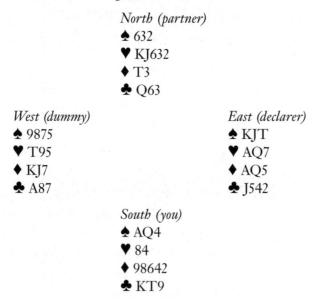

North (partner)
♠ 632
♥ KJ632
♦ T3
♣ Q63

West (dummy)
♠ 9875
♥ T95
♦ KJ7
♣ A87

East (declarer)
♠ KJT
♥ AQ7
♦ AQ5
♣ J542

South (you)
♠ AQ4
♥ 84
♦ 98642
♣ KT9

The bidding went like this:

East	South	West	North
One no trump	Pass	Two clubs	Pass
Two diamonds	Pass	Two no trump	Pass
Three no trump	Pass	Pass	Pass

The play might go like this. You lead the 4 of diamonds, declarer plays low from dummy, and your partner plays the 10, which declarer wins with the queen. Declarer tries a club that loses to your partner's queen.

This is the biggest play of the hand right here. What card your partner chooses to lead determines whether or not you're going to set the hand. She's going to be mighty tempted to switch to a heart—her good, long suit and the weakest suit in dummy—but she must have discipline and trust you. She must play a diamond despite her nice hearts. It doesn't matter how declarer then plays the diamonds because after your partner's lead, he only has one more diamond stopper. When you *get in* (get the lead), you'll take it out and then when you get in again, you'll have the setting tricks in your remaining two diamonds. If your partner were to switch to a heart instead of returning your diamond, however, you wouldn't have enough remaining entries to take out declarer's two diamond stoppers, and he would probably make the hand.

> **TRICKS OF THE TRADE**
>
> Goren says that every time the defense leads a new suit it amounts to losing a half trick on average!

Furthermore, when she switches, it will tell a savvy declarer that she (his RHO) has the heart honors and, if declarer plays low from his hand, you won't have a card high enough to keep the 10 from winning the trick on the board. This gives him an additional winner with the 10 on the board and an additional entry to the board (the 10 he wins with this trick) to finesse through her.

When Leading from a Weak Suit, You Must Have Entries

Your diamond suit is admittedly a weak five-card suit. However, you have entries in other suits that will allow you to get in and set up your diamonds. If you have a Yarborough or a hand without more than one entry, you should *not* lead the diamond because it will give your partner a false hope that your opponents can be set up. And they can't if there's no way you can get the lead to take advantage of your long suit. So if you were without the ace–queen of spades and the king of clubs you would lead something else, even though, as the cards lie, any other lead would be harmful.

Leading with Top Connecting Honors

Another potential lead is the top connecting honors. But in no trump this is often not a good lead unless they're internal connecting honors—like KJTx, leading the jack, or a three-card sequence, like QJTx. Why? Because you give up a possible trick if opponents have the ace, which they probably do.

What would you lead against a no trump contract with the following club holding?

♣ KQ74

You have two choices from the two rules you've learned: do you lead the top connecting honor, or do you lead fourth from longest and strongest? The answer: lead fourth. You give up a potential trick if you lead the king. Your partner might have the ace or jack. If she has the ace, she can take the trick and return it and you might get four club tricks off the top if they split 4–3–3–3. If she has the jack, it will either force out the ace or she can return it to you.

What would you lead from the following club holding against a no trump contract?

♣ KJT4

In this instance, you should lead the top connecting honor, the jack. Why? Because with your king on top of the jack–10, whichever card you force out—be it the ace or the queen—makes the remaining two of the top three honors outstanding, which should result in a trick.

Standard Leads Against No Trump Contracts

The following list shows the standard opening leads when defending against a no trump contract. The standard lead is bold and underlined:

xx	xxx**x**
xxx	xxx**x**x
A**K**Jx	A**Q**Jx
A**J**T9	A**T**9x
KQJx	K**Q**T9
K**J**Tx	K**T**9x
QJTx	Q**T**9x
JT9x	**T**9xx

One lead here is a departure from the norm, so it bears explaining. It's the lead of the queen from the holding of KQT9. Normally you'd think you'd lead the king or the 9, but you lead the queen to ask your partner to jettison the jack if she has it.

If you lead the queen and she has the jack, she'll know that you're leading from this specific holding. Otherwise, the lead of the queen in a no trump defense would promise a holding of QJT. But if she has the jack you can't be leading from that, so you must be leading from KQT9. She must drop the jack to keep from *blocking* your suit. Leading the queen has the further advantage of allowing you to continue the suit. If declarer has the ace-jack, he might not take the ace (called "holding up" the ace), hoping you will continue leading the suit with the queen and thereby allowing her to get two tricks—both the ace and the jack. So if your partner plays the jack when you lead the queen, it allows you to continue the suit without worrying about giving declarer a trick he otherwise wouldn't get.

DEFINITION

You **block** your partner's suit when your partner has several good cards remaining in a suit but you must take the trick because your only card in that suit is higher ranking than the remaining cards in her suit. This results in partner having no way to get the lead back into partner's hand to allow her to cash her tricks.

If she holds Jxx in the suit, and you hold the king and follow with the queen, it will be taken by the ace. If you get in again and lead the 10, your partner will be forced to overtake with her jack because it's the only card she has left in the suit. Now you can't win the 9 unless you have another entry into your hand. But if she plays the jack at your first play of the queen, your remaining cards are all good tricks after the ace is played. Playing the jack when partner leads the queen has the added advantage of allowing the leader to continue leading the suit without fear that opener has the ace and the jack, which would allow her to take two tricks—the jack in addition to the ace—for one more trick than she would get if you didn't lead the king after you led the queen.

One of the purposes of a standard lead is that it tells your partner what you have in your hand. If she sees you lead the 10, for example, she'll know that it promises the 9 and denies the jack. If you lead the king, it means that you have either the ace or the queen and jack along with it. But one thing to notice about these standard leads is that none of them consists of *top connecting honors when you only have two connecting honors*, which is a standard lead against a suit contract (as you'll see shortly). However, top connecting honors of three in a row is a good defensive lead against a no trump contract.

Opening Leads Against Suit Contracts

When you're on lead against a suit contract, your defense is substantially different than when you're on lead against a no trump contract. When defending against no trump, you're trying to set up a long suit. You can be patient to try to develop this suit.

When defending against a suit contract, however, you must take your tricks when you can. Because declarer has the ability to ruff aces and kings, you have to take them before declarer has been able to create a void in his hand, which renders your ace or king valueless.

When defending against a suit contract, however, you have different ways of attacking, only one of which involves setting up a long suit.

ALERT

Setting up a long nontrump suit is a very rare defensive tactic because it relies on declarer running out of trump and you getting the lead to set up your suit. It happens, but not often.

When defending against a suit contract, you often have to take your tricks before declarer can get rid of losers and ruff your winners. If you have the ace–king–queen of a suit, for instance, they would be worth three cold tricks in no trump. If you're playing a suit contract and declarer has a void in that suit, the ace-king-queen are worthless.

The Best Lead Against a Suit: Ace-King

Louis Watson, author of the best book on play of the hand—called, not too surprisingly, *Watson's Classic Book on the Play of the Hand at Bridge (1971)*—says that the best lead against a suit contract is the king from the ace–king holding. This is a great lead for two reasons:

- It almost definitely wins you the first trick.

- It allows you to get a view of dummy before making your next lead. As you recall, dummy is turned face up after the opening lead. If you are able to lead a card that will take the trick, like king from ace-king, you can see the dummy before you make your second lead.

Unfortunately, it is not often that you're defending against a suit contract and you find yourself in the wonderful position of being able to lead from an ace–king.

Leading Your Partner's Suit

When you haven't bid and you don't have a good lead from your hand, leading your partner's suit is usually a good lead and is generally safe. There are two theories about whether or not you should lead your highest card in a suit.

For years, when I was playing with Nancy Kelly and we were playing Standard American and no systems (which is what you're learning here) we played that you always led the top of your partner's bid—and it worked wonderfully. Nobody else liked it, but it does give your partner an instant idea of where the other cards in her suit are.

But most experts insist that if you lead your partner's suit, the lead should be as follows:

- **Low from an honor.** So if you have Q72 you would lead the deuce.

- **High from a doubleton.** You're trying to get a ruff and you want to tell your partner that you only have two. Of course, she won't know until the next time the suit is led whether or not you were leading a singleton or doubleton.

- **A singleton.** This is a wonderful lead because if your partner has the ace, which is more likely if you lead her suit than if you're leading an unbid suit, you're almost always assured that she'll return it and you'll get a ruff. Again, she has to determine whether you led a singleton or doubleton, but if she comes to the correct conclusion, you'll start out with two tricks.

- **Middle card from three worthless.** This is called *MUD* for *middle-up-down*. It gives your partner *count*, which is an indication of whether you have an even or odd number of cards in the suit led. If you lead a lower or middle card and the next card you play in the suit is higher, it indicates that you have an odd number of cards in that suit.

There's one time when you shouldn't lead your partner's suit: when you have a lot of cards in it. If your partner bid hearts, for example, and you have five hearts in your hand, the likelihood is that declarer could be void and your heart lead will just turn the lead over to him without you taking a trick.

DEFINITION

Count tells your partner whether you have an even or odd number of cards in the suit led. Generally, if you have an even number of cards in a suit, you will play a high card first, then a low card. If you have an odd number of cards in the suit, you first play a low card and then one higher.

Top of Connecting Honors

You learned about this lead in the section on leads against no trump contracts. Against no trump, it's not a terrific lead unless you have a three-card sequence, like queen–jack–10. Top of two connecting honors is a better lead against a suit contract because it sets up a relatively sure trick. Remember, against suit contracts you always must be sensitive to taking your tricks in outside suits before declarer can ruff them. If your first lead is the king from king–queen and if declarer has the ace, you have a good chance of getting a trick with your queen before he can set up a side suit to rid himself of the loser in the led suit.

Leading a Singleton

The idea here is to create an instant void in your hand so that if the suit is led again before you're out of trump, you can ruff. However, it requires a firm partnership understanding that your partner will return your opening lead when she finally gets the lead herself.

When you're on defense and you're not on opening lead, if you get in you should *return* your partner's suit unless there's a very good reason not to do so.

You don't want to lead a singleton unless it has the possibility of giving you a trick you might not otherwise get. For example, if you have Q74 of trump, a singleton lead really doesn't do you much good because you have the queen protected by two. If you are forced to use a small trump, your queen will fall with the lead of the ace and the king—so you really haven't gained anything. If opponent leads his ace and king of trump (if he has them), your queen will be good. If you've trumped with your low trump first, however, he will capture your queen on his second lead, so you haven't really gained a trick. You only get one trick with your trump either way. That doesn't mean that you shouldn't lead a singleton when you have a holding like Qxx, however. There are several ways you could still get your queen even after you ruff.

TRICKS OF THE TRADE

There's little more frustrating than to lead a singleton, have your partner get the lead while you still have some trump in your hand, and see her lead a different suit. You sit there in helpless anguish while your brilliant lead becomes worthless.

Sometimes a lead of a singleton is a good lead; often it's not. If you have only small trump, it's okay because you might be able to take advantage of the trump.

That said, if your partner has bid the suit in which you hold a singleton, it's almost always the best lead you can make for obvious reasons.

Leading a Singleton Honor

This is a paradox that faces many players. Opponents have the contract and you have a singleton honor. Should you lead it? The answer is, unless your partner has bid the suit, *no*. You're going to have a good chance to win a trick with this card during the play of the hand if your opponents try a finesse. But if your partner has bid the suit, it's a terrific lead. Not only will it set up a ruff in your hand, but it will probably help to set up your partner's suit.

Fourth from Longest and Strongest

You learned about this in the section on leads against no trump, and it's a valid lead against a suit contract, too. It's a good, safe, standard lead.

Cards That Smile; Cards That Frown

On opening lead, the specific card you lead communicates specific information to your partner:

- **Leading a small card promises an honor in the suit being played, so it smiles.** So if you lead a deuce, 3, or 4, you're promising your partner that you have an honor in the suit, with one exception: if the next card you play in that suit is lower than the one you led (for example, if you lead the 4 and then play the 3), this tells your partner you led a doubleton.

- **Leading a middle card denies an honor, so it frowns.** So if you lead, for example, the 7, it tells your partner to forget about your having any help for her in this suit.

Leading Suits with Aces Against Suit Contracts

One of the oldest axioms in bridge is *never underlead an ace*. Why? Well, whenever you succumb to the temptation to underlead an ace you see the singleton king come up on the board and you feel like an idiot—which is what I'm trying to keep you from feeling like here.

However, it doesn't matter whether it's a singleton king or a singleton anything else. If you underlead an ace and declarer has a singleton in his hand or in the dummy, and if your partner doesn't have the king, you won't win your ace on this hand. You've just given up a trick.

If you wonder about not leading an ace, just remember this axiom: *Aces were created to take kings or Queens.* As a general rule, you shouldn't play your ace until you can use it to take a king or queen. If your ace happens to be the setting trick, however, you should take it immediately.

To make matters more confusing, *you shouldn't lead an ace!* So where does that leave you? It means that against a suit contract below the slam level you shouldn't lead a suit in which you have an ace unless you have the king to go with it. (And, in the event of having an ace–king combination, you should lead the king first.) Even if your partner has bid the suit, you shouldn't lead the ace! There will be more about this a few paragraphs later.

If you lead an ace on opening lead, often you'll set up a king–queen combination for your opponents. If you wait to take your ace when they play one of their honors to try to take a trick, you might get an extra trick (if, for example, your partner has the Jxx in the suit). You certainly will keep them from making both the king and the queen!

So here are the rules relating to opening leads of suits with aces:

- Don't underlead an ace.

- Don't lead an ace against a contract below the slam level unless you have the king (then lead the king first).

Now I'm going to explain why you shouldn't lead an ace even if your partner has bid the suit. You hold the following:

    ♠ AJ4
    ♥ 75
    ♦ 8643
    ♣ JT98

Your partner opens one spade. RHO overcalls two hearts. By now you should know that you should bid two spades with this hand, so you do. And then LHO bids three hearts, which is passed out. It's your lead. Do you remember the first thing you should do before leading? *Think!* What do you know?

1. How many spades does your partner have and how big is her hand? Answer: five with a minimum. If she had six she would have rebid them, even with a minimum hand.

2. How many spades do opponents have? The answer: five. Your partner has five spades and you have three spades. That leaves five.

3. Key question: You have the ace. Who has the king—your partner or your opponents? Because your partner has a minimum, probably 13 points, and you have 6 HCP, opponents have 20 to 21 points. In this situation, more than half of the time opponents will have the king of spades. Why? Because more than half the points outside of your hand belong to opponents, 21 for them, 13 for your partner.

TRICKS OF THE TRADE

If you have ace doubleton, the ace can be a very good lead against a suit contract. If your partner has the king and you lead the ace and follow with another card in the suit, she should know you're leading a doubleton and return the suit for ruff, giving you three tricks off the top.

So there are two definite negatives to leading your ace:

- More than half of the time your lead of the ace will make the king a definite winner for opponents, because by leading your ace you can't take their ling;

- You give them an easy ruff of a spade. Why? Because spades will split one of three ways: 3–2, 4–1, or 5–0. In the first situation, you help them get rid of spades quickly so they may ruff before starting to pull trump. In the second, you give them a void immediately and they can easily ruff before pulling trump. In the third, you lose the ace immediately with a ruff. In the first situation, if you lead the ace and then the king wins for them, they will have a void somewhere, which they can use to ruff a losing spade before you've had a chance to reduce their trump holding.

Leading an ace generally costs you half a trick. This is because if you don't lead the suit in which you have the ace, you might be able to lead trump, drive them out of trump where they have their short spades, and, as a result, end up taking three spades tricks. Often the shortness is in dummy where their short trump is.

In time and as your wisdom grows, you might find an instance when you should lead the ace. But for now you should adopt the following two rules:

- If you have at least three cards in the suit, don't lead an ace on opening lead.

- Don't underlead an ace on opening lead.

Period. End of story. Incidentally, I have not yet found the wisdom alluded to in the preceding paragraph and follow these rules religiously.

ALERT

The idea against underleading an ace is only applicable when you're defending against a suit contract. It doesn't apply when you're defending no trump contracts, when the preferred standard lead of your fourth from longest and strongest often requires you to underlead an ace.

Leading Trump

"When in doubt, lead trump," is another ancient axiom of bridge. Sometimes a trump lead is the best lead you can make. More often it's not. It's not a good lead when you or your partner are short in a suit and you'll want to ruff some tricks yourselves. It is a good lead in the following situations:

- When dummy might be short in a suit and declarer will want to ruff his losers.

- When you and your partner have a lot of HCP in outside suits.

The question is, how do you know? From the bidding! Following are situations in which a trump lead is advised.

- If *all* of the following are true:

  - You and your partner bid to game in a competitive auction.

  - The ultimate declarer doubles you for penalty.

  - His partner pulls the double and puts him in game in their suit.

  You should lead trump because from the bidding you can deduce that declarer has a substantial holding in your suit whereas his partner is short. Ergo, the point of playing the hand will be for declarer to ruff in dummy the losers he holds in your suit. If you get off to a trump lead, you'll be cutting down his ability to ruff.

- Your partner opens the bidding at one no trump, but the opponents end up playing in a suit contract. The reason here should be obvious. Your partner has a good high-card holding and opponents are going to try to ruff or cross-ruff the hand. You should lead a trump to cut down this ability.

- If you make a takeout double and your partner leaves it in for penalty. You probably have only one trump and you should lead it.

- You and your opponents bid only one suit each, each partnership establishing a trump fit between them, and opponents end up in a partscore contract. You'll want to drive them out of trump in the hand where they're short in your suit.

Leading Doubletons

If you're leading a doubleton, you lead the higher card, then play the lower card at your next opportunity. This tells your partner that you only have two. It's called *going high-low*. The lead of a worthless doubleton is one of the least desirable leads in bridge, but sometimes you have no choice.

The when-you-have-no-choice situation can appear if, for example, you're defending a heart contract and hold a hand like the following:

♠ AQ73
♥ Q72
♦ 83
♣ Q843

You don't want to underlead your ace–queen of spades, your queen of hearts, or your queen of clubs. So your least-harmful lead is the 8 of Diamonds.

However, except in special circumstances, you shouldn't lead a doubleton when it's headed by an honor, like Kx, Qx, or Jx. You've got an opportunity to win a trick with your honor, so there's no reason to give that up by leading high-low from the doubleton, unless your partner has *freely* bid the suit.

DEFINITION

To bid a suit **freely** means that partner wasn't forced to bid it because you made some sort of forcing bid, like a takeout double.

If your partner has freely bid the suit, the lead of the king from Kx can be very profitable in two situations:

- If your partner has the ace, a presumable prospect, you should win the king. She'll win your next lead of your remaining card in the suit with her ace and return the suit for a possible ruff by you.

- If she's lacking the ace, in all probability she'll have the queen or queen–jack combination, so you'll be setting up her hand to win tricks by driving out opponents' ace.

Standard Leads Against Suit Contracts

The following list shows standard leads when you are on opening lead against a suit contract. The standard lead is bold and underlined:

Xx	xxx**X**
x**X**x	xxx**X**x
A**K**x	**T**9x
KQx	K**J**Tx
QJx	K**T**9x
JT9	Q**T**9x
KQT9	

Note the difference between opening leads against suit contracts and opening leads against no trump contracts (discussed earlier in this chapter). In a no trump defense, leading top connecting honors when you only have two connecting honors isn't a good lead. But against a suit contract top connecting honors of two connecting honors is a very good lead.

Note also that when you have the ace–king in a suit, you lead the king, not the ace. The only time you don't do this is if your ace–king is a doubleton. If you lead the ace and then the king, you're telling your partner that you're now void in the suit; so if she gets in before trump is pulled, you might be able to get a ruff if she leads the suit. The converse is that if you lead the king and then the ace, you're promising her that you have at least one more card in the suit.

Also, note the difference in standard lead when you hold KQT9. In no trump defense, you lead the queen, asking your partner to jettison her jack if she has it. Against a suit contract, you lead the king. Against a suit contract, you're trying to take your tricks before declarer can ruff them, so you're not trying to set up a long suit, as you would be if your were defending a no trump contract. Also, against a suit contract you're not so concerned about blocking and unblocking.

Leads Against Slams

If you're playing against a grand slam and you have an ace, it's probably going to be ruffed. Why would anybody in their right mind make a contract to take all the tricks without an ace unless that ace was of no concern to them?

The only reason the ace would be of no concern to them is if they're void in that suit. If you lead an ace, you're probably going to have it ruffed immediately. If so, you might be setting up a suit for them containing the king and queen, giving them a better chance of making their contract. Don't lead an ace against a grand slam contract in a suit for this reason.

To elaborate a little further on this, they might have to make a ruffing finesse to make the contract if they don't know where the ace is. Look at the following spade holding in a contract of seven hearts by East:

Partner
♠ 76432

West
♠ KQJT9

East (declarer)
♠ void

You
♠ A85

If you lead the ace on opening lead, you set up West's spades. If you don't lead the ace and East has a loser, he has to jettison it on West's spades. You're going to set the contract because East will have to take a ruffing finesse and it will lose.

However, against a small slam, many people like to lead an ace, figuring that then they only need one trick—probably not a good idea. Remember, aces were created to take kings and queens. You're not going to take a king or queen if you lead the ace, so even against a slam the lead of an ace is not a good idea unless it's the only trick in your hand and you can't see where you and your partner will take another trick. In that event, you better take your trick while you can.

But it's generally better to keep declarer in the dark as to who has the ace. You'll probably get to take it later and, if declarer doesn't know where it is, he might make a mistake if he has to guess on the location of an honor without knowing who has the ace. Look at the following hand:

♠ 975
♥ T632
♦ 84
♣ A842

You're defending against a contract of six diamonds and are on lead. Let's look at the entire club holding:

Partner
♣ Q74

West
♣ 532

East (declarer)
♣ KJT6

You
♣ A98

Declarer is probably going to have to guess the location of the ace and the queen. Without any clue, he'll have to lead from the board into his hand. If partner plays low and he guesses correctly and plays the jack, you'll be forced to play the ace and he'll make his slam. If he guesses incorrectly and plays the king, you win it with your ace and your partner should get the queen and you'll set him.

If you lead the ace at your first lead, however, you take this guess away from him. His king will then be a cold trick, and he'll probably correctly conclude from your lead that your partner has the queen. This illustrates why the opening lead of an ace is generally not a good idea, even against slam bids.

Leads Against Slams When Your Partner Doubles

A double of a slam by your partner should only be made as a lead-directing device. The reward of an extra 50 or 100 points simply isn't worth the penalty of having your opponents make a slam doubled. This is what the doubler, your beloved partner, is asking you to do when she doubles a slam:

- Lead the first suit bid by dummy if dummy has bid a nontrump suit.

- If dummy hasn't bid a suit other than trump but declarer has, lead the suit bid by declarer.

- If opponents have bid no other suit but trump, lead anything but trump.

- If you or your partner have bid a suit, don't lead it!

The Least You Need to Know

- When defending a no trump contract, generally the best lead is fourth from your longest and strongest suit.
- A double of a no trump contract asks for a specific lead.
- Don't lead or underlead an ace when defending a suit contract.
- Lead trump if you think opponents will have to ruff losers to make the contract.
- Leading a low card against a suit contract promises an honor in the suit.

In the Trenches: Defense After the Opening Lead

In This Chapter

- Signals: attitude and count
- Rule of 11
- Second hand low
- Third hand high
- Unblocking

Defense, for me, is the most fun part of bridge. You have to communicate with your partner, without speaking, through the cards you play. When you click and get together to set a contract, it's just a wonderful feeling.

Play by Opening Leader's Partner to First Trick

The card played by the partner of the player making the opening lead to the first trick can set the tone for the entire defense of the hand. The player making the opening lead—I'll call her opening leader—is doing the best she can by paying attention to the bidding and correlating the bidding to her hand.

But she's leading with only the bidding as her knowledge. After she leads, the dummy is exposed and everyone knows where 26 of the 52 cards in the deck are located—the 13 in their hand and the 13 in dummy. If your partner is on opening lead, your first opportunity to communicate with her is in your play to her lead. There are two ways to communicate with your partner when she makes the opening lead. You can either give her *count* or you can give her *attitude*.

Cards That Convey Your Attitude

In Chapter 22, I explained that opening leader can use cards that frown and cards that smile by the denomination of the card she leads. Playing a small card promises an honor in the suit being played, so it smiles. Playing a middle card, such as a 7, denies an honor, so it frowns. However, when playing to your partner's opening lead, you indicate your pleasure or displeasure in just the opposite manner:

- A small card played to your partner's opening lead frowns because it says that you don't like the suit and have no help in it.

- A high card played to your partner's opening lead smiles because it tells her that you do like this suit and probably have an honor in it.

Count

Count is the number of cards you have in the suit your partner led, usually limited to telling her whether you have an even or odd number of cards. Some players prefer to have count, rather than attitude, indicated on the first trick. This is the way you indicate count:

- If your first two cards played to the trick are low to high, you have an odd number of cards in the suit. So if your first card is the 3 and your next card is the 7, you have an odd number of cards in the suit—probably three or five.

- If your first two cards played to the trick are high to low, you have an even number of cards in the suit. So if your first card is the 7 and your next card is the 3, you have an even number of cards in the suit—probably two or four.

> **TRICKS OF THE TRADE**
>
> Whether your first play to your partner's trick conveys count or attitude is strictly a function of your partnership agreement. Before you start playing, make certain you have this understood. There is no right or wrong. The important thing is that you agree.

Rule of 11

The rule of 11 applies when your partner has led fourth from longest and strongest. You, as opening leader's partner, simply subtract the value of her opening lead from 11. That tells you how many higher cards are in all three hands other than opening leader's hand. To help make sense of this, take a look at the following hands:

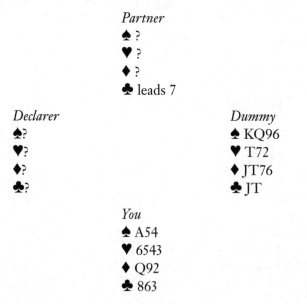

Partner
♠ ?
♥ ?
♦ ?
♣ leads 7

Declarer
♠?
♥?
♦?
♣?

Dummy
♠ KQ96
♥ T72
♦ JT76
♣ JT

You
♠ A54
♥ 6543
♦ Q92
♣ 863

Your partner leads the 7 of clubs through dummy to you. What's the club holding? Before you look at the answer, try to figure it out. Your partner led fourth from longest and strongest, so you should have knowledge of the configuration of the club holding by using the rule of 11. Have you figured it out?

Subtract 7 from 11. You get 4. That means that there are only four cards higher than the 7 of clubs in the three hands other than opening leader's hand. That includes your own hand. So you have one card higher than the 7 (the 8). That leaves three cards higher than the 7 in declarer's hand and dummy's hand combined. You can see that dummy has two cards higher than the 7. That means that declarer only has one card higher than the 7 in his hand. Following are the actual hands:

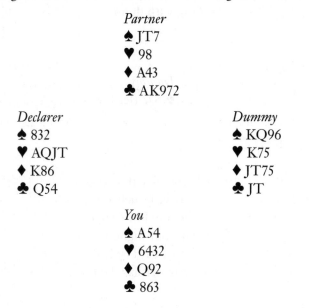

Partner
♠ JT7
♥ 98
♦ A43
♣ AK972

Declarer
♠ 832
♥ AQJT
♦ K86
♣ Q54

Dummy
♠ KQ96
♥ K75
♦ JT75
♣ JT

You
♠ A54
♥ 6432
♦ Q92
♣ 863

Contract: Two no trump

Opening Lead: 7 of clubs

The rule of 11 works. I'm not going to explain how or why, but it does. If you can rely on your partner to lead fourth from longest and strongest, you can determine where most of the cards are by using it. Assuming that the one card declarer holds in his hand that is higher than the 7 of clubs is not the ace, when you get in with your ace of spades and return the 6 of clubs, your partner is going to win four club tricks. That's because when she plays her ace and king, the other two honors will fall and the rest of her clubs will be good. Your partnership will be cemented.

Second Hand Low

"Second hand low" is an axiom that's probably as old as the game. It means that when you're defending and the lead is from your right (in other words, you're the second player to play to the trick), you play a low card unless the card led is an honor or there's some other good reason to play high. The reason is that it puts declarer on the guess as to where the high cards are. Your partner will have the last play, and declarer won't know what she has until she plays. If you play high, it simply takes this obligation to guess away from her.

Unless there's a reason to play high, playing high by second hand just gives away a trick uselessly. Look at the following holding with dummy as your RHO and on lead:

	Partner	
	♠ ?	
Dummy		*Dummy*
♠ ?		♠ 852 (leads deuce)
	You	
	♠ Q76	

Opponents lead the deuce from dummy. If you play the queen, it will probably lose to the ace or king. What's the point of going up with such a high card when declarer has to play behind you and your partner plays behind him? He doesn't know which hand has the missing cards. If you voluntarily play your highest card, it removes the guess from him. If you play high, he *knows* where that card is! It just goes against common sense. Whenever you're second hand, your partner has the last play. Keep declarer in the dark until your partner plays.

This might seem elementary, but you should always put declarer to the guess. The time when most people are tempted to play high as second hand is when they hold an ace, and the king is in the dummy to their left. Look at this holding:

	Partner	
	♠ ?	
Dummy		*Declarer*
♠ KJ7		♠ leads 4
	You	
	♠ A832	

Declarer leads low to the king–jack. If you go up with the ace, it makes the king a winner for sure. Worse, it takes the guess on the queen away from him. If you play low, declarer must guess both the ace and the queen. If he guesses you for the queen and your partner for the ace, he'll play the jack and your partner will win the queen. You'll end up with two tricks: your ace and your partner's queen. If you play the ace, you take part of this guess away from him and give him a sure trick with the king. If your partner has the doubleton queen, you'll be giving opponents two club tricks by going up high as second hand, if declarer then plays for the drop.

When to Play High in Second Hand

Sometimes you must go against the second-hand-low axiom and play high. This occurs when you have connecting honors and to play low could give your opponents a deep finesse and a gift trick. Look at the following hand, where you're holding second hand, playing behind declarer:

Partner
♠ ?

Dummy
♠ AT7

Declarer
♠ leads 4

You
♠ QJ7

Declarer, sitting as your RHO, leads a low spade. You're not sure, but there's a good possibility declarer has the king of spades. If you play low, he could play the 10 of spades, which will win the trick if declarer has the king. Then declarer plays the ace and goes back to his hand for the king and you have lost all three spade tricks.

However, if you play high as second hand here, and go up with your jack, you force out the ace. That way you have a third-round winner in your queen because it's protected by the 7 of spades and you're sitting behind the king.

But there's an exception to this rule, too. If you're sitting with the following, you should not go up with the jack:

Partner
♠ ?

Dummy
♠ AKT

Declarer
♠ leads 4

You
♠ QJ7

Why? Because dummy has both the ace and the king. Declarer thus has the ability to finesse twice. In the preceding example the ace and king were in different hands, one in dummy and one in declarer, so the queen-jack may only be finessed once. Here, with the ace and king both in dummy with the 10, declarer can play the 10 and come back and finesse again, so splitting your honors doesn't accomplish here what it does in the prior hand. If you go up with the jack, declarer might be able to figure out that you also had the queen, and he'll just come back to his hand to finesse you again. He has absolutely nothing to lose to come back to his hand and try another finesse, because if you have a doubleton it will fall.

If you don't have a doubleton, but your partner has the queen, he's going to lose it anyway unless it was a queen doubleton. But that's unlikely because why would you voluntarily play the jack if your partner is short in the suit? That would mean you have several cards in the suit. It just doesn't make sense. So if you play the jack, he's definitely going to come back to his hand and finesse again. In this instance, you should go low and hope that declarer will figure you don't have both the queen and the jack (or you would have played the jack) and will go up with the king. You don't have much to gain by going up with the jack here, and you have a trick to gain if you go low and declarer guesses wrong.

Covering an Honor

Generally, if the person on lead leads an honor, second hand should play a higher honor (called "covering an honor") if she has it in her hand. There are exceptions to this rule, however. Second hand should not cover an honor in the following circumstances:

If the honor is led from a sequence. Consider the following holding in dummy, your RHO:

<u>**Hand 1:**</u>

Partner
♠ ?

Declarer
♠ ?

Dummy
♠ QJ73 (on lead)

You
♠ K64

<u>**Hand 2:**</u>

Partner
♠ ?

Declarer
♠ ?

Dummy
♠ JT3 (on lead)

You
♠ Q87

In both instances, dummy holds honors in sequence, so if you hold the king in Hand 1, or the queen in Hand 2, you should *not* cover the honor the first time it's led. If your partner can take the trick, she will. If she can't take the trick, you can cover the second honor. You will have lost nothing because the only way you will have a trick in the first hand is if your partner has Txx. And if she does, you protect her by covering the second honor. In the second hand, if your partner can't take the first trick, you're out of luck in this suit because opponents have four of the top five honors. It's just a matter of time before they capture yours.

If your honor is going to be good if you don't cover it. This occurs when declarer only has a certain number of times he can finesse you, and you have more cards than that to protect your honor. This generally applies when you're playing no trump or trump is the suit that is led. The reason is that if you give away three tricks in a non-trump suit in a suit contract, declarer will probably be able to trump his fourth card. Consider the following:

Partner
♠ ?

Declarer   *Dummy*
♠ ?   ♠ Q5 (leads Queen)

You
♠ K743

Defending no trump, or if this is a trump lead, you would be foolish to cover the queen if it's led because you can protect your king. Look what happens. The queen is led. You play low and the queen wins. Then the 5 is led and you go low again. Declarer wins with the jack. Declarer plays the ace. You can discard your third card and retain your king. The only way declarer can get your king is if you voluntarily play it.

Which Honors to Cover

In defending a suit contract, if you're in a situation that calls for you to cover an honor, you should cover *any* honor with your honor. So if the jack or 10 *empty*, meaning it's the top of several unconnected cards, is on the board and the jack or 10 is led, you should cover if you have the king.

Why? Look at the following:

Hand 1:

Partner
♠ JT6

Declarer   *Dummy*
♠ A982   ♠ Q5 (leads Queen)

You
♠ K743

Hand 2:

Partner
♠ T96

Declarer
♠ AJ82

Dummy
♠ Q5 (leads Queen)

You
♠ K743

Hand 1: If you don't cover the honor, declarer gets two spade tricks he'd never get. Your partner is sitting with the jack and the 10, both of which will be winners if you cover the queen. If you don't cover the queen, declarer will let it ride and your partner can't take it. The queen will emerge as a winner in addition to declarer's ace. If you cover the queen, declarer takes the ace and your partner's jack and 10 are now the two highest cards in the suit.

Hand 2: This is a very common occurrence. If you don't cover the queen immediately, declarer makes three spade tricks because the queen wins, then he finesses the king and the ace wins, too. If you cover, it makes his jack good, but then your partner takes the 10. So if you cover, you save a trick.

Third Hand High

"Third hand high" is another axiom that's been around since creation. It means that if you're the third player to play to the trick and your partner leads low, you play as high a card as you can as long as it's higher than the card played by dummy.

Bottom of a Sequence

You should play the bottom card of your highest sequence. For example, your partner led the 3 of clubs and your RHO plays low, and you hold the following:

♣ QJ75

You should play the jack. If opponents take the trick with the king, it indicates to your partner that you might have the queen. However, if you were to play the queen it would absolutely promise your partner that you did *not* have the jack.

Finesse Against Dummy When You Can

Look at the following holding. This is a situation that occurs again and again. Even good players misplay it:

Partner (on lead)
♦ 3

Declarer   *Dummy*
♦ ?   ♦ K54 plays the 4

You
♦ AJT

What do you play? If declarer has the queen, he'll take the trick. If declarer's queen is a singleton, you won't ever get your ace. Should you play your ace or play low, hoping your partner has the queen? If your partner has the queen, you can wait until she gets the lead again. She'll lead through the king again, and the king will never win a trick. If you play your ace, you make the king a sure trick. What to do?

Answer: Your partner led fourth from longest and strongest. That means that she has a maximum of five diamonds. You have three. Dummy has three. Declarer must have at least two. That means you should play the 10 because you should still get your ace, even if declarer has the queen.

If you're playing in a suit contract and you think that declarer has a singleton honor, however, you should play your ace. This would occur if, in the above situation, your partner had led the deuce and both you and dummy had four diamonds instead of three each. That pretty much marks the suit as 4–4–4–1, with declarer having the singleton. In this instance, play your ace while you can.

Unblocking in No Trump

When defending a no trump contract, especially one in game, you are working with fewer HCP than your opponents. When you know your partner is trying to set up a long suit, you sometimes have to *unblock*, which means that you discard a high card, maybe a potential winner, in order to enable your partner to run her long suit. To help you understand this concept, let's look at a hand where you're defending a contract of three no trump:

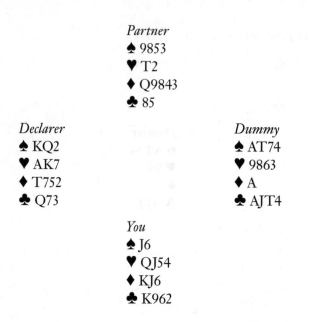

Partner
♠ 9853
♥ T2
♦ Q9843
♣ 85

Declarer
♠ KQ2
♥ AK7
♦ T752
♣ Q73

Dummy
♠ AT74
♥ 9863
♦ A
♣ AJT4

You
♠ J6
♥ QJ54
♦ KJ6
♣ K962

Your partner leads the 4 of diamonds. Dummy plays the singleton ace. You must unblock by discarding the jack of diamonds when you might otherwise be tempted to play the 6.

If you were to play the 6 on the first trick, then when you subsequently get on lead with your king of clubs you will play your king of diamonds, which wins. Then you return your last remaining diamond: the jack. That's the only entry into your partner's hand. But if your partner overtakes with the queen, declarer has the suit stopped with his 10.

Following is the layout of the cards if you originally play the 6 and then win the losing club finesse (after your opponent wins the ace of diamonds, he goes to his hand with a heart and then leads the queen of clubs, which you win with your king), after you have cashed your king of diamonds:

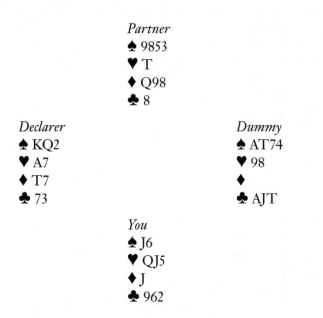

Partner
♠ 9853
♥ T
♦ Q98
♣ 8

Declarer
♠ KQ2
♥ A7
♦ T7
♣ 73

Dummy
♠ AT74
♥ 98
♦
♣ AJT

You
♠ J6
♥ QJ5
♦ J
♣ 962

You lead the jack of diamonds. If your partner lets it ride, there's no other way into her hand to allow her to cash her two remaining diamonds winners. So she has to overtake, which leaves declarer's 10 of diamonds as the highest card outstanding in the suit. He takes your partner's diamond lead and cashes his remaining winning tricks to make the contract. But look at how the cards lay if you originally play the jack of diamonds under the ace in dummy on your partner's opening lead:

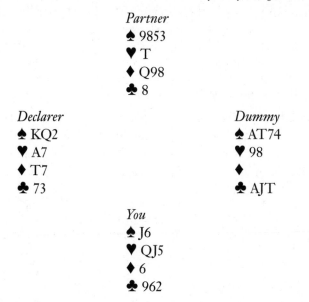

Partner
♠ 9853
♥ T
♦ Q98
♣ 8

Declarer
♠ KQ2
♥ A7
♦ T7
♣ 73

Dummy
♠ AT74
♥ 98
♦
♣ AJT

You
♠ J6
♥ QJ5
♦ 6
♣ 962

See what a big difference that makes? After you take your king of diamonds, you now lead your 6 of diamonds through declarer's 10. Declarer can't win because if he plays low, your partner will win the trick with the 8 and then pull declarer's 10 with his queen. If declarer plays his 10, your partner wins with her queen and runs her remaining diamonds winners.

To recap: If you unblock on your partner's opening lead by discarding your jack and keeping your little 6, you defeat the contract. If you just discard the 6 on her opening lead, you can't defeat the contract.

As an additional bonus to the discard of the jack instead of the 6, it signals your partner to continue the suit because you have help.

The opportunity to unblock usually arises in the following circumstances:

- When you have three cards in your partner's suit

- When you also have high cards in your partner's long suit, but only one low card. You must preserve that low card as an entry back into your partner's hand.

What Card to Return to Your Partner

When defending a no trump contract, there's another unblocking rule you should follow when you hold three cards in your partner's suit headed by the ace (commonly called "three to the ace"). After you win the ace, you should lead your highest card back to her. For example, if your original holding was ace–honor–low and you took the trick with the ace, return the honor, not the low card. This has several desirable effects:

- It leads through declarer and possibly finesses him.

- It informs your partner where the missing high cards in the suit are located. If you take the ace and return the 10, she should know that you don't have the cards in between the ace and the 10. So she can mentally remove the cards she sees in dummy and the cards she sees in her own hand and place the missing cards in declarer's hand.

- It unblocks your suit for your partner. If you lead low and your partner wins and returns a lower card than your remaining honor, you win, but can't get back to her.

Return Lead with Four Cards in Your Partner's Suit

When you have four cards in your partner's suit, and you know that your partner has led fourth from longest and strongest, you need not be too concerned with unblocking. That is because you and your partner have the majority of the cards in the suit between you.

When you have three cards in your partner's suit, it's important that you return your highest card, as explained in the preceding section. However, what card should you return when you started out with four cards in your partner's suit?

The answer is that you should return the card you would have led had you been on lead—the card that was originally your fourth highest. Look at the following holding between you and your partner defending a no trump contract:

Partner (on lead)	*You*
♣ KT652	♣ Q743

Your partner leads the 5; you play the queen, which loses to the ace. Declarer loses a finesse to you. What card do you now play to return to your partner? You return the 3, the card that was your fourth highest in the suit originally. Now, if you have agreed that when you have three cards you return the highest remaining card, your partner knows that you started with either four or two cards in her suit. Why? Because the 3 is the lowest outstanding card in the suit. If you had three cards in the suit, you would have returned a higher card.

Now your partner should be able to determine the exact holding in her suit by looking at dummy and looking at the card you returned. Your partner wins with the 10 and comes back with the king, thereby dropping opponents' remaining jack. What card do you play now? Here's another unblocking situation, and you must be alert for it. If you were to just play low now, you have the 7 and the 4 left; your 7 will take your partner's next lead, which will be the 6. Here's the holding after your partner gets in with the 10:

Partner	*You*
♣ K62	♣ 74

When your partner leads the king, you have to choose between playing the 7 and the 4. Here's the holding if you play the 4 on her king:

Partner	*You*
♣ 62	♣ 7

When your partner leads the 6 next, your only remaining card is the 7, which will win the trick. Now you're out of clubs while your partner is sitting across from you with a good club trick in her hand and no entry.

As you can see, this is an unblocking situation. When your partner leads her king, you drop your 7 of clubs and retain your 4. Here's the holding if you play the 7 on her king instead of the 4:

Partner	*You*
♣ 62	♣ 4

Then when she leads her 6, you play your 4, leaving her in the lead to cash her deuce and set the contract.

Leading After the Opening Lead

Ah, those axioms. Here's another, in iambic meter, that generally holds you in good stead:

> When the dummy's on the right,
>
> Lead the weakest suit in sight!

If you get the lead after the opening lead, and you're sitting in front of declarer so that the dummy is your RHO, you have the advantage that you don't have on opening lead of seeing the cards in dummy. In this situation, lead the suit in which dummy is weakest.

Another rule if dummy is on your right is that it's unwise to lead into a tenace composed of honors, like the ace–queen, in dummy. Look at the following holding in dummy after you win the opening trick with your singleton king of clubs, so you can't return your partner's lead:

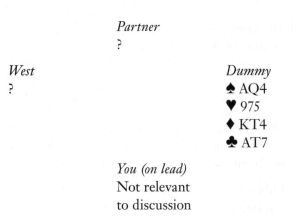

Partner
?

West   *Dummy*
?   ♠ AQ4
                                                        ♥ 975
                                                        ♦ KT4
                                                        ♣ AT7

You (on lead)
Not relevant
to discussion

If you lead a spade, you take the guess on a possible finesse from declarer and put your partner in a terrible spot. If she has the king, it renders it fairly useless because the queen will win if she ducks and the ace will take it if she plays the king.

If you lead a diamond, it once again removes a possible guess from declarer. You might not know where the ace is. If your partner has it, declarer won't know where it is, either. Why make life easier for him? If you lead a diamond, he'll play low and your partner will have to either play the ace (making the king good) or duck (making the king good).

Hearts is the weakest suit in sight, and that's what you should lead because you're leading through declarer. If he has broken honors, he has to guess what to play with no help from dummy. As an example, look at the actual heart holding:

Partner
♥ AT6

Declarer   *Dummy*
♥ KJ2   ♥ 975

You
♥ Q843

You lead the 3 of hearts. What's declarer to do? Play the jack? Play the king? Play low? If he plays low, your partner will win with any card higher than the 9. If he plays the jack and your partner has the queen, he's going to lose. If he plays the king and your partner has the ace, he's going to lose. As the cards lay, his correct play is the jack, which will force out your partner's ace. But he has to guess. Make him.

The Holdup

I introduced the holdup—the refusal to win a trick—in Chapter 20 as a tool to use as declarer to cut off communication between defenders' hands. It's also useful in defense to keep declarer from getting to the spot where his long suit is located. Look at the following hand:

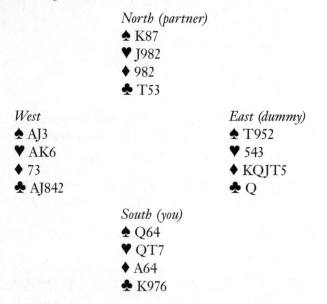

North (partner)
♠ K87
♥ J982
♦ 982
♣ T53

West
♠ AJ3
♥ AK6
♦ 73
♣ AJ842

East (dummy)
♠ T952
♥ 543
♦ KQJT5
♣ Q

South (you)
♠ Q64
♥ QT7
♦ A64
♣ K976

West reached an optimistic contract of three no trump and your partner led the deuce of hearts. West took your queen with his ace. It's clear that the only chance he has to make this hand is to set up his diamonds and take four diamond tricks. He should take two club tricks and with the three tricks he has with the ace–king of hearts and the ace of spades, that would make his contract.

If he leads low to his king of diamonds and you take it with your ace immediately, he'll get the lead right back on whatever you lead next and will get back over to dummy and run his diamonds.

But if you hold up on his diamonds, it's unlikely he'll be able to get back there after you take your ace of diamonds. Let's look at it. He takes the ace of hearts and leads low to the king of diamonds, which you allow him to take. He then leads the queen of diamonds, which you also allow him to win. When he leads the jack, you're forced to take it because your ace is the only remaining diamond in your hand. Now the hands look like this:

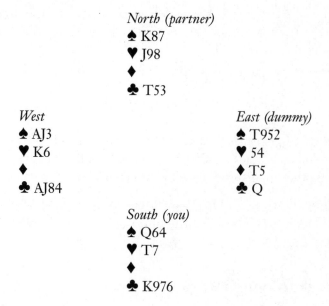

North (partner)
♠ K87
♥ J98
♦
♣ T53

West
♠ AJ3
♥ K6
♦
♣ AJ84

East (dummy)
♠ T952
♥ 54
♦ T5
♣ Q

South (you)
♠ Q64
♥ T7
♦
♣ K976

So far he's taken three tricks and you've taken one. He can take two more clubs, a heart, and a spade—maybe two. Unless he can get to the dummy to cash his two good diamonds, he's history. As you can see, there's no way he can now get to the board. By holding up and not taking your ace of diamonds until the third lead of diamonds, you destroyed his transportation to the board and assured the defeat of the contract. Had you taken your ace of diamonds at the first trick, making his contract would have been a piece of cake.

Signals

When a suit is led and you have no more cards in it, you can use the situation as an opportunity to communicate to your partner what you have in your hand, and what you want her to lead if she gets the lead.

High-Card Discard Is Encouraging

There are several methods of discarding to communicate with your partner. The standard way is to discard a high card in a suit you want her to lead. Look at the following holding in your hand:

♠
♥ KQ92
♦ 872
♣ 752

Spades is trump and your opponent is pulling trump. Your partner still has one spade in her hand, so your opponent leads another high spade to pull your partner's last trump. You should use this opportunity to tell your partner about your hand.

A good discard here would be the 9 of hearts, telling your partner that if she gets the lead you want her to lead hearts. Discarding a high card in a suit that wasn't led tells your partner that you like that suit.

Low-Card Discard Is Discouraging

If you discard a low card, you discourage your partner from leading that suit. So if you were to discard the deuce of clubs or the deuce of diamonds, you'd be telling your partner that you don't want her to lead those suits because you don't have much in them. If you discard your deuce of clubs, however, she can't tell which of the other two suits you want led. So if you can discard high without harming your holding, you should make an encouraging discard.

Sometimes, however, it's inconvenient to discard a high card, and it's better to discourage another suit, implying that you like your good suit. Let's assume that the hands look like this:

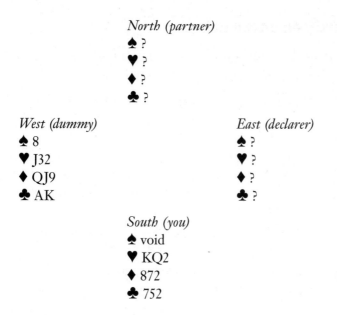

North (partner)
♠ ?
♥ ?
♦ ?
♣ ?

West (dummy)
♠ 8
♥ J32
♦ QJ9
♣ AK

East (declarer)
♠ ?
♥ ?
♦ ?
♣ ?

South (you)
♠ void
♥ KQ2
♦ 872
♣ 752

East is declarer and is pulling trump. As mentioned, there's still one out in your partner's hand, so East leads the ace of spades. What do you discard?

You don't want to discard the queen of hearts, because that's an extremely important card that you can't intelligently give up. You can't discard the deuce of hearts because that would be discouraging.

You clearly wouldn't want her to lead a club with the ace and king on the board. However, there's a good way in this hand to tell her to lead a heart without throwing away a good hearts trick: you should discard the deuce of diamonds. That tells her that you don't like diamonds. Your partner can look at the dummy and determine that you clearly shouldn't like clubs much, either. So by discarding the low diamond in your hand, you're telling her that you want her to lead a heart.

The Least You Need to Know

- If you give attitude to your partner's opening lead, a low card tells her you don't like the suit and a high card says you do like the suit.

- If you give count to your partner's opening lead, your first two plays are high to low to show an even number of cards in the suit. If your first two cards are low to high, you show an odd number of cards in the suit.

- Using the rule of 11, if your partner leads fourth from longest and strongest, you subtract the number of the card she leads from 11 and the result is the number of cards higher than the card led in the three hands other than opening leader's hand.

- If you're second hand, you should generally play low, unless you're covering an honor.

- If you're third hand, you should generally play high.

Guide to Bids and Responses

Opening Bids

Opening Bid	Requirements
One of a suit	13–21 points, at least five cards in a major suit, at least three cards in a minor suit.
One no trump	15–17 HCP; no singletons or voids, and not more than two doubletons.
Two diamonds, two hearts, two spades	At least 22 points, at least five cards in the suit or a guarantee of at least nine tricks if opening a major and ten tricks if opening a minor.
Two clubs	Same as above, or 22–24 points with no five–card suit except clubs.
Two no trump	20–21 HCP, no singletons or voids, and not more than two doubletons.
Three of a suit	A seven-card suit; a suit headed by at least the queen–10; 4–9 HCP; no outside ace; not more than one outside king; when opening in a minor suit, no four-card major.
Three no trump	25–26 HCP; no singletons or voids, and not more than two doubletons.
Four in a suit	At least eight cards in length; at least two of the top four honors in your long suit; 4–9 HCP; no outside ace; only one outside king; if opening a minor suit, no four-card major.
Five in a suit	Must be clubs or diamonds, Eight- or nine-card suit, suit must be headed by at least two of the top four honors, 4–9 HCP, no outside ace, not more than one outside king.

Responses to Partner's Opening Bid

Opening Bid	Holding	Response
One of a suit	0–5 points	Pass
	6–16 points	One of a higher-ranking four-card suit at the one level
	10–16 points plus a five-card major or four-card minor	Two of the long suit
One of a major	6–9 points with at least three cards in opener's suit	Two of opener's suit
	6–9 points w/o a higher-ranking four-card suit or at least three cards in opener's suit, no singletons or voids	One no trump
	10–12 points and three or four cards in opener's suit	Three of opener's suit
	13–15 HCP, balanced hand, stoppers in the three unbid suits, no four-card higher-ranking major	Two no trump
	16–18 HCP, balanced hand, stoppers in the three unbid suits, no four-card higher-ranking major	Three no trump
	16 or more points, does not deny four cards in opener's suit, can be totally unbalanced	Jump shift
	6–10 points, five cards in opener's suit, at least one singleton or void	Jump to game
One of a minor	6–9 points, no four-card major, five cards in opener's suit	Two of opener's suit
	10–12 points, no four-card major, five cards in opener's suit	Three of opener's suit
	12–15 HCP, no four-card major, stoppers in all suits unbid by opener	Two no trump
	16–18 HCP, no four-card major, stoppers in all suits unbid by opener	Three no trump

Opening Bid	Holding	Response
One no trump	0–7 HCP	Pass
	0–7 HCP, at least five cards in either hearts or spades, or six cards in diamonds	Two of long suit
	8–9 points; no four-card major	Two no trump
	8+ points; at least one four-card major	Two clubs (Stayman)
	10+ points; five-card major	Two clubs, then jump to three of your suit if partner doesn't bid your suit; jump to four in your suit if she bids your suit
	9+ points, a six-card major	Jump to game in your suit
	10–14 HCP, no four-card major	Three no trump
	15–16 HCP, no four-card major	Four no trump (quantitative, not forcing)
	17–19 HCP, no four-card major	Six no trump
	20+ HCP, no four-card major	Seven no trump
	6–7 HCP, broken six-card minor with nothing outside	Jump to three of minor
Two no trump	0–4 HCP	Pass
	5–10 HCP; no four-card major, no singletons or voids	Three no trump
	11–13 HCP, no trump distribution	Four no trump
	14–15 HCP, no trump distribution	Six no trump
	16+ HCP, no trump distribution	Seven no trump
	5+ HCP, four-card major	Three clubs (Stayman)
	5+ points, six-card major	Four of your major
Two diamonds, two hearts, or two spades (Strong)	Five-card suit headed by king-jack	Bid the five-card suit
	3+ points, at least one king, three-card support for your partner's suit	Raise partner's suit one level
	0+ points, no five-card suit, less than three-card support for your partner's suit	Two no trump

Responses to Partner's Opening Bid

Opening Bid	Holding	Response
Two Clubs	0+ points; no five-card suit; less than three-card support for your partner's suit	2 Diamonds
	4+ points; five-card suit headed by king-jack	Bid the five-card suit at two level
Three of a suit	0–14 points; no support for your partner's suit	Pass, partner is weak
	7–14 points; support for your partner's suit	Raise partner's suit
	0–6 points	Pass
	15+ points; a good five-card suit; no support for your partner's suit	Bid your long suit (forcing)
Four in a minor	Less than extra values	Pass
	Extra values	Bid game or explore for slam
Four in a major	Less than extra values	Pass
	Extra values	Explore for slam if your hand justifies it; remember, your partner is weak, even though the opening bid is game

Opener's Rebid After Opening One of a Suit

Opener's Bid	Holding	Response
One of a new suit at the one level	13–15 points, four cards in a suit higher ranking than the suit bid by responder	One of your higher-ranking suit
	13–15 points, less than six cards in your suit; balanced hand	One no trump in responder's suit
	13–15 points, six cards in your suit	Rebid your suit at the two level
	13–15 points, less than six cards in your suit, a four-card suit lower ranking than your opening suit	Bid your lower-ranking four-card suit at the two level
	13–15 points; less than six cards in your suit, but four-card support for your partner's suit	Raise partner's suit at the two level
	18–19 points, all unbid suits stopped	Two no trump
	20–21 points, all unbid suits stopped	Three no trump
	16–18 points, six-card opening suit	Jump to three of opening suit
	17+ points, five cards in opening suit, four cards in higher-ranking suit	Reverse to four-card suit
	19+ points, a second biddable suit	Jump shift to second suit
	16–19 points, four cards in your partner's major suit bid	Jump to three of partner's major suit
	20+ points, four-card support for your partner's major suit bid	Jump to game in partner's suit

Opener's Bid	Holding	Response
New suit at two level without jumping	13–15 points, five-card opening suit, less than three cards in your partner's major suit bid or less than four cards in your partner's minor suit bid; unbid suits stopped; no singletons or voids	Two no trump
	Same, but with support for your partner's suit	Raise partner's suit
	16–19 points, support for your partner's major suit	Jump raise partner's suit
	16–19 points, no support for your partner's suit, unbid suits stopped	Three no trump
	17+ points; five cards in opening suit; four cards in higher ranking suit	Reverse to four- card suit
	19+ points, a second biddable suit	Jump shift to second suit
One no trump	13–15 points, balanced hand	Pass
	13–15 points, a singleton or void	Two of a lower ranking suit
	13–15 points, six-card suit or a good five-card suit if your hand is unbalanced	Rebid your opening suit at the two level
	16–18 points, no singleton or void	Two no trump
	16–18 points, six-card suit	Jump rebid your suit at the three level
	17+ points, unbalanced	Reverse
	19+ points, unbalanced	Jump shift
	19+ points, no singleton or void	Three no trump
Two no trump after major suit opening	13–15 points, six-card suit	Four of your suit
	13–15 points, five-card suit	Three no trump
	16+ points	Bid a new suit (forcing) for a slam invitation
Two no trump after a minor suit opening	13–17 points, balanced	Three no trump or four in a suit
	18+ points, balanced	Four no trump (quantitative) four in a suit as a slam invitation

Opener's Bid	Holding	Response
Three no trump	13–15 points, balanced	Pass
	13–15 points, a singleton or void	Four in a suit
	16+ points, balanced	Four no trump (quantitative)
	16+ points, a singleton or void	Four in a suit as a slam invitation
Jump shift	13–15 points, five-card opening suit	Lowest–no trump bid available
	13–15 points, six-card suit	Rebid opening suit
	16+ points	Jump to three no trump
One level raise of your suit	13–15 points	Pass
	16–19 points	Raise to three level if a major suit, two no trump if a minor
	20+ points	Jump to game in your suit if a major, bid three no trump if a minor
Jump raise of your major suit	13–19 points	Four of your suit (game)
	20+ points	Four no trump (Blackwood)
Jump raise of your minor suit	13–15 points, unbid suits stopped	Three no trump
	13–19 points unbalanced	Four of suit, or new suit, or pass
	20+ points	Explore slam
Three no trump after major suit opening	13–15 points	Four of your suit (game)
	16+ points	Four no trump (Blackwood)
Three no trump after minor suit opening	13–15 points	Pass
	16+ points, no singletons or voids	Bid slam or explore slam

Other Bridge Variations

This book has concentrated on how to play rubber bridge, which is by far the most popular version of the game. However, there are other forms of bridge that are just as much fun.

Duplicate Bridge

In duplicate bridge, everybody plays the same hands. Duplicate is played by eight players or more. In tournaments, there are thousands of players. After bidding, the hands are played in the same way, but the cards aren't put in the middle of the table when playing to each trick, as is done in rubber bridge.

In duplicate, each player plays his card on the table in front of him. When the trick is completed, each player keeps the card in front of him, placing it face down horizontally if he wins the trick or vertically if the opponents win the trick.

When the hand concludes, each player takes his cards and places them in a duplicate board, which has spaces for each of the four hands: North, East, West, and South. After a certain number of boards is played—usually between two and five—all boards are passed to the next lower-ranking table.

The players sitting North-South remain stationary. The players sitting East-West move to the next higher-ranking table after the set of boards is played. Players move up. Boards move down.

At the end of the evening all East-West pairs have played the same hands and all North-South pairs have played the same hands. Scoring is based on how your scores on each hand compare with the scores of the other players who played the hands. For example, if you bid and make a small slam but everyone else bids and makes a grand slam on that hand, you get the worst score on the hand: zero.

It's very competitive. One of the big advantages is that winning doesn't depend on the luck of the deal because everyone plays the same cards. If you have a Yarborough, every player sitting in your seat will have to play that Yarborough. Whoever does the best with it will have the highest score for that board.

Chicago

Chicago, also known as Four-deal bridge, is a very popular type of bridge that shortens the normal game of rubber bridge. Instead of playing until one pair wins two games—which can last a long time if one pair does a lot of defensive bidding—Chicago consists of one round of four hands, scored as follows:

1. For the first hand, neither pair is vulnerable.

2. For the second and third hands, dealer's pair is vulnerable.

3. For the fourth hand, both pairs are vulnerable.

Cards are dealt and played. The deal rotates to the left, as in rubber bridge. At the end of the fourth round, after each player has dealt once, the scores are added and a winner is determined.

You may play as many rounds as you like, and you may either change partners or not, as you like, after each round.

A nonvulnerable game gets a 300-point bonus above the line. A vulnerable game gets a 500-point bonus above the line. A partscore on the first three hands gets a 50-point bonus. If you get a partscore on the fourth hand, you get a 100-point bonus.

Resources

Bridge on the Internet

You can play bridge with live people on the internet without leaving your living room. You play with people all over the world, and games are available 24 hours a day, 7 days a week.

Players range from beginners to experts. You can join games on various levels: beginner, intermediate, advanced, or expert. You can also join any table you want and just watch, without playing.

Here are four online bridge games:

- BridgeBase (bridgebase.com)
- Microsoft (zone.msn.com/en/bridge/default) You must access this website using Internet Explorer.
- OKbridge (okbridge.com)
- Swan Games (swangames.com)

100 honors   Four of the top five cards in the trump suit in one hand. A player holding 100 honors receives a bonus of 100 points above the line.

150 honors   All five of the top honors in the trump suit in one hand. A player holding 150 honors receives a bonus of 150 points above the line.

150 aces   All four aces in one hand when the hand is played in no trump. A player holding 150 aces receives a bonus of 150 points above the line.

4–3–3–3   Description of a totally balanced hand, with four cards in one suit and three cards in the other three suits.

above the line   Points entered on the scoresheet above the horizontal line for overtricks, bonuses, and penalties. These points don't count toward making game.

attitude   A signal to your partner telling her whether you like the suit she led or not. A high card generally indicates you like the suit; a low card generally indicates you don't like the suit and discourages her from continuing it if she retains the lead.

auction   A series of bids between the partnerships to obtain the contract.

balancing   To make a bid or double at a low level to keep the auction from being passed out after opponents have stopped bidding and there have been two consecutive passes.

below the line   Points entered on the scoresheet below the horizontal line indicating the points scored for exactly the number of tricks bid and made.

bid   Any call made by a player that predicts the number of tricks the player's pair will take in a specified trump or in no trump.

Blackwood   A conventional bid in which the bid of four no trump asks partner to respond with the number of aces in her hand. A response of five clubs means zero aces, five diamonds means one ace, five hearts means two aces, and five spades means three aces.

block   You block your partner's suit when your partner has several good cards remaining in a suit but you must take the trick because your only card in the suit is higher ranking than the remaining cards in your partner's suit, and there's no way back into your partner's hand to allow her to cash her tricks.

board   Another name for the exposed hand in dummy.

body cards   8s, 9s, and 10s.

book   The first six tricks taken by the declaring side. *Defenders' book* is the number of tricks required to be taken, after which the next trick won by defenders will set the contract.

bypass   Failing to bid a lower-ranking suit or a suit at a lower level to, instead, bid a higher-ranking suit or a suit at a higher level when bidding the lower-ranking suit or the suit at a lower level would be the standard bid.

call   Any bid, double, redouble, or pass.

Cappelletti   A conventional overcall in defense against a no trump opening by opponents. Double is penalty, two clubs shows a one-suited hand, two diamonds shows 5–5 in the majors, two hearts shows five hearts and an undesignated five-card minor, two spades shows five spades and an undesignated five-card minor (*see* Hamilton, Pottage). This name is used on the East Coast and in major portions of America.

cheaper minor   A bid of the lowest unbid minor suit available at the time of responder's second call. This is a standard method of making a weak response to a strong two-clubs opening bid.

clubs   The lowest ranking of the four suits in a deck of cards.

cold   To be able to make a contract easily with no chance of failure.

competing   To make a bid to contest with opponents without implying to your partner that you're interested in contracting for game.

competition   When both pairs are bidding to get the contract.

connecting honor   A holding of two consecutive honor cards in the same suit, like king–queen or jack–10.

contract   The commitment of the declaring side to win a specified number of tricks with a specified suit as trump or with no trump.

conventional bid   A bid with a defined meaning other than the standard meaning.

count   An indication of an even or odd number of cards in your hand by discarding high to low to indicate an even number of cards in the suit led, and low to high to indicate an odd number of cards in the suit led.

cover   Play by second or third hand of a higher card over the card played by opponent.

crossruff   The ability to ruff losers in different suits in the hands of both partners.

cue-bid   A bid of opponents' suit that conveys something to your partner other than a holding in that suit.

dealer   The person who distributes the cards in clockwise order; the player with the first opportunity to make a call.

declarer   The player who is playing the hand with her partner as dummy.

deuce   The two card of each suit.

diamonds   The second lowest ranking of the four suits.

direct seat   The player sitting as the LHO of opening bidder.

discard   The play of a nontrump card not of the suit led.

distribution points   Points in counting the hand for voids, singletons, and doubletons.

D0PI   Double = Zero, Pass = One. A response to Blackwood over interference telling your partner how many aces you have in your hand.

double   A call by an opponent of declarer that increases the value of tricks or undertricks made by declarer.

doubleton   Any total holding in a suit that is exactly two cards in length.

doubling into game   A double of a partial score that, if unsuccessful, will result in opponents getting at least 100 points below the line when they wouldn't have gotten 100 points below the line without the double.

down   Any hand that doesn't make the contracted number of tricks; synonymous with set. *See* undertricks.

down the line   To bid the higher-ranking suits of equal length first.

drawing trump   For declarer to lead trump until the opponents no longer have any trump in either of their hands.

drop-dead bid   A bid that asks your partner to pass and allow the bidder to play the hand in the bid made by the drop-dead bidder.

duck   To not take a trick when you have a high card that would enable you to win that trick.

dummy   The hand that belongs to declarer's partner. Dummy is always played face up on the table.

duplicate   The form of tournament bridge where each player plays the same hand as the other players sitting in the same direction (North, South, East, or West). This is accomplished by the hands being dealt into boards and the boards are passed from table to table. North-South remain stationary but the East-West pair moves after each round. Each table is numbered. The boards are passed to the next lower-numbered table and the pairs move to the next higher-numbered table. At the end of the game, each North-South pair has played the same hands and each East-West pair has played the same hands.

empty   No support for an honor, as in "jack empty," meaning a holding of a jack with several lower-ranking cards.

end play   To put the opponents in the lead in a situation in which anything led will gain you a trick.

entry   A card that allows a partner to get the lead into a specific hand by leading to it.

equal vulnerability   When both sides have the same vulnerability.

establish   To set up a suit in which a player may play the remaining cards as winners without any danger of losing them to a higher card or a trump.

extra values   Points in excess of a minimum opening bid.

favorable vulnerability   When your pair is not vulnerable and your opponents are vulnerable.

feature   An ace, king, or queen–jack in a suit in response to an asking bid of two no trump by responder when you have opened with a Weak Two-bid.

finesse   Any play that depends on finding a specific card in a specific place.

first seat or position   The dealer, the first person to have an opportunity to make a bid on the hand.

first-round control   When a card or absence of cards in your hand assures you of the ability to take the trick the first time a particular suit is led. An ace or a void constitutes first-round control in a nontrump suit in a trump contract.

fit   When a partnership has the majority of cards in a suit between the two hands.

five-card major   A system of bidding in which you can't open the bidding with one of a suit in a major suit unless you hold at least five cards in the suit. Also describes a major suit in which you have five cards, as in "I did not have a five-card major."

follow suit   Playing a card of the same suit that is led.

forcing bid   A bid that forces a player's partner to bid again, regardless of the quality of the holding in her hand.

forcing no trump   Because a two-level overcall is game forcing in Two-over-One, if responder has enough points but no suit to bid, she bids one no trump, which is "forcing" on opener to bid once more.

fourth from longest and strongest   The fourth-highest card in your longest suit. A preferred opening lead when defending against a no trump contract.

fourth seat or position   The player to dealer's right, the fourth player to have an opportunity to bid in the bidding rotation.

free bid   A bid made by a player with no obligation to bid.

game   Obtaining 100 points below the line in one hand or a succession of hands before the opposing pair obtains 100 points below the line in the same hands.

game forcing   A bid made by a player that requires her partner to keep bidding until the pair has bid a game.

get in   To get the lead.

grand slam   Bidding and making all 13 tricks.

Hamilton   A conventional overcall in defense against a no trump opening by opponents. Double is penalty, two clubs shows a one-suited hand, two diamonds shows 5–5 in the majors, two hearts shows five hearts and an undesignated five-card minor, two spades shows five spades and an undesignated five-card minor (*see* Cappelletti, Pottage). This name is used in California.

HCP   High-card points. *See* entry following **hearts**.

hearts   The second-ranked suit in the deck of cards.

high-card points   Total points in a hand determined by adding up 4 points for each ace, 3 points for each king, 2 points for each queen, and 1 point for each jack.

high-low   Discarding a higher card at your first opportunity, and a lower card of the same suit at your second opportunity, generally to indicate an even number of cards in the suit led.

hit   Another term for double. Sometimes called *smash*, *bend*, or *hammer*.

hold up   To refuse to take a trick you have the capability to take.

honors   Aces, kings, queens, jacks, and 10s.

interference   A bid made by opponents of the opening bidder.

invitational bid   A bid asking your partner to bid again, but not requiring her to, generally to game or slam if she has a certain number of points in her hand or to pass if she does not have that number of points in her hand.

Jacoby transfer   A response of two diamonds or two hearts to a no trump–opening bid requiring partner to bid the next higher suit.

jump   To skip a level of bidding and bid the same suit.

jump shift   To skip a level of bidding and change suits.

jump overcall   To skip a level of bidding and bid a new suit after an opening bid by opponents.

kibitz   To watch a game as a spectator without being a participant.

Landy   A conventional overcall in defense against a no trump opening by opponents. Double is penalty, showing at least 15 HCPs. Two clubs shows two five-card majors. Two diamonds, hearts, or spades shows you have a good suit in the suit bid, almost surely six or more, and the expectation that you can take six or more tricks.

lead   The first card to be played to a trick.

lead up   To lead to a higher card.

lead-directing double   A double, generally of a conventional bid, made not for penalty but to tell your partner what suit to lead if she has the opening lead.

leading through strength   An opening lead of a suit bid by dummy or any lead of a suit bid by leader's LHO, or a lead by dummy's RHO through a strong suit exposed by dummy.

LHO   Left-hand opponent.

limit raise   A jump raise in the suit first bid by partner at responder's first opportunity to bid, showing at least three cards in the suit and between 10 to 12 points.

loser   A card that will not take a trick if led.

major suits   Spades and hearts.

making   Taking the number of tricks declarer contracted to take.

marked card   A card that is known to be in a certain hand because of previous play or bidding.

maximum   The highest level of a known bidding range.

Michael's cue-bid   Bidding the same suit opener bid in the direct seat or after two passes, showing 5–5 in the majors.

minimum   The lower level of a known bidding range.

minor suits   Diamonds and clubs.

Moysian fit   A 4–3 fit in the trump suit between you and partner.

natural bid   A bid that indicates a holding in the suit bid or in no trump if no trump is bid; a nonconventional bid.

New Minor Forcing   If your partner opens and you respond by bidding a higher-ranking major suit and your partner rebids one no trump, and the suit you bid first is a five-card major with invitational values, you can bid two of the unbid minor suit. This shows that your one-level major suit is a five-card suit with at least 10 HCPs. Your bid of the unbid minor suit is a conventional bid that says nothing about that suit; you may bid it even if you are void.

no trump   A contract where there is no trump suit.

off the top   To take all the tricks you need or can get without allowing the opponents to get the lead.

on   Continuing to play a system after an interfering bid by opponents or after your partner has made an overcall instead of an opening bid. *See also* systems on.

onside   A card that's in a position that if you take a finesse, it will win.

open   The first bid made on a hand.

opening lead   The first lead in the play of the hand, made by declarer's LHO.

opening light   To open a hand with less than 13 points.

outside suit   A nontrump suit.

overcall   The first bid made by opponents of the opening bidder.

overtrick   Tricks scored beyond the contracted bid.

partial   Bidding and making a contract less than game.

partial stopper   A card that, in combination with a holding in partner's hand, might stop opponents from running a suit—like Qx or Jxx.

partscore   The score received for bidding and making a contract less than game.

pass   Declining to make a bid, double, or redouble when it's your turn.

passed hand   A hand that doesn't have a bid and doesn't make a bid.

passout seat   After bidding has commenced, the position of the player sitting after two consecutive passes.

play for the drop   To lead high-ranking cards hoping that a missing high card, lower ranking than the cards you lead, will have to be played because holder is short in the suit, rather than finessing for it.

point count   The total of the points in your hand.

Pottage   A conventional overcall in defense against a no trump opening by opponents. Double is penalty, two clubs shows a one-suited hand, two diamonds shows 5–5 in the majors, two hearts shows five hearts and an undesignated five-card minor, two spades shows five spades and an undesignated five-card minor. This name is used in Europe. (*See* Cappelletti, Hamilton)

preempt   A weak bid showing a long suit and not many high-card points.

preemptive jump shift   A bid and system that promises that a jump shift by responder shows a long suit and a weak hand, generally a hand with at least six cards in the suit bid and less than 6 points in the hand.

pulling trump   *See* drawing trump.

quantitative bid   A bid, usually no trump, that is not conventional and asks partner to bid slam if she's at the maximum but to pass if she isn't at the maximum.

quick tricks   A high-card holding that generally promises that it will win a trick, like an ace or a king–queen of the same suit.

renege (revoke)   Failure to follow suit when you are able to follow suit.

reopening double   A part of the negative double system in which the opening bidder doubles at his first rebid opportunity if his LHO has overcalled, partner has passed and RHO has passed, and opening bidder has shortness in the overcalled suit with support for all unbid suits.

reverse Drury   When your partner opens one of a major in third or fourth seat, you need a way to show your good hand. If you have a limit raise for partner's major, bid two clubs. This is artificial, stating that you have a maximum passed hand with at least three-card support. If partner has opened light, without a full opening hand, she rebids her suit at the two level. If she has a full opener, she bids a new suit.

responder   Partner of the first person to bid on a hand.

response   The bid that opening bidder's partner makes.

restricted choice   A theory that states that in the play of the hand, if one of your opponents drops an honor, you should play his partner for the other honor.

return   A standard lead by the partner of the opening leader, to lead the suit led by opening leader at partner's first opportunity.

reverse   When opener rebids a suit at the twp level that is higher ranking than the suit with which she opened at the one level. Responder may also reverse.

RHO   Right-hand opponent.

RONF   An acronym for *Raise is the Only NonForcing* bid. A response to a Weak Two opening bid in which a raise of partner's opening suit may be passed, but any other bid by responder is forcing on partner to bid again for one round.

rubber   The unit of measurement for home or "party" bridge. The first pair to win two games ends the rubber, and the winner is the pair with the most points scored during play of the rubber.

ruff   To win a nontrump trick by playing a trump.

ruffing finesse   A finesse taken into a void, with the intention of ruffing if the card led is covered by leader's LHO, or discarding another suit if the card led is not covered.

rule of 2, 3, and 4   A system used to determine when to open a preemptive hand. With unfavorable vulnerability you may open by overbidding your hand by two tricks. With equal vulnerability you may open by overbidding your hand by three tricks. With favorable vulnerability, you may open by overbidding your hand by four tricks.

rule of 11   If partner leads fourth from longest and strongest, you subtract the number of the card she leads from 11 and the result is the number of cards higher than the card led in the three hands other than opening leader's hand.

run   To set up a long suit and take all the remaining cards in the suit without fear of losing a trick by opponents playing a higher card or trumping.

sacrifice   A bid you make with no hope of making the contract to keep your opponents from making a game, generally to keep them from making a vulnerable game.

safety play   To intentionally lose a trick in order to retain an entry.

second hand low   A familiar rule in play of the hand, that the hand immediately to the left of the leader should play a low card.

second seat or position   Dealer's LHO, the player with the second opportunity to make a call.

secondary suit   A long or strong nontrump suit in which you hope to take tricks after pulling trump.

sequence   A consecutive series of cards three or more in a row.

set   To fail to make a contract.

set up   To establish a suit in which a player may play the remaining cards as winners without any danger of losing them to a higher card or a trump.

shortage points   Points added to your HCP for short suits. Also called distribution points.

shuffling   The process of mixing the cards after each hand.

sign-off bid   A bid that indicates to the partner that the bidder does not want any more bidding.

signals   Plays of certain cards to communicate a specific holding of cards in your hand.

simple raise   To raise your partner's first-bid suit one level at your first opportunity to bid.

singleton   A suit that has only one card in it.

slam   Contracting for 12 or 13 tricks.

slow shows   A metaphor meaning that keeping the bidding low and bidding slowly shows a good hand.

sluff   To discard a card in a suit not led because you are void in the suit led.

small slam   Bidding and making 12 tricks.

spades   The highest ranking of the four suits in a deck of cards.

splinter   A double jump shift showing a singleton or void, an opening hand, and promising four cards in partner's suit.

spot cards   The cards from 2 to 10. For example, some bridge players will refer to a card as the "9 spot," instead of just the 9.

Standard American   A system of bidding and play taught in this book.

standard leads   A list of leads that are considered normal and understood as conveying the same information to all players.

Stayman convention   A conventional bid where a response of two or three clubs to partner's opening bid of one or two no trump asks partner to bid her lowest-ranking four-card major or to bid diamonds at the lowest level available to deny holding a four-card major.

stiff   A singleton.

stopper   A card in a suit that will take a trick and protect against opponents running the suit.

strain   Spades, hearts, diamonds, clubs, or no trump.

strip   To take away the opponents' cards in a suit that they can safely lead without giving you a trick.

strip and end play   A method of playing a hand to force opponents to lead into a tenace or give declarer a ruff and a sluff.

Strong Two   An opening bid at the two level that requires a partner to keep the bidding open until game has been bid or opening bidder has rebid his opening suit. *See* two demand.

support   Help in terms of the number of cards in the suit bid by partner. If partner has shown a five-card suit, support should be three cards. If partner has shown a six-card suit, support should be at least two cards. If partner has bid a second suit, promising only four cards, support must be at least four cards.

system   A method of bidding where certain bids mean certain things.

systems on An agreement between partners that a system they are playing will continue to be played even if opponents interfere or if a bid is made as an overcall or response and not as an opening bid.

takeout double A double of opponents' last bid suit asking partner to bid her longest suit and implying four cards in any unbid major.

tenace A holding of two cards, one of which is two levels below the other.

tenace position When there is only one card outstanding remaining between a holding of two cards.

third hand high A familiar rule in play of the hand, that the partner of the player making the lead of a low card should play the highest card possible in the suit led.

third seat or position The dealer's partner, the player with the third opportunity to make a call.

tight A holding of only the specified cards. *King–queen tight* means you hold only the king and the queen in that suit and no other cards.

top connecting honors A standard lead of the highest of two sequential honors.

transportation The ability to get the lead back and forth between a pair's two hands.

trick The play of four cards, one card by each player, in rotation.

trump The suit in which the hand is played, which for that hand becomes the most powerful suit in the deck.

two demand An opening bid at the two level that requires a partner to keep the bidding open until game has been bid or opening bidder has rebid his opening suit. *See* strong two.

Two-over-One system A very popular system that is used by almost all tournament players is one called the Two-over-One system. In this system, when a player makes a Two-over-One response (such as one diamond — pass — two clubs) she promises enough points that the partnership can make a game. Because of this, all subsequent bidding is game forcing, even if it sounds weak.

unblock To discard a higher card and retain a lower card to allow partner to remain in the lead and run a suit.

underlead To lead a lower-ranking card than another card you have in your hand.

unfavorable vulnerability When you are vulnerable and your opponents are not vulnerable.

unilateral bid A bid by a player without regard to what the player's partner has bid or not bid.

Unusual no trump   When opponents open at the one level, an immediate jump overcall of two no trump shows you have two five-card suits: either both minors, if opponents opened a major, or hearts and the other minor, if opponents opened a minor suit.

up the line   Bidding the lower-ranking of suits of equal length first.

void   A suit in which a player holds no cards.

vulnerable   A pair who has won a game and is subject to greater penalties for undertricks and greater rewards for bidding and making games.

waiting bid   A bid that communicates nothing about the suit to the partner who has made a strong opening bid, but just keeps the bidding open so partner may make a rebid.

Weak Two   A modern bidding convention in which an opening bid in diamonds, hearts, or spades at the two level shows a long suit and a weak hand.

Western cue-bid   The opponents have bid a suit, but your side is marked with most of the high-card points. If your side has found a minor suit fit and if it is clear that your side does not have a major suit contract available, a cue-bid of the opponents' suit does not show a control, as do many cue-bids. It instead says, "I think we can make three no trump if you have a stopper in their suit." So a three-level cue-bid of their suit asks partner to bid three no trump with a stopper in opponents' suit.

winner   A card that will definitely win a trick, used in evaluating your hand after the contract has been made but before you start play as declarer in no trump.

Yarborough   A balanced 4–3–3–3 hand containing no card higher than a 9.

Index